WHAT THEY TOLD YOU IN HISTORY CLASS

VOLUME ONE

Indus Khamit Kush

COVER DESIGN & CONCEPT: *ACT Graphix*
COVER FONTS: *Industrial Fonts & Graphix*

**Library of Congress Cataloging-in-Publication Data
Card Number 99-163580**

Published
by

A&B PUBLISHERS GROUP
1000 Atlantic Avenue
Brooklyn, New York,
11238
(718) 783-7808

97 98 99 00 01 6 5 4 3 2 1

Manufactured and Printed in the United States

Dedication & Acknowledgement

To the one Source, who goes by infinite names.

To the Shrines and the highly elevated Ancestors
who served as the major sources of inspiration
for all of us.

To my family for their support.

To those scholars mentioned in this book who have
sacrificed so much in the interest of truth, and to those
not mentioned who have contributed to the struggles
and advancement of our people.

To Thomas Powell for his friendship
and editorial assistance.

To Dr. Jack Felder for his insightful foreword.

To friends and associates for their
valuable assistance.

Contents

Foreword 1

Preface...5

Racist Quotes-Past and Present 10

Presidents...10

    The First President of the United States
    was a 'Black' Man, a Moor 13

    The Original Statue of Liberty
    was a 'Black' Woman 17

Actors / Famous People 19

Sports Figures 23

Political Figures 25

'Naturally Inferior'...26

'Inferior' Physical Characteristics.......................27

'Natural' Enslavement...31

'Inferior' Black Race...35

'Superior' White Race...37

'Inferior' Black 'Civilization' 40

'Superior 'White [European] Civilization...........42

'Inferior' Intelligence 44

Scientific Racism..45

Extermination...48

Creators of the Human Race 53
Creators of Civilization 75
The Foundations of White Supremacy 113
    Greece (and Rome) originated Civilization ...113
Creators of Greek Philosophy 113
The African Origins of the "Greek Miracle" 122
Before Greece and Rome 123
The African Origins of "Greek Philosophy" 139
'Stolen Legacy' 183
Creators of Religion 209
The Foundations of White Supremacy 219
Judeo-Christian Tradition Gave the World
    The True Religion & Concept of God 219
White People "Worshiped" Black [Deities] 222
The First Gods (Deities) of Antiquity
    were Black 223
Jesus Christ, the Son of God, was Black 228
The Mother of God was Black 232
The World's Earliest Messiahs 237
Moses was Blacj 241
Enoch, the First Perfect Human Being
    was Black 243
St. Maurice, the legendary Black "Savior,"
    of White Germany 248
Creators of Christianity 261
The Founding Fathers of the Church 282
The First Martyrs 282
Black Popes 283
Conclusion 285

Foreword

Black people must remember the White western world has committed a crime against science. Because starting about five hundred years ago when they colonized most of the non-White world, they conspired to re-write the history of non-Whites to imply that the millions and millions of non-White people did not contribute anything to world development and civilization.

Science is classified knowledge obtained from systematic observation, study and experiments. Therefore, history is a science. For example, we have carbon 14 dating of fossils, DNA testing and the scientific investigation of other similar artifacts. And yet, they deliberately falsified and ignored the scientific evidence pointing to the African Origins of Civilization.

Dr. Jack Felder

There is wide spread belief in our society that some races contribution to mankind is not as significant or important as others and that this somehow determine their present day value. Race, therefore, becomes the critical ingredient as to whether that race should be tolerated, eradicated. Is not the most important U. S. government building called the White House? And If you rearrange the letters in AMERICA , does it not spell (I-Am-Race)?

Have we forgotten that the framers of the U. S. constitution owned Black slaves? Have we also forgotten that the first 12 presidents of the United States also owned slaves ? Now, as parents knowing the true nature of the U. S. ruling class don't encourage our children and race to read books by historians that tell the truth, then we are committing a crime. We are neglecting the "higher" education about our people and why they are important to us and to humanity.

I have known Indus Khamit-Kush for a number of years, and when he came up with What They Never Told You In History Class, it was a stroke of genius. This book is absolute must reading for all Black people now! Why? Because it is a road map for Black people; it tells you where you came from, where you are, and where you are going. It is also a compass and a time clock that points in the direction of our freedom, and tells us the time of day, today, yesterday, and TOMORROW. They have a saying in Black Africa, "if you don't know where you are going, any old road will do." Well this book is giving you the right road to follow. Therefore, if we fail as a race of people in the future we will not have any excuse.

Brother Kush is pointing the way! Brother Kush and I have had some extensive conversations about the plight of Black people in the new millennium. One of the things he hopes to achieve in his new edition is to dispel the myth of White supremacy and Black inferiority at its roots. He wants Black people to know that we had a complete history thousands of years before White people were civilized and before some White people got the upper hand, then wrote us out of history. They enslaved us and we became war captives. However, even during enslavement of some Africans in the Americas, we still had great civilizations operating in Sudan, Ethiopia, etc. which were never enslaved or colonized by White people.

One of the high points in his new edition of the book is this – he deals with the Black African origin of Christianity. Many Black Christians don't know that at least three Popes were Black. There were three Roman Emperors who were Black also. They know that the month of July was named after Julius Caesar and August was named after the Black Roman Emperor Septimus. Or when we say amen after praying, we are just giving praise to the great pharaoh "A-men-Ra." The man was so great during his time that every prayer had to end with his name and even today almost 3,000 years later, every prayer ends with his name.

During the time of Christ there was no Middle East. It was created by Europeans in order to write Black people out of the Holy Land. They have called Black people Nubians, Lydians, Phoenicians, to cause confusion in their real racial make-up as Black People.

Remember, adherents to White supremacy got the upper hand and colonized most of the non-White world. The biggest damage was that they colonized the writings or re-writing of world history. They wrote the achievement of so-called colored people out of history and claimed all the real achievements for themselves.

Those who classified themselves as White know that the Black Egyptians invented the alphabet and the Black Arabs invented the Arabic number system (zero to nine) which the whole White world uses today. Do you think White people will teach you that in their school system? Now today almost the year 2000 B. C., most Black People believe God waited 1610 years to come to the White king of England, King James 1st (1601-1625) who had questionable sexual preference for members of the same sex and a decided preference for intoxicating liquids.

In addition, he was a racist who got Shakespeare to translate and re-write the Hebrew bible for the English speaking world. Remember, it does not say the Holy Bible; it says the King James Version of the Holy Bible. Please get and read the Original Holy Bible (Aramaic Bible or at least the Hebrew Bible or Greek bible). Well, I am turning all of you over to my strong African Brother Kush. Hold on to your seats for the ride of your life for Black African truth and justice, a pointer to our liberation.

Your brother, Dr. Jack Felder

Preface

This book is the first completely new revision of *What They Never Told You In History Class* in over fifteen years. It contains a wealth of new information that has never been included in any previous edition.

Also, it surveys the great works of Joel A. Rogers, John Jackson, Yosef ben-Jochannan, Cheikh Anta Diop, Gerald Massey, Count Volney, Geoffrey Higgins, Martin Bernal, George G. M. James' *Stolen Legacy* and the contributing writers of *Journal of African Civilizations* headed by Ivan Van Sertima with a special mention to the outstanding scholarship done by Professor John Henrik Clarke. The incredible facts unearthed by this illustrious group of men - and the ancestors - have put all of us in their debt.

In the millennium, the most important issue will still be the race question. Not surprisingly, technology will provide White supremacy with greater weapons of destruction to minds of the non-White population throughout the world. The basic implication for Blacks is that we do not have "a history" of any real significance to the rest of the world. We are in effect a non-essential factor in the forward advance of civilization. Thus in a time of crisis or surplus Black people are likely to be an expendable and disposable commodity based on our lack of contributions to mankind.

But does this perception have any basis in truth? *What They Never Told You In History Class* attempts, in its own small way, to help to re-establish Africa's rightful place in history. Though despised and rejected, we are a living history of "Creators, Originators and Innovators." *Out of Africa* came *Humanity and Civilization*, a fact that changes the "reality" of White supremacists for theirs is a different world-view of history.

Professor Martin Bernal, a formidable British academician with a chair at Cornell University, reveals their basic premise which states that from the north came the White Indo-Europeans known as "Aryans," and they "conquered Greece and endowed it with civilization." In addition, there was "the widespread belief that Greece represented the formative stage of later European civilization" which relates to the "popular philosophical arguments that people living in cold climates achieved the greatest intelligence and morality." "Racism," argues Bernal, "still fuels the academic neglect of Egyptian [read African]...influence on Greek culture."

Many scholars are wedded to the inherent supremacy of the White European for political as well as economic reasons. According to this award winning Cornell professor, "people [Western scholars and scientists] are feeling constrained to assert their belief in the absolute superiority of European culture. Certainly when it comes to grant giving, you cannot get a grant unless you support this line." As we can see, these scholars cannot afford the luxury of writing the Truth. The "hype" of Global White Supremacy has become the primary reason for their continued existence. The *Truth* is no longer an issue as long as the "hype" survives and flourishes.

In fact, the "hype" is used to control and exploit others - to give White skin advantages and privileges over non-Whites in America and throughout the world. Is it not a pity that their belief in their own "hype" is so limited that none of them feel confident enough to compete with others on fair and equal terms without any unearned advantages or privileges?

If White supremacy could be viewed as a religion, it would be absolute heresy to imply any origins of western or European civilization from a Black source. No one wants to hear about Africa's contributions to civilization especially not the White supremacist.

Western scholars cannot accept that "Out of the Dark Continent" came the "Light of Civilization"! The African [Black] origins of [White] Europe is too much for the average White supremacist to bear. How can their mind set accept the reality that "the parent of civilization and the cradle of the arts, is a Black nation instead of a White one. The Egyptian origins of Greek Civilization rocks the very foundation of Western Civilization.

That Africa left the indelible mark of civilization on Greece and thereby on Europe is a fact that their conditioned mind-sets cannot accept, evidence not withstanding. White Supremacy must be upheld at all costs. It is like asking an American Nazi to accept the fact that Hitler had Jewish roots, if he had them. It would simply be too hard for a Nazi to imagine given the fact that they have been programmed in the complete opposite direction. So, too, with the White supremacist in America and throughout the world.

Which leads to a very unsettling question for them: What is the White childhood of Europe [Greece] doing in a Black cradle

[Egypt]? Without this particular primacy the very foundation of White Supremacy cannot stand. Dr. Clarke has often said that "the Europeans monopolized information"; one might also include the very perception of "reality" itself. Thus civilization was started by the White man in the "person" of Greece and Rome. And, of course, they should also be credited with creating the one and only "true religion" from the White Judeo-Christian tradition. This is but another manifestation of White superiority. Given their twisted perception of reality it should come as no surprise that "God is White" too. It was through the superior intellect and spiritual insight of the White European that civilization and religion could be achieved for the rest of the non-White world.

Therefore, the innate inferiority of Black people is self-evident having been completely absent in any elevation of man from barbarism to civilization.

This stereotype has far-reaching consequences. A fact that has been clearly illustrated in a *Newsweek* article entitled, "You Can't High-Jump If the Bar is Set Low," by Connie Leslie. It reported on a scientific experiment done by Claude Steele, a professor of social psychology at Stanford University "who demonstrated that some Blacks suffer from 'stereotype vulnerability' which in simple terms means that if you, by word or deed, tell kids they're part of a group that can't succeed, they won't. "Over time," Steele told *Newsweek*, "the pressure from 'stereotype vulnerability' can push Black students to stop identifying with achievement in school."

Steele argues that when Blacks (or any other group) are confronted with a Stereotype about their intellectual skills before they take tests, they tend to perform according to the stereotype. Change the expectations, however, and Steele finds that Blacks score as high as White students taking the same test.

Arthur A. Schomburg Founder of the Schomberg Center for Research in Harlem, New York.

What *They Never Told You In History Class* will change their perception and knowledge of "his-story," and greater success will follow. Because it's one thing to say that we are "equal," it's quite something else to prove it. This book attempts to record –

and prove - our magnificent "History of Success" so that we can indeed repeat history.

"The Schomburg Center for Research in Black Culture, New York City represents the largest collection of Black literature and artifacts for research in the world.

Arthur A. Schomburg: Born in San Juan, Puerto Rico on January 24, 1874, Schomburg quickly learned the importance of having an awareness of one's cultural roots. Young Puerto Rican students in the literary club to which Schomburg belonged were assigned books about Latin American history and the history of Puerto Rico itself.

When, however, Schomburg inquired about books about his own African past, his teacher told him that no such a thing as Black history existed! The seed of concern was thereby planted."

New National Black Monitor, July 8, 1982

Essence Magazine (August, 1992) tells us:

"Our Children are in trouble"

by Jill Nelson

What does "Black" mean to you?

Can we make it mean something to them

One of the greatest historians of our modern era, the late John Henrik Clarke, recalled that during his youth he had inquired about the history of his people, and a well-meaning southern liberal gave this response. He said, "I'm sorry John but you came from A Race That Had No History."

The celebrated anthropologist L. S. B. Leakey, (*Progress and Evolution of Man in Africa*) once wrote that:

"In every country that one is drawn into a conversation about Africa, the question is regularly asked by people but what has Africa contributed to world progress."

And, back during the sixties, James J. Kilpatrick then a reporter-editor for the Richmond [Va.] *NEWS LEADER* and a contributor to other conservative publications, demanded to know from James Baldwin during a television interview that was charged with hostility,

Essence Magazine (August, 1982) tells us:

"OUR CHILDREN ARE IN TROUBLE"

our teenagers are becoming strangers, striking out against society — and us

BY JILL NELSON

WHAT DOES "BLACK" MEAN TO YOU?

CAN WE MAKE IT MEAN SOMETHING TO THEM?

what Negroes had contributed to civilization.

What Mr. Kilpatrick tried to insinuate was this:

"History" Proves that

White people are Superior.

Because when you read it, anybody who was anything from Aristotle to Einstein was White.

Therefore, Black People are destined to be inferiors, since no one from the Black race seems to have done anything really important.

Fortunately, however...

"HIS-STORY" is not necessarily the ..."WHOLE-STORY."

Presidents

George Washington

Thomas Jefferson

Abraham Lincoln

Theodore Roosevelt

Shipped the Slaves to [the] West Indies in exchange for some rum and sundries.

U. S. President: George Washington in a letter addressed to a captain John Thompson on July 2, 1766. He sold a slave named Tom for liquor.

I advance as a suspicion only that the Blacks…are inferior to Whites both in body and mind. Never yet could I find that a Black had uttered a thought above the level of plain narration…ever saw an elementary tract of painting or sculpture.

U. S. President: Thomas Jefferson

I have no purpose to introduce political and social equality between the White and Black races…that I am not nor ever have been in favor of making voters or jurors of negroes, nor of qualifying them to hold office nor to intermarry with White people; and I will say in addition to this that there is a physical difference between the two which, in my judgment, will probably forever forbid their living together upon the footing of a perfect equality, and in as much as it becomes a necessity that there must be a difference , I am in favor of the race to which I belong having the superior position.

U. S. President: Abraham Lincoln, debate with Stephen Douglas, Charleston, 1858

Now as to the negroes! I entirely agree with you that as a race and in the mass they are altogether inferior to the White.

U. S. President: Theodore Roosevelt, letter to Novelist Owen Wister, 1906

It was the administration of Woodrow Wilson, however, which took the most drastic action against Negroes…It was in Wilson's administration and with his express approval that federal civil service workers were segregated by race in their employment, with separate eating and toilet facilities. When a Negro leader protested this segregation, Wilson all but ordered him out of his office because his language was 'insulting.'

U. S. President: Woodrow Wilson, *Atlantic Monthly* LXXXVII (January 1901) as cited in *Race, The History of an Idea in America*, Thomas F. Gossett, 1963

Woodrow Wilson

William Howard Taft began his administration in 1909 by assuring the White South that he would appoint no federal officials in their region who would be offensive to them, and of course the White South knew what he meant.

U. S. President: William Howard Taft, *The Life and Times of William Howard Taft*, Henry F. Pringle, 1939

William Howard Taft

…(I have) a strong feeling of repugnance when I think of the negro being made our political equal and I would be glad they could be colonized, sent to heaven, or got rid of in any decent way…

U. S. President: James A. Garfield, letter to Jacob D. Cox, July 26, 1865

Woodrow Wilson said that the Negroes in the South had been 'a host of dusky children untimely put out of school.' Conditions had approached the stage of 'ruin' until 'at last the Whites who were the real citizens got control again.'

James A. Garfield

U. S. President: Woodrow Wilson, *Atlantic Monthly* LXXXVII (January 1901) as cited in *Race, The History of an Idea in America*, Thomas F. Gossett, 1963

As one who had lived in the South, he wanted to be sure to make it clear that social equality of political and economic opportunity did not mean necessarily that everyone has to mingle socially – or that a negro should court my daughter.

Dwight Eisenhower

U. S. President: Dwight D. Eisenhower, quoted from *Eisenhower, The President Nobody Knew* by Arthur Larson (New York, 1968). The remark was made to Larson 1956

I want folks to walk down the hall at the Justice Department and look in the door and see a nigger sitting there.

Lyndon B. Johnson

Ronald Reagan

Richard M. Nixon

U. S. President: Lyndon B. Johnson, a remark made to Thurgood Marshall

...Blacks are genetically less intelligent than Whites...

U. S. President: Ronald Reagan, a belief reported by Ernest W. Lefever a nominee of Mr. Reagan for Assistant Secretary of State for Humanitarian Affairs according to both of his brothers John and Donald [*New York Times*, June 4, 1981]

America's Blacks could only marginally benefit from federal programs because 'Blacks are genetically inferior to Whites'

U. S. President: Richard Nixon, a belief expressed by Mr. Nixon according to one of his top advisors, John D. Ehrlickman [*New York Times*, December 11, 1981]

Several past presidents and slave-owners are on America's paper currencies: George Washington ($1), Thomas Jefferson ($2), Alexander Hamilton ($10), Andrew jackson ($20), Ulysses Grant ($50) and Benjamin Franklin ($100).

Grant, the 18 th president, was the last U.S. President to own slaves.

The Nuwaubian Moors Newsletter (Ed. 1, Vol. 16, October 19, 1997) shocked the world with this incredible revelation:

The First President Of The United States Was A "Black" Man, A Moor

They boldly proclaimed that:

George Washington was not the First President of the United States. He was the 9th. The real first President of the United States was John Hanson who understood the importance of the war and was concerned."

"He served as president from 1781-1782 A. D. In fact, he sent 800 pounds of sterling silver, by his brother Samuel Hanson, to George Washington to provide the troops with shoes...

They tried so hard to cover the true Moorish identity of John Hanson because of his great accomplishments as a leader. Since Euro-Americans have their roots in England, it must be very hard to accept the fact that the true *"father"* and founder of The United States of America was a Moor...

The Many Faces of John Hanson

Mulatto John Hanson

John Hanson
The 1 st President

They even have a bronze statue of John Hanson, at Statutary Hall in the White House, it looks just like the original picture.

By the way only the greatest *"Americans"* are placed in this hall.

John Hanson was described as a man of action with great organizational abilities. He organized two riflemen groups that were the first to join General George Washington during the revolutionary war. **He also appointed George Washington as general.** John Hanson was the assemblyman for Charles County in Maryland and was chairman of the Frederick County on two committees: The Committee of Observation and The Committee of Correspondence.

Upon his death, he was eulogized by the **Maryland Gazette, on November 21, 1783 A. D.** and I quote:

'Thus was ended the career of America's greatest statesman. While hitherto practically unknown to our people, and this is true as to nearly all generations that have lived since his day, this great handiwork, the nation which he helped to establish, remains as a fitting tribute to his memory. It is doubtful if there has ever lived on this side of the Atlantic, a nobler character or shrewder statesman. One would search in vain to find a more powerful personage or a more aggressive leader, in the annals of American history...(author's italics)'

Abraham Lincoln, the supposed 16th president, said John Hanson should be honored equally with George Washington."

The article maintained that:

"They try to hide the true identity of John Hanson...They'll show you a mulatto looking person who is Europeanized or Euro-American while the real John Hanson, the original picture is buried; but if you go on the Internet, which they don't expect "Black" people to have, if you go to the

The Library Of Congress **website (lcweb2.loc.gov)**, which you can find under **"American Memories"** under **Dagurerreotype** pictures, which is an early photographic process with an image made of a light sensitive silver metallic plate, will you see that he is unmistakably a Moor..."

The Great Seal of the United States Was Designed By John Hanson

Make note the seal, called the Great Seal, used first by John Hanson is the same seal used by Bill Clinton.

This seal along with the signature of the President is necessary to conclude the law by a Supreme Court decision...He [George Washington] also recognized that without the official seal he was not technically president and called an emergency session of Congress and only after George Washington accepted all conditions, laws, rules, and authority under the first President John Hanson was he given the seal. This was under resolution drawn up by Thomas Jefferson.

John Hanson statue

So, in actuality George Washington was the 9th president of The United States and the 1st president under the Constitution.

Proof of this can be seen on a bronze medallion that on one side shows Washington reviewing his troops, and on the other side shows

John Hanson's caption:

"First President Under The Articles Of Confederation."

The medallion was made by Congress on the 200th anniversary of the Surrender of Cornwallis."

The article contained a heading which stated that:

The Great Seal of the U. S.

John Hanson
false bust

[

Seen also on the back of the ($1) one dollar bill]

Also, according to *The Nuwaubian Moors Newsletter* :

> "...what most of you don't know is that **George Washington was a freemason** as were 14 other of your most prominent presidents including: James Monroe, Andrew Jackson, James Polk, James Buchanan, James Garfield, William Mckinley, Theodore Roosevelt, William Howard Taft, Warren Harding, Franklin D. Roosevelt, Lyndon B. Johnson, Gerald R. Ford, Jimmy Carter and George Bush to name a few.

NEW YORK TIMES, SUNDAY, MARCH 29, 1998

An Ancient Body of Men

Freemasons trace their origin back to the medieval guilds of stone masons, attributing their symbol of square and compass to that craft. Although lodges, which are made up of at least seven masons, were established prior to the 18th century, the first Grand Lodge was established in 1717 in England. There are lodges in nearly every country and about 5 million members worldwide, with about 2.9 million American and 350,000 British masons.

FAMOUS MASONS, PAST AND PRESENT

Louis Armstrong	Casanova	Clark Gable	Roy Rogers
Neil Armstrong	Marc Chagall	Guiseppe Garibaldi	Nathan Meyer Rothschild
John Jacob Astor	Walter P. Chrysler	John Glenn	David Sarnoff
Mustapha Attaturk	Sir Winston Churchill	Harry Houdini	Sir Walter Scott
Stephen Austin	Ty Cobb	Sam Houston	Peter Sellers
Irving Berlin	Buffalo Bill	Al Jolson	Jan Sibelius
Simon Bolivar	Edward VII	Rudyard Kipling	Joseph Smith
Ernest Borgnine	Edward VIII	Fiorello La Guardia	John Philip Sousa
James Boswell	Duke Ellington	Charles Lindbergh	Stendhal
Omar Bradley	Douglas Fairbanks Sr.	Franz Liszt	Harry Truman
William J. Bratton	W. C. Fields	Harold Lloyd	Jonathan Swift
Robert Burns	Sir Alexander Fleming	Douglas MacArthur	Voltaire
Eddie Cantor	Gerald Ford	George Marshall	John Wayne
	Samuel Colt	Wolfgang Amadeus Mozart	George Washington
	Davy Crockett	Rupert Murdoch	The Duke of Wellington
	Cecil B. DeMille	Robert Peary	Oscar Wilde
	Sir Arthur Conan Doyle	Theodore Roosevelt	Darryl Zanuck
	Henry Ford	Franklin D. Roosevelt	Florenz Ziegfeld
	Benjamin Franklin	Paul Revere	

George Washington in his freemason's apron.

Sources: Grand Lodge of the State of New York, "The Concise History of Freemasonry"

Who? Me a Mason? Britain Sees Threat

by WARREN HOGE

LONDON

FREEMASONRY, the mysterious and ritualistic fraternal society that began in Britain more than 350 years ago, has only one secret left–its membership list-and now the Government is trying to make it public.

Jack Straw, the Home Secretary, demanded this month that judges who are Masons be publicly identified. He said that if he doesn't get voluntary compliance the Government will pass a law compelling them to reveal lodge membership.

For centuries, Freemasons an oath listings the punishments revealing the names of member breaking other confidences. mason's throat would be cut, tongue torn from his mouth...

THE ORIGINAL STATUE OF LIBERTY

WAS A BLACK WOMAN

Dr. Jack Felder, a biochemist, educator, author and historian, asked this startling question in a New York newspaper, the *Daily Challenge* (July 16, 1990):

> Did you know that the original Statue of Liberty was to have been a Black woman being liberated from slavery with broken chains in her hands and at her feet and that she also had a dark Negroid face?

Felder continues:

> The idea of building a statue to the liberation of African slaves in the U. S. was first broached in 1865 near Versailles, France by Edouard Rene Lefebvré de Laboulaye. Laboulaye was an internationally renowned jurist and author of a three-volume history of the United States.

> One of Laboulaye's dinner guests was Frederic Auguste Bartholdi, a young sculptor with the freedom of man. Bartholdi took on this job of building the Statue of Liberty…

According to this insightful author:

> Laboulaye's concern as expressed in the May 1984 issue of the airline magazine *Pam Am Clipper* was for "a monument to send as a gift to abolitionists in recognition of the end of slavery in the U. S."

> Moreover, it is a known fact that Bartholdi used Egypt as his principal inspiration for the Statue of Liberty.

In his thought-provoking monograph on this subject entitled, *From the Statue of Liberty (Liberation) to the Statue of Bigotry,* Dr. Felder cites Bartholdi's words:

> "Colossal statuary does not consist simply in making an enormous statue. It ought to produce an emotion in the breast of the spectator, not because of its volume, but because its size is in keeping with the idea it interprets… "
> (p 11)

In the newspaper article, Felder writes that:

> Eventually, Bartholdi built a model faithful to the wishes of de Laboulaye with broken chains at her feet and a broken

chain in her left hand and a distinctly Negroid face. The broken chains were to indicate the broken chains of slavery.

In addition, Dr. Felder lists several sources to substantiate his claims. For example, he maintains that:

"1. Proof and documents supporting the fact that the first and original Statue of Liberty was a Black woman breaking the chains at her feet and in her hand. Go to the Museum of the City of New York. Fifth Avenue and 103rd Street...

2. Check with Suzanne Nakasian, director of the Statue of Liberty – Ellis Island Foundation's National Ethnic Campaign. Nakasian has said that the African-Americans' direct connection to Lady Liberty is unknown to the majority of Americans, Black or White and this fact is not an accident.

3. You can check at the archive in Washington D. C. and ask for a photo-copy of the letter that...the French historian, Edouard Rene Lefebvré de Laboulaye sent to president Abraham Lincoln...

4. You can check with the French Mission at the U. N. and ask for some original French material on the Statue of Liberty, including Bartholdi's original model.

Pictures for the Original [Black] Statue of Liberty

[Source: From the *Statue of Liberty* by Dr. Jack Felder]

The inspiration for the Statue of Liberation for Edouard Rene Lefebvre De Laboulaye in America was the LIberation of the African Slave in 1863.

Actors / Famous People

Mainstream America is depending on you – counting on you – to draw your sword and fight for them. These people [mainstream America] have previously little time or resources to battle [the] misguided propaganda of...Blacks who raise a militant fist with one hand while they seek preference with the other...We've reached that point in time when our national social policy originates on 'Oprah.' I say it's time to pull the plug...

Actor: Charlton Heston speech delivered before the conservative *Free Congress Foundation* in Washington D. C., 1998 transcript obtained by the Violence Policy Center

I believe in White supremacy until the Blacks are educated to a point of responsibility, I don't believe in giving authority and positions of leadership and judgment to irresponsible people.

Actor: John Wayne, Interview in *Playboy*, May 1971

...but there are some things inborn in you...My father was once stabbed by a Negro.

Actress: Farrah Fawcett-Major, In reference to her admitted prejudice against Blacks, which she was trying to overcome, *National Enquirer*, August 1, 1977

It is now entirely clear to me that, as his cranial structures and hair type prove, Lassalle is descended from the Negroes who joined Moses' flight from Egypt (that is, assuming his mother, or his paternal grandmother, did not cross with a nigger). Now this union of Jewry and Germanism with the negro-like basic substance must necessarily result in a remarkable product. The officiousness of the fellow is also nigger-like.

Philosopher: Karl Marx, Letter to Friedrich Engels, 1862

Stephen, if it weren't for you wretched Britishers, we wouldn't have any Negroes in this country anyway; we wouldn't have this mess!

Evangelist: Billy Graham in a letter to Stephen Olford, 1940

The Negro is a child, and with children nothing can be done without the use of authority. With regard to the Negroes then, I have the formula: I am your brother, it is true, but your elder brother.

Missionary: Albert Schweitzer, M. D., *On the Edge of Primeval Forest*, 1961

Hegel called Africa: the land where men are children.

Philosopher: Hegel as quoted by John Corry, *New York Times*, March 1985

I can summarize my attitude about employing more negroes very simply – I think it (integration, open housing and jobs) is a wonderful idea for somebody else, somewhere else...I feel the negroes have already made enough progress to last the next 100 years...

Billionaire: Howard Hughes, Memorandum to Robert Meheu, April 1968.

"Myth" turned into Reality!

[Keep "inferiors" segregated.]

At this movie theater in the segregated South,
Black patrons had to use a separate entrance
leading to a "crow's nest"—a balcony upstairs

Putting "Ideas" into practice
Keeping "inferiors" segregate

...the phenomenal performance of the Blacks in Berlin worried many people besides the Führer...Unnamed 'medical authorities' quoted as saying that the emergence of the Blacks had introduced a new factor into sport; colored athletes were claimed to have abnormal muscular qualities, different from those of White men, and in particular an 'elongated heel' which gave them extra spring and therefore an unfair advantage. Because of this, it was suggested, future Olympiads would have to be split into two sections, one for Blacks and one for Whites. (Hurst-Davis, 1986)

Scholar: Jan Nederveen Pieterse, *White on Black, Images of Africa and Blacks in Western Popular Culture*, 1992

The history of this Expedition is the history of the past [rather than the future] in reference to the heated visions of philanthropists for the railroad Christianization of

Africa, and the abolition of the Slave Trade...Between the civilized European and the barbarous African there is a great gulf set...To change the customs even of civilized...men...is...a most difficult and slow proceeding; but to do this by ignorant and savage races, is a work which, like the progressive changes of the globe itself, requires a stretch of years that dazzles in the looking at.

Author: Charles Dickens, *The Niger Expedition, Works*, 20 Vols., 1903

The negroid streak creeps northward to define the Nordic race. Already the Italians have the souls of Blackamoors. Raise the bars of immigration and permit only Scandinavians, Teutons, Anglo-Saxons and Celts to enter I believe at last in the White man's burden. We (Nordics) are as far above the modern Frenchman as he is above the Negro.

Author: F Scott Fitzgerald, in a letter dated, 1921

Under the South's so-called Jim Crow laws, Blacks were restricted to "separate but equal" facilities everywhere—even in parking lots—during much of the 20th century.

Sports Figures

I once had a nigger working for me. He couldn't do the job, I had to put him in the mail room...[I] would never hire another nigger, I'd rather have a trained monkey working for me than a nigger.

Major League Sports Owner: Marge Schott, owner of the Cincinnati Reds, made these statements as reported by Mr. Jones, a former employee, in the *New York Times* (November 26, 1992)

I think people; are afraid to speak out on the subject. White people have to have White heroes. I myself can't equate to Black heroes. I'll be truthful. I respect them, but I need White people. It's in me and I think the Cavaliers have too many Blacks.

Major League Sports Owner: Ted Stepien, former owner of the Cleveland Cavaliers [a professional basketball team], *New York Times* December 6, 1982

Blacks make better athletes than Whites because they were 'bred to be that way.' He added that the difference between Whites and Blacks 'goes all the way back to the Civil War, when during the slave period the slave owner would breed his big Black with his big woman so that they could have a big kid. That's where it all started.'

He also said that if more Blacks become coaches that 'there's not going to be anything left for the White people.' 'I mean, all the players are Black,' he said. 'The only thing that the Whites control is the coaching jobs.'

CBS Sports commentator: Jimmy (the Greek) Snyder, statements made in an impromptu encounter with a reporting team from *WRC-TV*, an *NBC*-owned and-operated station, as reported in the *New York Times*, (January 15, 1986)

Al Campanis, the Los Angeles Dodgers' vice president of player personnel, suggested on national television to Ted Koppel that Blacks might not be qualified to be managers or hold executive positions in baseball because they lack 'the necessities ' to manage in the major leagues.

Vice-President, the Los Angeles Dodgers: Al Campanis made this response when asked by Ted Koppel, the host of *Nightline*, the *ABC* News program, why the majors had no Blacks in executive positions as reported in the *New York Times* (April 8, 1987)

> 'Blacks have different muscles that react in different ways.'

Golf legend: Jack Nicklaus made this statement as reported by S. L. Price in *Sports Illustrated* (December 12, 1997, Vol. 87, Issue 23).

> David Halberstam, a Miami Heat radio announcer, made a bizarre connection between modern basketball and Thomas Jefferson's slaves.

Radio Announcer: David Halberstam as reported in the *New York Times* (April 1997)

> The muscle structure of the Black athlete typically is more suited for certain positions in football and basketball.

Educator: Dale Lick, a former candidate for the presidency of Michigan State in 1993, made this statement according to S. L. Price in an article entitled, "ATHLETES-Physiology; The Bell Curve," *Sports Illustrated* (December 12, 1997, Vol. 87, Issue 23).

> Fuzzy Zoeller, a golf professional, called Tiger Woods a 'little boy'… at the Augusta National Club.

Professional Golf Player: Fuzzy Zoeller made remark on the heels of Wood's victory at the Master [April 1997] and the 50-year anniversary celebration of Jackie Robinson's breaking the baseball color line as reported in the *New York Times* (April 1997)

> Amcasts, which sell ads for thousands of radio stations and is a division of Katz Radio Group, warned companies against buying too many ads on Black…radio stations because 'advertisers should want prospects, not suspects,' according to the internal company memo.

> "When it comes to delivering prospects, not suspects, the urbans deliver the largest amount of listeners who turn out to be the least likely to purchase," buying too many ads on ethnic stations would mean losing "the more important 'White' segment of the population;" and advertisers can reach "all the ethnics you need without even using an ethnic station…"

Advertising Agency: *Amcasts*, an advertising agency, which encouraged advertisers to minimize or eliminate advertising in Black and Hispanic radio stations.

Goodyear television ad, which makes fun of a Black man's lips and compares them to tires.

Corporation: Goodyear Tire and Rubber company ad aired in Latin America as reported in *Jet* magazine January 12, 1998

Jeff Gralnick, called a Somali warlord "an educated jungle bunny." He is also reported to have referred to the Somali people as "the rest of the jungle bunnies out there are not like him at all. They're illiterate."

TV Producer: Jeff Gralnick, an executive producer of *NBC's Nightly News.* as quoted in the *Amsterdam News* (October 23, 1993)

The morning talk show had decided to interview well-known Black Americans for a story on the racial elements for the Sprewell Case. Kevin Cosgrove went to two talent bookers for *Good Morning America* and said, "The bosses want spades for the Sprewell segment," according to the *New York Daily News*.

Television producer: Kevin Cosgrove, senior producer *ABC's Good Morning America*, as cited in *Jet* magazine, January 12, 1998

Political Figures

Why increase the sons of Africa, by planting them in America, where we have so fair an opportunity by excluding all Black and tawnys, of increasing the lovely White and red.

Statesman: Benjamin Franklin, *Observations Concerning the Increase of Mankind*, 1753

I got a wire from the Reverend Doctor King in New York. He was getting ready to get the Nobel Prize – he was the last one in the world who should ever have received it...I held him in complete contempt because of the things he said and because of his conduct. (He) said he never criticized the FBI. I said "Mr. King" – I never called him reverend – "Stop right there. You're lying."

Director of the Federal Bureau of Investigations: J. Edgar Hoover, statement made in 1964

I can't understand it. I can't understand it. I never did think Martin Luther King was a good American, anyhow.

U. S. Vice-President: Spiro T. Agnew, remark to an aide following riots after assassination of Dr. King.

... because of differences in intelligence 'integration of the Blacks and Whites...is less likely to result in accommodation that it is in perpetual friction, as the incapable are placed consciously by government side by side with the capable'.

Presidential Advisor: Pat Buchanan, one of the architects of Nixon's southern strategy, submitted a memo with this suggestion to Nixon reported by Larry A. Greene in his review of the book, *The Bell Curve Debate: History, Documents, Origins*, edited by Russell Jacoby and Naomi Glauberman in *Telos* magazine, (December 1996)

Naturally Inferior"

The permanent, natural inferiority of the Negro was the true and only defense of slavery...

Journalist: Edward A. Pollard, The Lost Cause Regained, 1868

France is and remains by far the most terrible enemy. This people which is basically becoming more and more negrified constitutes in its tie with the aims of Jewish world domination an enduring danger for the existence of the White race in Europe. For the contamination by Negro blood on the Rhine in the heart of Europe is just as much in keeping with the perverted sadistic thirst for vengeance of this hereditary enemy of our people as is the ice-cold calculation of the Jew thus to begin bastardizing the European continent at its core and to deprive the White race of the foundation for a sovereign existence through infection with lower humanity.

Dictator: Adolph Hitler, German Chancellor

The new U. S. constitution reemphasized Black inferiority by deeming that for political representation, each slave would only count as three fifths of a human being.

U. S. Constitution: Cited in Black Profiles in Courage, Kareem Abdul Jabbar and Alan Steinberg, 1996

No rational man, cognizant of the facts, believes that the average negro is the equal ...of the average White man.

Biologist: Thomas Huxley, *Emancipation, Black and White*, 1865

Voltaire believed that the gap between White and Black could not be bridged…

Philosopher: Voltaire, well-known French philosopher, "Essay sur les Mousers," 1829 as cited in *White on Black, Images of Africa and Blacks in Western Popular Culture*, Jan Nederveen Pieterse, 1992

In his *Notes on Virginia* (1786), he [Jefferson] set down his reasons for believing that the Negro is condemned by nature to an inferior status.

U. S. President: Thomas Jefferson, 1786 as cited in *White on Black, Images of Africa and Blacks in Western Popular Culture*, Jan Nederveen Pieterse, 1992

Charles S. Coon attributed Black inferiority to the fact that Blacks were a newer, less evolved race…

Scientist: Charles S. Coon, as cited by Larry A. Greene in Telos magazine, (December 1996)

To Nathaniel Southgate Shaler, Blacks were an 'alien folk' deserving of disenfranchisement and dispersal over the U. S. to avoid burdening any one section.

Professor: Southgate Shaler, dean of the Lawrence School at Harvard, "the Negro Problem," *Atlantic*, 1884

…In 1798, Secretary of War Henry Knox specifically pro-hibited ' Negroes, Mulattos, and Indians' from joining the marines (a ban that lasted, amazingly, until 1942)…

Secretary of War: Henry Knox, 1798 as cited in *Black Profiles in Courage*, Kareem Abdul Jabbar and Alan Steinberg, 1996

"Inferior" Physical Characteristics

…the Negro was anatomically much closer to the ape than the White.

Professor: Dr. S. T. von Sommerring, a German professor of med-icine as reported in William Stanton's, *The Leopard's Spots: Scientific Attitudes Toward Race in America, 1815-1859*, 1960

Orang-Outangs [monkeys] did not seem at all inferior in the intellectual faculties to many of the Negro race …

Author: Edward Long in his book *Essay Concerning Human Understanding*

Innately "Inferior" ???

By the end of the 18th century, Charles White could write that Blacks were an intermediate species between Whites and apes…

Doctor: Charles White, advocate of the polygenic origin [of man] theory, as reported in Larry A. Greene's review of the book, "The Bell Curve Debate: History, Documents, Origins," edited by Russell Jacoby and Naomi Glauberman in Telos magazine, (December 1996) White supremacy can come in many forms. Here is one of its most direct and basic representations.

Athletics Director: Charles Cavagnaro statement made on UNLV's campus at a staff meeting quoted by a Las Vegas television station and newspaper from unnamed sources as reported in *Jet* magazine, (June 15, 1998)

Charles Cavagnaro, athletics director, at the University of Nevada, Las Vegas called Black Football players 'monkeys' and 'apes.'

Karen Stevenson, the first Black woman to win the so-called "Rhodes Scholar" award, reported that while in Russia a Soviet citizen was shocked to find out that she was attending a university. He called her 'a sub-species.' Someone else on the streets of Russia called her 'a monkey'.

Rhodes Scholar: Karen Stevenson as reported in *Ebony* Magazine, (December 1979)

It is clear that the scoundrel, the ape, the beast, the Black man are near equivalents in the minds of the men who were fighting to free the slaves as well as to save the Union.

Author: M. Fabre 'Popular Civil War propaganda: the case of patriotic covers.' *Journal of American culture*, summer, 1980 as cited in *White on Black, Images of Africa and Blacks in Western Popular Culture*, Jan Nederveen Pieterse, 1992

White argues, occupy a different 'station' on the chain from the Whites. in his opinion, the Negro is an intermediate species between the White man and the ape.

Doctor: Charles White as cited in *Race, The History of an Idea in America*, Thomas F. Gossett, 1963

The lips of rapists and murderers he [Lombrosos] found to be 'fleshy, swollen and protruding as in negroes.' The teeth were usually huge, irregular, and far apart, as in gorillas and orang-utans...He found the upper limbs of criminals generally longer, 'ape-like character.' The palms were prone to have simian creases, the toes farther apart, as in apes that use the toes for climbing trees, and the 'the foot is often flat, as the Negroes'.

Author: M. Fabre 'Popular Civil War propaganda: the case of patriotic covers.' *Journal of American culture*, summer, 1980 as cited in *White on Black, Images of Africa and Blacks in Western Popular Culture*, Jan Nederveen Pieterse, 1992

Negroes, says White, are closer to apes than they are to White Europeans. 'In whatever respect the African differs from the Europeans,' he declares, 'the particularity brings him nearer to the ape.'

Doctor: Charles White as cited in Race, The History of an Idea in America, Thomas F. Gossett, 1963

Jefferson argues, first of all, that the Negro is ugly, he asks whether the blushes, those 'fine mixtures of red and White,' which lend to the 'expressions of every passion' in the White race are not superior to the 'eternal monotony, - that immovable veil of Black which covers the emotions of the other race?' In addition, the Negroes have 'a very strong and disagreeable odor.' The 'flowing hair' and 'more elegant symmetry of form, says Jefferson, convinces the Negroes themselves that the Whites are more beautiful.

U. S. President: Thomas Jefferson, *Notes on Virginia*, 1786 as cited in *Race, The History of an Idea in America*, Thomas F. Gossett, 1963

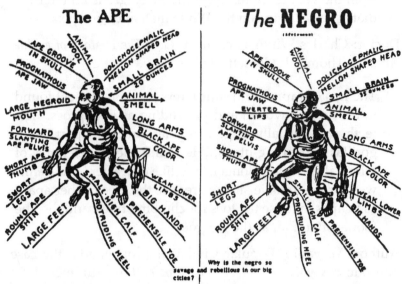

Scientists Say Negro Still In Ape Stage

Races Positively Not Equal

OFFBASE

BLACKS ENRAGED BY MONKEY BUSINESS AT AT&T

A drawing that used a monkey to depict Africans, while characters from other countries were represented by humans, has focused attention on the fragile relationship between African-Americans and corporate America. The illustration, published in the September issue of *Focus*, AT&T's employee magazine, draws attention to the racial insensitivity that often exists beneath the veneer of model corporate diversity.

In October, faced with demonstrations at its Manhattan headquarters and the ire of many of its own employees, AT&T folded the magazine. A month earlier, the magazine's staff issued an internal memo of apology and ended its relationship with Michael Moran, the Madison, N.J., freelance illustrator who did the work.

In the aftermath of the scandal, AT&T has pledged to redouble its efforts to make workers more sensitive to race and gender issues. After meeting with executive director Benjamin F. Chavis Jr. and other NAACP officials, AT&T chairman and CEO Robert E. Allen sent a letter to all employees announcing a new push for company-wide diversity. Allen also met with Southern Christian Leadership Conference president Joseph Lowery and the Congressional Black Caucus.

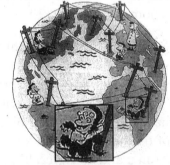

Most observers consider these responses consistent with AT&T's record of commitment to diversity. Nearly 15% of the company's workers and 8.6% of its managers in the United States are black. And AT&T is one of the few major corporations that did not lose a disproportionate share of black employees during recent job cuts, according to a *Wall Street Journal* analysis of Equal Employment Opportunity Commission records (see "Gee, Blacks Really Did Lose More Jobs" below). But what alarms many observers is this: If this can happen at AT&T, which was cited as one of BE's "Best Places For Blacks To Work" (cover story, Feb. 1992), what can African-Americans expect from the rest of corporate America?   —A.E. Jr.

"Natural" Enslavement

God has put into every White man's hand a whip to flog the Black man.

Essayist-Historian: Thomas Carole

A Black skin means membership in a race of men which has never created a civilization of any kind. There is something natural in the subordination of an inferior race even to the point of enslavement of the inferior race…

Scholar: John Burgess, respected as the dean of academic scholars, *The Slant of the Pen* (Racism in Children, Books), edited by Roy Preiswerk

It is race, is it not? That puts the hundred millions of India under the dominion of a remote island in the north of Europe. Race avails much, if that be true, which is alleged, that all Celts are Catholics, and all Saxons are Protestants; that Celts love unity of power, and Saxons the representative principle. Race is a controlling influence in the Jew, who for two millenniums, under every climate, has preserved the same character and employments. Race in the negro is of appalling importance.

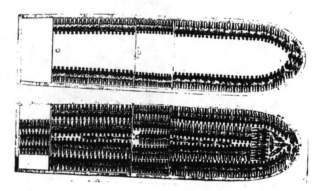

Slave ships

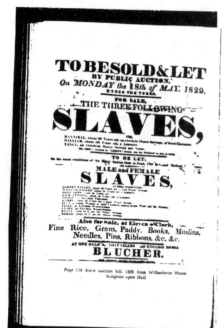

Posters offering slaves for sale

Author: Ralph Waldo Emerson, a famous and well-known American writer, *English Traits*, 1903

Documents proved that in the free states" the condition of the African, instead of being improved,' had become worse...In the states which had 'retained the ancient relation' between the races, Negroes had 'improved greatly in every respect—in number, comfort, intelligence, and morals...In short, slavery was necessary to preserve the Negro race and the annexation of Texas necessary to preserve slavery.

Politician: Secretary John C. Calhoun, as reported in William Stanton's, *The Leopard's Spots: Scientific Attitudes Toward Race in America, 1815-1859*, 1960

Anyone could easily see that the Negro was not the White's equal, and almost everyone did.

Scientist: Professor Samuel G. Morton, a professor of anatomy and author of Crania Americana as reported in *William Stanton's, The Leopard's Spots: Scientific Attitudes Toward Race in America, 1815-1859*, 1960

Let White Men rule!

The struggle for life and the survival of the fittest were 'applicable to the races of men also. The destiny of weaker varieties was either extinction…or else…relegation to a subordinate place in the economy of nature.'

Scientist: Joseph le Conte, "The Race Problem in the South," from the book, *The Black Image in the Mind* by George M. Fredrickson, 1971

'The personnel crisis.'
Caption: 'The true maid. Batoualette, very practical ashtray during drinks.'
Fantasio, 1 Nov. 1929

It's not that their dedication is less. In fact it's greater. They lack the intellectual capacity to succeed, and it's taking them down the tubes…one of the best things (slave traders) did for you was to drag your ancestors over here in chains.

Chairman: William K. Coors, former chairman of Adolph Coors Brewing Co., as told to a group of minority business owners attending a seminar (*Jet* magazine, April 19, 1984)

The Negro deprived of the support of stronger races he still relapses into savagery…

Professor: Franklin Henry Giddings of Columbia University, from the book *The Black Image in the White Mind* by George M. Fredrickson, 1971

In 1725 James Houston, a physician for the royal Africa Company on the West African coast, wrote in his notebook: 'their natural Temper is barbarously cruel...As for their Customs they exactly resemble their Fellow Creatures and Natives, the Monkeys.'

Doctor: J. Houston, *Some new and accurate observations...of the Coast of Guinea...for the advantage of Great Britain in general, and the Royal African Company in particular*, 1725

The most of them are as near beasts as may be, setting their souls aside.

Author: Richard Ligon who wrote of the slaves in Barbados in 1657

The cause of humanity would be far more beneficial by the (African slave) trade and servitude regulated and reformed, than by the total destruction of both or either.

Political theorist: Edmund Burke, *Works of,* 1866

Charles Lyell, who had recently paid him a visit in Mobile during his second tour of the United States, had expressed the opinion that through slavery the Negro could be civilized and perhaps even 'brought up to the Caucasian standard.'

Scientist: Charles Lyell, author of the *Principles of Geology,* expressed this view to Dr. J. C. Nott in 1847

The Negro race was a race of children. It was the duty of the South to protect them faithfully from the ravages of a freedom they were not equipped to endure.

Scholar: De Bow, "Nature and Destiny of the Negro," *Review X,* 1851

...the Secretary added that 'so far from bettering' the condition of the African race, changing the relation between the races of the South would 'render it far worse.' To the African, freedom would be 'a curse instead of a blessing.'

Politician: Secretary John C. Calhoun, as reported in *William Stanton's, The Leopard's Spots: Scientific Attitudes Toward Race in America, 1815-1859,* 1960

Samuel Cartwright found Black flight from plantations not to be an indication of discontent but a disease:

'drapetomania,' which drove them to seek freedom.

Scientist: Samuel Cartwright as cited in Larry A. Greene's review of the book, *The Bell Curve Debate: History, Documents, Origins,* edited by Russell Jacoby and Naomi Glauberman in *Telos* magazine, (December 1996)

He remarked that statistics on insanity from the census had been published in America and in Europe and that 'throughout the civilized world' word had gone forth that, according to American experience, slavery was 'more than ten-fold more favorable to mental health than freedom.' Slaves were consoled with the assurance that though they were denied liberty, they were 'not bound with insane delusions, nor cursed in idiocy' as their free brethren were.

Doctor: Dr. Edward Jarvis' statement that was published in the American Journal of the Medical Sciences, 1843 as reported in *William Stanton's, The Leopard's Spots: Scientific Attitudes Toward Race in America, 1815-1859,* 1960

This book says Black people are stupid!

The "Inferior" Black Race

E. L. Thorndike, one of the pioneers of mental testing, explained that 'the apparent mental attainments of children of inferior races may be due to lack of inhibition and so witness precisely to a deficiency in mental growth.

Scientist: E. L. Thorndike, a pioneer of mental testing, *Educational Psychology,* 1903 as cited in *Race, The History of an Idea in America,* Thomas F. Gossett, 1963

The minds of primitive races had all the limitations of the minds of children, except that their childhood of intellect was permanent.

Social Scientist: Herbert Spencer, a legendary social scientist in the field of sociology, "The Comparative Psychology of Man, Read Before the Anthropological Institute, June 22, 1875," in *Essays: Scientific, Political, and Speculative,* (3rd ed., 3 vols.; London, 1878

Primitive races, he declared, were in an early evolutionary stage, something like that of an arrested childhood.

They should thus be given tender and sympathetic treatment by their...elders.

Professor: G. Stanley Hall, founded the *American Journal of Psychology, Adolescence,* 1904

Jung writes: 'he [the Black] reminds us – in not so much our conscious but our unconscious mind – not only of childhood but of our prehistory, which would take us back not more than twelve hundred years so far as the Germanic races are concerned.'

Psychologist: C. G. Jung, a legendary psychoanalyst of the West

Both scientific and popular thought supported the view that Whites were civilized and rational, while members of other races were savage, irrational, and sensual.

J. D'Emilio and E. B. Freedman, *Intimate matters: A history of sexuality in America,* 1989

Thomas Nelson Page, stated his opinions more calmly but had a similar low opinion of Negroes. He maintained that 'the negroes *as a race* have never exhibited any capacity to advance that as a race they are inferior'.

Author: Thomas Nelson Page, "The Negro Problem," *Atlantic Monthly,* LIV, 1884

'The civilization that we as White secreted in Europe and America' could not have developed apart from the genetic endowments of the creating people.'

Political Advisor: Sam Francis, longtime friend and informal adviser to Pat Buchanan, explanation of the basis of the European cultural achievement as reported by Larry A. Greene, *Telos* magazine, (December 1996)

...in view of the Black's laws advanced civilization, of the Black man's being a child, especially a Child of Nature – affectionate, spontaneous, with sometimes the capricious and somehow innocent cruelty of children.

Scientist: Sandra Gilman, *Racial Stereotypes,* 1964

The "Superior" white race
[THE SUPERIORITY OF THE WHITE EUROPEAN RACE IN INTELLIGENCE & CIVILIZATION]

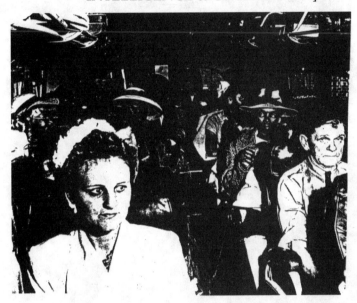

"Inferiors " to the back of the bus

"Superiors: to the front

We come among the Africans as members of a superior race and servants of a government that desires to elevate the more degraded portions of the human family.

Doctor: Dr. Livingston of the famous statement, "Dr. Livingston, I presume," Elpseth Husley, *Livingston* 1974

It is European techniques, European examples, and European ideas, which have shaken the non-European world out of its past out of barbarism in Africa.

Professor: Hugh Trevor-Roper, *The Rise of Christian Europe* (Thames & Hudson, London, 1966)

Europe is the light of the world and the ark of knowledge: upon the welfare of Europe, hangs the destiny of the most remote and savage people.

Historians: P. J. Marshall, and G. Williams, *the Great Map of mankind: British perception of the world in the age of Enlightenment*, London, 1982.

Let White Men Rule!

Osborn attributed nearly all of mankind's achievements to the Nordic race. The 'Nordic tide which flowed into Italy' produced Raphael, Leonardo da Vinci, Galileo, Titian, Giotto, Donatello, Botticelli, Andrea del Satro, Petrarch, and Tasso.

Scientist: Dr. Henry Fairfield Osborn, paleontologist and president of the American Museum of Natural History, 1908 as cited in *Race, The History of an Idea in America,* Thomas F. Gossett, 1963

> I am sure that no one who has had the privilege of mixing in the society of the abler men of any great capital, or who is acquainted with the biographies of the heroes of history…can doubt the existence of grand human animals, of natures pre-eminently noble, of individuals born to be kings of men.

Scientist: Francis Galton, early leader of the "eugenics" movement, coined the word "nature and nurture," *Hereditary Genius: an Inquiry into Its laws and Consequences* (rev. ed., 1891) as quoted in *Race*

> …the superiority of a race cannot be preserved without pride of blood and an uncompromising attitude toward the lower races.

Author: Ross, "The Cause of Race, Superiority; Annals, American Academy, Political and Social Science," XVIII, July 1901 as cited in *Race, The History of an Idea in America,* Thomas F. Gossett, 1963

> Race is everything. Literature, science, art, in a word, civilization, depend on it.

Professor: Dr, Robert Knox, a professor of anatomy at Edinburgh College of Surgeons, *The Races of Men: A Fragment,* 1850

> Africa, earth's second-largest continent, contains…just under 750 million people … with about one-third of this number descended from Hamites and Semites, who are part of the "White race." The early history of Africa is concerned only with the Hamitic and Semitic peoples. Though the Negro, the Bushman and the Hottentot also lived on the continent, they did to step upon the stage of history until their relatively recent discovery by Europeans. As such the history of Africa remains chiefly the purview of the "White" (Caucasoid) man.

Zoologist: Robert E. Kuttner, "A Short History of the Peoples of Africa," *The Barnes Review,* January/February 1999

"Inferior" Black "Civilization"

It will be seen that, when we classify mankind by color, the only primary race that has not made a creative contribution to any civilizations is the Black Race.

Historian: Arnold Toynbee, *A Short of History*, 1934

I am apt to suspect the negroes...to be naturally inferior to the White. There never was a civilized nation of any other complexion than White, nor even any individual eminent either in action or speculation. No ingenious manufactures amongst them, no arts, no sciences...

Philosopher: David Hume, *Essays and Treatises on several subjects*, London: 1753

...in England...the child can demonstrate to you that a negro is not a man...

Philosopher: John Locke in his work, *An Essay concerning Human Understanding*

[Negroes are]...incapable of contemplating any objective entity such as God or Law...Nothing remotely human is to be found in their [the Negroes'] character. Extensive reports by missionaries confirm this and Mohammedanism seems to be the only thing which can, in some measure, bring them nearer to a civilized condition.

Philosopher: Hegel as quoted by Robin Horton and Ruth Finnegan eds. from *Hegel Senstuttgut*, 1961

...no other people other than Caucasians had ever developed a great civilization...

Scientist: Professor Samuel G. Morton, a professor of anatomy and author of Crania Americana as reported in William Stanton's, *The Leopard's Spots: Scientific Attitudes Toward Race in America, 1815-1859*

Almost all civilized peoples belong to the White race. The people of other races have remained savage or barbarian, like the men of prehistoric times.

Professor: Charles Seignobos, University of Paris, *History of Ancient Civilization*

Chambers argues that man began as a Negro, passed through Malay, Indian, and Mongolian phases, and finally emerged as a Caucasian. 'The leading characters...of the various races of mankind are simply representations of the development of the highest, or Caucasian type.

Scholar: Robert Chambers, Vestiges of the Natural History of Creation, 1844

However long man has been on earth, he argued, "we know nothing beyond his modern history, commencing with that of Egypt." In this period, the Negro had created no civilization, had always been a slave.

Doctor: Dr. Josiah Clark expressed to General O. O. Howard, superintendent of the Freedman's Bureau, 1866

Images of the World from the point of view of European boy's adventures.
Drawing by Hans Borrebach, The Hague, 1950's.

In no area were Caucasians in debt to Negro contributions. In instances when Hamites were engulfed by large Negro tribes, the mixed products were considered inferior by the purer Hamites...

Scientist: Robert E. Kuttner, "A Short History of the Peoples of Africa," *The Barnes Review*, January/February 1999

[Dr. White professed] one of the earliest, and surely the most amiable, of the innumerable paeans to the 'White European,' the Caucasian, the Aryan, the Teuton, that these groups, lost in admiring wonder at their own magnificent gifts, have crooned to themselves over the last two centuries. None would doubt the White European's intellectual magnificence—surely superior to that of 'every other man,' he intoned.

Where else shall we find, he asked, that nobly arched head, containing such a quantity of brain...? Where that variety of features, and fullness of expression; those long, flowing, graceful ring-lets; that majestic beard, those rosy cheeks and coral lips? Where that...noble gait? On what other quarter of the globe shall we find the blush that overspreads those soft features of the beautiful women of Europe, that emblem of modesty, of delicate feelings...?

Doctor: Dr. Charles White, a prominent surgeon, as reported in William Stanton's, The Leopard's Spots: Scientific Attitudes Toward Race in America, 1815-1859, 1960

Superior White [European] Civilization

...no other people other than Caucasians had ever developed a great civilization...

Scientist: Professor Samuel G. Morton, a professor of anatomy and author of Crania Americana as reported in *William Stanton's, The Leopard's Spots: Scientific Attitudes Toward Race in America, 1815-1859*, 1960

Almost all civilized peoples belong to the White race. The people of other races have remained savage or barbarian, like the men of prehistoric times.

Professor: Charles Seignobos, University of Paris, *History of Ancient Civilization*

If Africa was the cradle of mankind, it was only an indifferent kindergarten. Europe and Asia were our principal schools.

Professor: Charles Coon, University of Pennsylvania, *The Origin of Races*

'The civilization that we as White secreted in Europe and America could not have developed apart from the genetic endowments of the creating people.'

Political Advisor: Sam Francis, longtime friend and informal adviser to Pat Buchanan, explanation of the basis of the European cultural achievement as reported by Larry A. Greene, *Telos* magazine, (December 1996)

The Negro race was a race of children. It was the duty of the South to protect them faithfully from the ravages of a freedom they were not equipped to endure.

Scholar: De Bow, "Nature and Destiny of the Negro," *Review X*, 1851

[Dr. White professed] one of the earliest, and surely the most amiable, of the innumerable paeans to the 'White European,' the Caucasian, the Aryan, the Teuton, that these groups, lost in admiring wonder at their own magnificent gifts, have crooned to themselves over the last two centuries. None would doubt the White European's intellectual magnificence—surely superior to that of 'every other man,' he intoned.

Where else shall we find, he asked, that nobly arched head, containing such a quantity of brain...? Where that variety of features, and fullness of expression; those long, flowing, graceful ring-lets; that majestic beard, those rosy cheeks and coral lips? Where that...noble gait? On what other quarter of the globe shall we find the blush that overspreads [those] soft features of the beautiful women of Europe, that emblem of modesty, of delicate feelings...?

Doctor: Dr. Charles White, a prominent surgeon, as reported in *William Stanton's, The Leopard's Spots: Scientific Attitudes Toward Race in American, 1815-1859*, 1960

[The] 'structure of the European, whatever...the cause,' was 'superior' to that of the other races of men, or, at least 'farther removed for the brute creation.' He rested his proof on the differences between the European and the African, because these races, [occupy] 'opposites extremes of the scale...'

Professor: Dr. John Augustine Smith, lecturer in anatomy and surgery in the College of Physicians and Surgeons of the University of New York

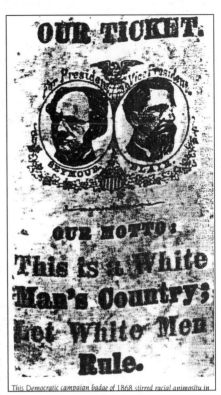

This Democratic campaign badge of 1868 stirred racial animosity in

This Democratic campaign badge of 1868 stirred racial animosity in the North (New York Public Library, Schomberg center for Research in Black Culture

"Inferior" Intelligence

> The African race is greatly inferior to the Caucasian in general intellectual [capacity]…

Journalist: Theodore Parker, for the book *John Weiss, Life and Correspondence of Theodore Parker*, New York 1864

> Having demonstrated that the negro and the Caucasian are widely different in characteristics, due to a deficiency in the negro Brain, a deficiency that is hereditary … we are forced to conclude that it is useless to try to elevate the Negro by education or otherwise.

Doctor: Dr. Robert Bennett Bean, "Some Racial Peculiarities of the Negro Brain." *American Journal of Anatomy*, September 1906

> We may concede it as a matter of a fact that (the Negro race) is inferior…

Congressman: Owen Lovejoy, 1860

> The negro is not the equal of the White man…

Congressman: Representative James Brooks of New York from a speech delivered in December 18, 1867

OTHERS TAKE THEIR HISTORY SERIOUSLY . WHY DON'T WE?

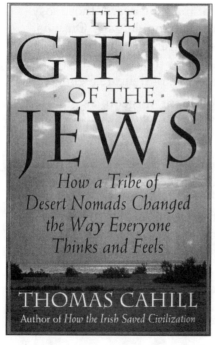

Scientific Racism

[Inferior Intelligence]

The Black variety is the lowest and lies at the bottom of the ladder. The animal character lent to its basic form imposes its destiny from the moment of conception. It never leaves the most restricted intellectual zones…its faculties for thinking are mediocre or even nonexistent…

Scientist: J. Arthur de Gobineau, Oeuvres, 1983

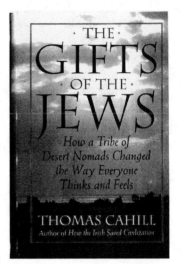

[Negroes were]…in reason much inferior,' and 'in imagination they are dull, tasteless, and anomalous.'

U. S. President: Thomas Jefferson, *Notes on Virginia*, 1786 as cited in *Race, The History of an Idea in America*, Thomas F. Gossett, 1963

In his *Observation on the Feeling of the Beautiful and Sublime* (1764), Kant elaborates on Hume's essay in section 4, entitled "Of National Characteristics, So Far As They Depend upon the Distinct Feeling of the Beautiful and Sublime." Kant first claims that 'so fundamental is the difference between [the Black and White] races of man …it appears to be as great in regard to mental capacities as in color.

Philosopher: Emmanuel Kant, legendary philosopher, as cited *Race, Writing and Differences* by Louis Gates Jr.

Rushton believes Blacks are genetically programmed to be of low intelligence, high criminality, and hyper-sexuality.

Professor: Professor Rushton Ontario University, as quoted by Larry A. Greene in *Telos* magazine, (December 1996)

Whites are more intelligent than Negroes; intelligence is overwhelmingly the result of genetic inheritance rather than environmental influence…

Scientist: Professor A. R. Jensen, a noted University of California at Berkeley psychologist, as reported in the *Saturday Review* magazine (May 17, 1969) entitled, "Race and Intelligence: The findings of R. Jensen by J. Cass

Since [the] negro intelligence is naturally…low…let's give Blacks cash incentives not to breed.

Professor: William Shockley of Stanford University, a Nobel prize winner in physics, as reported in the *National Review* magazine (December 7, 1973) entitled, "Lesser Breeds."

> On the problems of Black people, Jensen fretted about..."the genetic enslavement of a substantial segment of our population."

Professor: Professor Leon J. Kamin reported on A. R. Jensen's work in the *New York Times* Book Review, June 9, 1985

> I do not see why people should have the right to have children... if one did have a licensing scheme the first child might be admitted on rather easy terms. If the parents were genetically unfavorable, they might be allowed to have only one child ... that seems to me the sort of practical problem that is raised by our new knowledge of biology.

Scientist: Nobel Prize winner, Francis H. C. Crick as reported by Professor Daniel J. Kevles, a science historian at California Institute of Technology, in the book *In the Name of Eugenics*

> 'Blacks... are not academically competitive with Whites in selective institutions, ' ...failure is not looked upon with disgrace.'

Professor: Texas Professor Lino Graglia who argued that the university should drop affirmative action, as reported by Scott Baldauf in the *Christian Science Monitor* (September 9, 1997, Vol. 89 Issue 206)

> [Blacks] scorn...hard work and academic achievement...despite substantial progress over the past few decades [Blacks] continue to show conspicuous evidence of ...failure in schools and college

Author Dinesh D'Souza, *The End of Racism*, 1995

> In a highly developed information society and a highly educated society such as Japan, the people require politics that bravely faces problems. In the United States, because there are a considerable number of Blacks...the (intellectual) level is low.

Japanese Prime Minister: Yasuhiro Nakasone, the Prime Minister, made this statement that was quoted in two Japanese newspapers, the Yomiuri Shimbun and Tokyo Shimbun, as reported in the *New York Times* (September 24, 1988)

Because they were incapable of higher education, their schools should be limited to instruction in the lower trades, since 'as a race they are capable of taking pride in handiwork.

Scholar: cited in *Race, The History of an Idea in America*, Thomas F. Gossett, 1963

In 1856, Gratiolet in France advanced the theory that in Negroes the coronal suture of the skull closes at an early age, gripping the brain in a prison and arresting its growth. For this reason, although young Negro children are as intelligent as White children, at the age of thirteen or fourteen they begin to fall behind because their skulls prevent their intellectual development.

Scholar: Gratiolet in *Race, The History of an Idea in America*, Thomas F. Gossett, 1963

Louis Agassiz, Harvard's eminent naturalist, confirmed Morton's general claim by declaring that development of the brain of an adult Negro 'never gets beyond that observable in the Caucasian in boyhood.

Scientist: Professor Louis Agassiz, professor of natural history at Neuchâtel, from a lecture given in Charleston, 1848 as cited John Hope Franklin

Having demonstrated that the negro and the Caucasian are widely different in characteristics, due to a deficiency in the negro Brain, a deficiency that is hereditary ... we are forced to conclude that it is useless to try to elevate the Negro by education or otherwise.

Doctor: Dr. Robert Bennett Bean, "Some Racial Peculiarities of the Negro Brain." *American Journal of Anatomy*, September 1906

Gladden sympathizes with a White southern educator who speaks of the 'unexampled difficulties' of educating the 'morally undeveloped' Negroes who are 'a race, a thousand years behind...'

Scholar: Professor Gladden cited in *Race, The History of an Idea in America*, Thomas F. Gossett, 1963

Extermination

If a race has no history, if it has no worthwhile tradition it becomes a negligible factor in the thought of the world, and it stands in danger of being exterminated.

Historian: Carter G. Woodson

New York Times, December 8, 1999

1,000 Rally to Condemn Shooting of Unarmed Man by Police"

Armadou Diallo ...from Guinea, West Africa...never been in trouble with the law...unarmed when died...'41 bullets'...'four officers... everyone interviewed said they believed that the police officers had judged Mr. Diallo as a criminal because of the color of his skin.' "

THE VIOLENT REBIRTH OF THE KLAN

Bill Wilkinson (center, at Klan rally in Alabama) is leader of the K.K.K.'s most notorious branch.

At some future period, not very distant as measured by centuries, the civilized races of man will almost certainly replace the savage races throughout the world.

Scientist: Charles Darwin, *The Descent of Man*, 1871

We should so far yield to the evident designs and purposes of Providence,' as to be both willing and anxious to see the negroes, like the Indians and all other effete and dingy-hued races, gradually exterminated from the face of the whole earth.

Author: Hinton R. Helper, author of *Nojoque*, 1867

Professor R. B. Cartell...concludes that savages, including the whole Negro race, should on account of their low mentality and unpleasant nature, be painlessly exterminated.

Professor: B. Cartell, transmitted by Lord Raglan, *The Origin of Civilization*

Benjamin Franklin later expressed a rather similar idea, declaring in this Autobiography that rum was 'the appointed means' of fulfilling 'the design of Providence to extirpate these savages in order to make room for the cultivators of the earth.'

Revolutionary Figure: Benjamin Franklin, *The Autobiography of Benjamin Franklin: A Restoration of a "Fair Copy"* by Max Farrand, 1949

According to Karl and Frederick Hoffman, the ultimate end for Blacks, who were the least evolved and least able to survive in the racial struggle for existence, was extinction.

Scholars: Karl and Frederick Hoffman as quoted by Larry A. Greene in *Telos* magazine, (December 1996)

All things point to the fact that the Negro as a race is reverting to barbarism with the inordinate criminality and degradation of that state. It seems, moreover, that he is doomed at no distant day to ultimate extinction.

Professor: Paul B. Barringer, Chairmen at University of Virginia who made this prediction at a conference in 1970

What progress the Negro had made he showed to the discipline of slavery. As a free man, the Negro showed a strong tendency, which was probably ineradicable, to return to his naturally savage state. Convinced that the Negroes were a dying race, Shaler recommended that they be scattered over the United States...

Professor: Southgate Shaler, dean of the Lawrence School at Harvard, "the Negro Problem" *Atlantic*, 1884

White Police Accused Of Sexually Brutalizing Black Man With Toilet Plunger

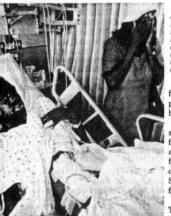

◄ Abner Louima lays hand-cuffed to his bed at Coney Island Hospital in New York as his wife, Micheline, stands by his bedside. Louima says police officers beat and sodomized him while in custody at a Brooklyn, NY, police station after he was arrested outside a nightclub.

▲ New York Police Officers (l-r) Justin Volpe, Thomas Bruder and Thomas Wiese were arrested and charged in connection with the sexual brutal attack of a Haitian immigrant in New York.

A Haitian immigrant who was arrested in a nightclub fight in New York accused White officers of taking him into a station house bathroom and sexually brutalizing him with the handle of a toilet plunger.

"They said, 'Take this, nigger,' and stuck the stick in my rear end," said 30-year-old Abner Louima in an interview from the hospital, where he was listed in critical condition after surgery to repair a puncture in his small intestine and an injury to his bladder.

The investigation into Louima's arrest intensified after doctors confirmed that the injuries appeared to have been caused by a blunt instrument.

Officer Justin Volpe, 25, surrendered to internal affairs and was charged with aggravated sexual abuse and first degree assault, police officials said. Officer Charles Schwarz was charged with first degree assault.

Also arrested were Officers Thomas Bruder and Thomas Wiese, who were each charged with assault and criminal possession of a weapon—a police radio with which he and Wiese allegedly beat Louima in their patrol car.

The NY Daily News reported that Louima identified two of the officers from photographs shown to him in his hospital bed.

"The alleged conduct involved is reprehensible, done by anyone at anytime," said Mayor Rudolph Giuliani. "Allegedly done by police officers, it's even more reprehensible."

Louima was one of two men who police said interfered with officers trying to break up a fight between two women outside a nightclub called Club Rendez-Vous in Brooklyn, NY. Both men were arrested on charges of assault, resisting arrest, disorderly conduct and obstructing justice. The charges against Louima have since been dropped.

Louima told the Daily News that the trouble began when he was handcuffed and put in a patrol car. When he protested, officers kicked him and beat him with police radios, he said.

Louima said at the 70th Precinct stationhouse in Brooklyn, officers pulled down his pants and led him to the bathroom, where they sodomized him with the plunger and then jammed the handle in his mouth. An ambulance took him to the hospital.

Louima says he plans to file a civil lawsuit against the city.

12

Upon meeting the states and people that favor this equality and amalgamation of the White and Black races, God will exterminate.... A man can not commit so great an offense against his race, against his country, against his God... as to give his daughter in marriage to a negro—a beast...

Publisher: Buckner H. Payne, *The Negro: What is His Ethnological Status*, 1867 on in 1848. See his "Nigger Question" written in 1849

There is nothing in the gradual diminution and destruction of a savage or inferior race in contact with a more civilized ... which is mysterious...The first gifts of civilization are naturally fatal to a barbarous [people]...

Philanthropist: Charles Loring Brace, *The Races of the Old World: A Manual of Ethnology*, New York, 1870

> If you should meet with a man who should say… that all men ought to have an equal chance to do the best they can for themselves on earth, then you might ask them whether he thought the Bushmen, Hottentots, or Australians were equal to the best educated and most cultivate White men. He would have to admit that he was not thinking of them at all.

Professor: William Graham Sumner, a professor of political science at Yale University and one of the founders of American sociology, *The Challenge of Facts and other Essays*, 1914

> If a nation with a more advanced, more specialized, or in any superior set of genes mingles with, instead of extermination, an inferior tribe, then commits racial suicide…[Without] elimination of the unfit, evolution amongst the higher forms does not, in fact, take place…

Scholar: Robert Pearson, a well-known eugenicist

> This would be a great land if only every Irishman would kill a Negro, and be hanged for it. I find this sentiment generally approved – sometimes with the qualification that they want Irish and negroes for servants, not being able to get any other…

Scholar: *Race, The History of an Idea in America*, Thomas F. Gossett, 1963

> It was Kidd's thesis that the Anglo-Saxon race, though it was the most profoundly altruistic of all the races, had a degenerating effect on the inferior races with which it came into contact. When confronted with the Anglo-Saxons, the inferior races tended naturally to die off. Nothing could stay this mighty law, this 'destiny which works itself out irresistible.' Whatever the Anglo-Saxons might intend, 'the weaker races disappear before the stronger through the effects of mere contact.'

Scholar: Benjamin Kidd, *Social Evolution*, 1894

WHAT AFRICA HAS CONTRIBUTED TO CIVILIZATION/MANKIND

CREATORS OF
THE HUMAN RACE
[The African Origins of Man]

The first Man and the first Woman were Black.

Newsweek magazine in an article entitled, "African Dreams," (September 23, 1991) informed us that:

"...scientific evidence...has been clear on

THE AFRICAN ORIGIN'S OF HUMANITY SINCE THE 1970's ..."

"In 1994, Cavil-Sforza, along with Paolo Menozzi and Albert Piazzas, published his magnum opus, *The History and Geography of Human Genes* - a sort of combination atlas and family tree. Cavalli-Sforza's genealogy **places Africans at the root of the tree**, with the **Europeans and Asians branching off from them...**"

"Mapping the Past," *Civilization*, Mar-Apr., 1996, p. 44

Michael Wood, the host of the television series *Legacy* calls

"...Africa the heartland of humanity"

"Scientists claim to have found **our common ancestor**—a woman who lived 200,000 years ago and left resilient genes that are **carried by all of mankind.**

Scientists are calling her *Eve*...

was more likely a dark-haired,

Black-skinned woman..."

Newsweek, "The Search for Adam & Eve," January 11, 1988

The New York Times in an article entitled. "Modern Man's Origin Linked To A Single Female Ancestor," on March 26, 1988 reported that:

"Calculations of the slow changes that have taken place in human DNA over the millennia indicate that

everyone alive today may be a descendant of a

single female ancestor who lived in Africa

140,000 to 280,000 years ago, scientists at the University at Berkeley have reported. The studies, led by Dr. Allan C. Wilson, support the view that modern man,

Homo sapiens, originated in Africa

about 200,000 years ago and later spread throughout the rest of the world.

Similarly, in the scientific magazine *Nature* (February 1986, Vol. 319, p. 493) this team of scientists primarily from Oxford University, Oxford cited C. Stringer's work, *Hominid Evolution* (Academic, N. Y. 1984, p. 55-83) in this way:

"The earliest fossils of...modern man (Homo sapiens) have been found in Africa at Omo in Ethiopia, Border Cave in **South Africa** and at Klasies River Mouth in South Africa."

In *Science* magazine (February 17, 1986) there is an article entitled *"Chromosome maps prove the origins of race"* which begin with this paragraph:

How did mankind develop into the dozens of races we know today? Fossil evidence indicates that

Homo sapiens [modern man]

started off in Africa,

and then spread into Europe Asia and the Americas...

On the front page of the Science section in the *New York Times* (Tuesday, October 30, 1984), John Wilford reports on the "Towering Reputation" of the famed scientific family—the Leakeys.

"The name Leakey is synonymous with the study of human origins." (Paleoanthropology). "They discovered and named the origin of bones of the first human tool-makers, Homo habilis, and dug up the most complete skeleton of a more recent ancestor, Homo erectus."

He credits them with this outstanding achievement:

"They proved beyond doubt
the African Origins of Man"

Dr. David W. Phillipson (Glasgow Museum and Art Galleries), Dr. Laural Phillipson wrote in *The Cambridge Encyclopedia of Africa* that:

The idea that humans first evolved in Africa is as old as the idea that they have evolved at all.

In 1871, Charles Darwin wrote, in the *Descent of Man*,

> it is somewhat more probable that our early progenitors lived on the African continent than elsewhere.

Cambridge University Cambridge, London 1981

As one writer puts it:

> "In this field, a person kicks over a stone in Africa, and we have to rewrite the textbooks."

"Bones subsequently discovered **in Africa** are believed to be from modern humans living there about 100,000 years ago. These bones ...

represent the earliest known modern humans.

> Before their discovery it was assumed that modern humans didn't evolve until 35,000 years ago,

> > which is when they first appear in the European fossil records. So Blacks were hardly the last to reach modernity...

Newsweek, "The Search for Adam & Eve," January 11, 1988

African Genius, a book by noted British historian Basil Davidson who explained that:

New York Times, September 22, 1994

New Fossils Take Science Close to Dawn of Humans

By JOHN NOBLE WILFORD

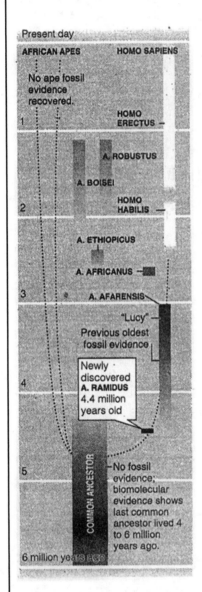

Present day

AFRICAN APES   HOMO SAPIENS

No ape fossil evidence recovered.

1

HOMO ERECTUS —

A. ROBUSTUS

A. BOISEI

HOMO HABILIS —

2

A. ETHIOPICUS

A. AFRICANUS —

3   A. AFARENSIS

"Lucy" —
Previous oldest fossil evidence

Newly discovered
A. RAMIDUS
4.4 million years old

4

COMMON ANCESTOR

5   No fossil evidence; biomolecular evidence shows last common ancestor lived 4 to 6 million years ago.

6 million years ago

Fossils found in Aramis, Ethiopia, are believed to be from the oldest known hominid species. This is one theory of the approximate timetable.

Source: Dr. Tim D. White, University of California at Berkeley.

Fossils of the oldest human ancestors have been discovered in Ethiopia, where these apelike creatures lived 4.4 million years ago on a forested flood plain. Not only do they represent an entirely new species, scientists said, but they also may well be the long-sought relatives who lived close to the fateful time when the lineages leading to modern apes and Homo sapiens went their separate ways.

"The discovery of these ancient fossils and their context signals a major step in our understanding of human origins," Dr. Tim D. White, a paleontologist at the University of California at Berkeley, said yesterday in an announcement of the findings.

In setting out to master their own continent, Africans made a first and crucial contribution to the general growth of mankind.

Most physical anthropologists seem now to have accepted that vital evolutionary steps which led from near-men towards *true men were taken in Africa:* in some recent words of Leakey's that it was

'the African continent which saw the emergence of the basic stock which eventually gave rise to man as we know him today'

Little, Brown and Company, Boston, London, 1969, p. 28

Science reporter John Noble Wilford's article entitled, "Humans' Earliest Footprints Discovered," provides additional verification of Africa's primacy in man's origins:

> "The earliest fossilized footprints of an anatomically modern human being have been discovered in 117,000-year-old sandstone on the shore of a South African lagoon, scientists reported yesterday.
>
>> Fossil bones may inspire paleontologists, and satisfy geneticists that they have

traced modern Homo Sapiens back to...Africa.

>> But nothing is more evocative of human ancestors than living, walking people than a trail of footprints."

New York Times, Friday, August 15, 1997

In the same article Wilford asserted that:

> Most paleoanthropologists, and especially geneticists, think this fateful transition occurred between 100,000 and 200,00 years ago. Geneticists think the **"African Eve," the one common ancestor of all living humans**, lived at about this time.

> "Indeed, all the remarkable advances made by these earlier species fade into insignificance beside the explosion of change wrought by *Homo sapiens sapiens* - the anatomically modern humans. No more than 70,000 years after **the first appearance of this species in Africa** (around 100,000 B. C.), *Homo sapiens sapiens* were to be found throughout virtually the entire habitable world.

> The fact of *Homo sapiens sapiens'* dominance is unquestioned. What remains unknown, however, is the way in which these early humans managed to achieve that dominance. Did these patently superior creatures, with their glittering accomplishments in tool-making and hunting, arise on the continent of Africa in 100,000 B. C. and spread across the world?"

"The Human Dawn," *Time Frame*, Time-Life Books, Virginia, 1990, p. 61

Mark Ridley, a lecturer in the department of zoology at the University of Oxford, in a review for the *New York Times* (August 27, 1997) of a book *Ecco Homo* by Noel T. Boaz provides a response to that question:

Most anthropologists think **humans originated** *in* eastern **Africa**

> - in Ethiopia, Kenya and Tanzania - where the main early human fossils have been found.

A similar point was made by Dr. M. G. Seelig:

"...the earliest race of beings were Negroid, it is but natural to believe that at one time these were universal, and that their birthplace must have had one common center, which must have been Africa. Throughout the whole world, where the ossified remains of earliest man have been found, we find the same type, which is Negroid."

Medicine, An Historical Outline, Williams I. Wilkins Company, Baltimore, 1925, p.15

"Sir Godfrey Higgins Esq. in his scholarly masterpiece entitled, *Anacalypsis* (Vol. I) declared:

"WE HAVE FOUND

The Black Complexion
OR SOMETHING RELATING
TO IT
WHENEVER

We Have Approached
The Origin of Nations

In the classic work, *A Book of the Beginnings*, Vol. II, Gerald Massey, clearly declares that:

"The most reasonable view on the evolutionary

theory...is that **the Black race is the most**

ancient and

that Africa is the primordial home."

Which is why Robert Ardrey aptly entitled his book, *African Genesis*. In it he pointed out that:

...not in Asia, was mankind born.

The New

New Debate Over Humankind's Ancestres

Biologists insist all human lineages track back to a woman in Africa 200,000 years ago.

By NATALIE ANGIER

SHE may no longer be called Eve, and her most imaginative and outspoken proponent may have died two months ago, but the provocative notion that our genes hold evidence of a mother of us all is growing ever more powerful.

By this theory on the origins of modern *Homo sapiens*, all 5.384 billion humans on Earth today can be traced to a woman who lived in Africa about 200,000 years ago, and who left an unmistakable if wraithlike signature on our DNA.

The woman was a member of a race of the first truly modern people, who, with their newly lightened skeletons, their more capacious brains and their softer brows, radiated out from their African homeland and overwhelmed or supplanted the many more primitive humans who were then living in Asia and Europe.

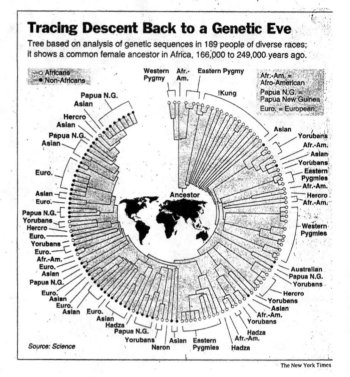

Tracing Descent Back to a Genetic Eve

Tree based on analysis of genetic sequences in 189 people of diverse races; it shows a common female ancestor in Africa, 166,000 to 249,000 years ago.

Source: Science

The New York Times

The home of our fathers was that African highland

reaching north from the Cape to the Lakes of the Nile.

New York: Dell Publishing Co., Inc., 1961, p. 11

From the evidence Prof. Jackson drew this logical conclusion in his scholarly work, *Man, God And Civilization*:

"Since there is overwhelming evidence that

the human race originated in Africa,

then all mankind has an African ancestry.

Hence, all men must be Negroes."

"Of one blood," said St. Paul, "God made all the races of the earth."

No matter how hard people try to get around it, they cannot escape their *origins* ... Africa.

Even Henry Fairfield Osborn, the late head of the American Museum of Natural History, said,

"Negroid stock is even *more ancient* than Caucasian or Mongolian."

Man, Rises to Parnassus, Princeton, N.J., 1928

Professor of Anatomy Sir Grafton Elliot Smith suggests that:

"There is still something to be said for **Darwin's** view that

Africa may have been

the original home of mankind."

To a scholar such as Griffith Taylor, *Environment and Race*, (London, 1927) the conclusion is clear:

"A major principle of ecology tells us that

the Negrito was therefore

the *earliest to develop*

of the five races."

The scientists called them ...

Homo-Habilis, Homo-Erectus, and

Hominids named Australopithecus.

Dr. Albert Churchward in his book, *Signs and Symbols of Primordial Man* stated

that *all* mankind

[Caucasians, Semites, Hamites and Indo-European Aryans included]

Originated from the "PYGMIES"

The New York Times (Friday, Nov. 10, 1972) reveals:

Skull Pushes Back Man's Origin

By Walter Sullivan

"Ancient bones found in Africa have been assembled into a skull that may extend man's immediate ancestry back more than one million years earlier than previously believed."

Professor Ashley Montagu, the author of **Man: His First Two Million Years: A Brief Introduction to Anthropology,** (New York, 1959) makes a similar point:

Skull Pushes Back Man's Origin

By Walter Sullivan
Ancient bones found in Africa have been assembled into a skull that may extend man's immediate ancestry back more than one million years earlier than previously believed.

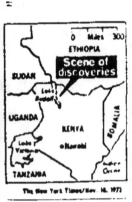

Richard Leakey with the skull, found in fragments

"Since **the ancestors of man** were almost certainly **tropical** animals of African origin, they were almost ... certainly **Black-skinned.**"

Therefore, Dr. Diop says:

"It can be concluded from the foregoing, that from 5 million years ago to the glacial thaw 10,000 years ago, **Africa** almost unilaterally peopled and **influenced the rest of the world.**"

In his work *Key to Culture*, Joseph McCabe, the English scholar, concludes:

"There is strong reason to think that

man was at first very dark of skin, woolly-haired and flat-nosed,

and, as he wandered into different climates, the branches of the race diverged and developed their characteristics."

From his monumental scholarly work, *Anacalypsis* (2 vols.), Sir Godfrey Higgins said in his own words:

"Now I suppose, that

man was originally a Negro,

and he traveled Westwards, gradually changing from the jet Black of India, through all the intermediate shades of Syria, Italy, France to the fair White and red of the maid of Holland and Britain."

The learned scholar Griffith Taylor, *Environment and Nation*, (Chicago, 1936) adds that

"**the Negritos**, or little Negroes, **were the first in Europe**, after the Neanderthal, a near-human Negroid type, and that

'the Negritos ' introduced their culture 'all over the world.'

The *original color* of primitive man was '*Black*,' he says." *Sex and Race*, Vol. I

The French historian, Professor Charles Seignobos, in his scholarly *History of Ancient Civilization*, indicated that:

"The *first civilized inhabitants of the Nile* and Tigris-Euphrates Valleys *were a dark-skinned people with short hair and prominent lips...*"

"**Herodotus**, of 447 B. C., said very clearly that the **People of** all that region of **Mesopotamia** and **India** were **Black**.

He called them Ethiopians. Moreover, **tropical man** is never White. He is most often **Black** or dark brown, with **flat nose**, frizzy or **woolly hair**, and protruding jaws. Thus when **the Christians chose**

Adam as their ancestor, they really chose a dark-skinned progenitor for the human race, even though the early Christians of Europe knowing no better represented Adam in their paintings as White." (J. A. Rogers, *Sex and Race, Vol. 1*)

"Cheikh Anta Diop," writes Dr. Leonard Jeffries, Jr., Professor of Africana Studies and Chairman of Black Studies at City College of New York, "presents the scientific and historical data for the **African origin of humanity.**"

Professor Jeffries also makes this point:

> "Two conclusions are evident from Diop's first chapter of Part I, 'Prehistory: Race and History and the Origin of Humanity and Racial Differentiation':
>
> 1.   '**Humanity born** at the latitude of the **Great Lakes** near the Equator is by necessity pigmented and African. This is substantiated by **GLOGER'S LAW** which states that warm-blooded animals are pigmented in hot and humid climates.
>
> 2.   *All* **races** are issued **from** the **African race** by direct relationships, and other continents were **peopled** from Africa
>
> at the Homo Erectus stage as well as the Homo Sapien stage which appeared about 150,000 years ago.' "

("Africa: Cradle of Humanity," *Nile Valley Civilizations*)

In the chapter entitled, *"Africa - The Beginnings,"* the English archaeologist Michael Carter in his book *Archaeology* said:

> **"*Africa* can perhaps be described as**
>
> *the cradle of mankind -*
>
> **the birthplace of man."**

Similarly, Dr. Diop declares:

> **"If mankind originated in Africa, it was necessari-**

ly negroid before becoming White through mutation and adaptation

at the end of the last glaciation in Europe in the Upper Paleolithic; and it is now more understandable why the Grimaldian negroids first occupied Europe for 10,000 years before Cro-Magnon Man - The prototype of the White race—appeared (around 2000) ."

("Africa: Cradle of Humanity," *Nile Valley Civilizations*)

Rene Verneau, former head of the Paleontological Institute of Paris, agrees:

"Recent discoveries seem to indicate that the **Negro** element *preceded* **the White and the Yellow everywhere.**"

Huxley Memorial lecture, 1924

The *New York Times* declared in a Friday, June 11, 1982 article that

"Ethiopia Bones Called Oldest Ancestor of Man

Fossil bones discovered in Ethiopia were reported yesterday to be from the oldest ancestor of man yet known, an ape-man who walked on two feet, had a small brain and lived four million years ago. The bones were 400,000 years *older* than the famous *'Lucy'* skeleton found in 1974.

The new fossil discovery was announced by Dr. J. Desmond Clark and Dr. Time D. White, anthropologists at the University of California at Berkeley."

Africa's role in human history is also aptly described in the April issue of *Science 84* magazine by its cover title -

SCIENCE 84

APRIL   **TWO DOLLARS**

**CREATING US
14 FOSSILS THAT TELL THE STORY
OF HUMAN EVOLUTION**

Boyce Rensberger, the senior editor who wrote the cover story, informs us that around April (1984) specimens of Man's Most Ancient Ancestors will be: " . . . brought to New York for an exhibition called, **'Ancestors Four Million Years of Humanity,'** at the American Museum of Natural History."

A survey of such specimens taken from the article by Boyce Rensberger entitled,

"Bones of Our Ancestors,"

clearly establishes Africa as

the Original Home of the First Man and

the Human Race.

Let us first begin with the specimen in the article called Sivapithecus (17 million - 8 million years ago):

> "According to one view the hominid lineage may trace its ancestry to Sivapithecus or its close relative Ramapithecus. ... An almost identical form lived in Kenya 17 million years ago."

Next, 'Australopithecus afarensis' (3.9 million years ago):

> "... this specimen represents the oldest known, generally accepted hominid, or member of human lineage ... It was found in Tanzania..."

> Then, we have 'Australopithecus africanus' (3 million-2 million years ago): "... the first example of A. africanus ever found came from a site called Taung in South Africa in 1924..."

Moving on we come to Homo habilis (2.2 million - 1.6 million years ago):

> foot, below, and the hand both from a 1.75 million year-old layer of Olduvai Gorge in Tanzania, confirm that H. Habilis walked upright..."

From here we go to Homo erectus (1.6 million - 0.4 million years ago):

> "... Homo erectus was the first species of human to

migrate out of **Africa**. This specimen, the **most complete** known and the **oldest** at 1.6 million years of age, was found in **Kenya** ... Homo erectus is the earliest hominid to have controlled fire..."

Lastly, we insert **Homo sapiens** (30,000—present):

"... There are ... finds in **southern Africa** that suggest **modern people appeared** there about **100,000 years ago**."

As one can see, all the specimens mentioned in the article were found in Africa.

"The African continent is no recent discovery; it is not a new world, like America or Australia...

while yet *Europe* was

the home of *wandering barbarians*,

one of the most wonderful civilizations

on record had begun to work out its destiny

on the banks of the Nile..."

(*History of Nations*, Vol. I 8 p. 1, 1906)

J. A. Rogers, *Africa's Gift to America*

"The opinion of that great scholar goes even further. It seems increasingly evident that *humanity* was *born in Africa*. In fact, the most important stock of human bones found up to now has been in South Africa."

Cheikh Anta Diop, *The African Origin of Civilization (Myth or Reality)*

Life Magazine's November 1981 article entitled:

The Top Paleoanthropologists Square-off

stated that, "Professor Donald Johnson came upon a human-like creature, in Ethiopia's Afar Triangle, that lived in Africa some 3.5 million years ago. The creature was called 'Lucy.' "

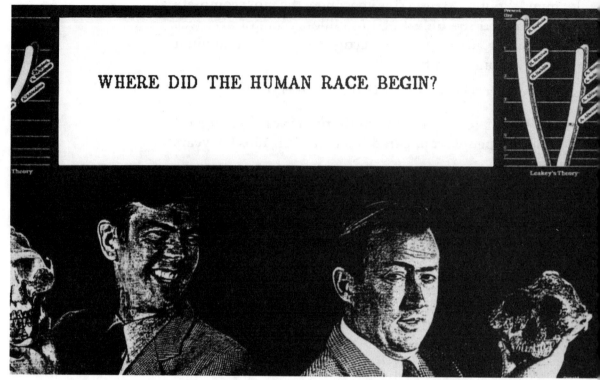

WHERE DID THE HUMAN RACE BEGIN?

Also, it referred to the fact that:

"Today it is generally agreed that evolution has two main branches. One branch leads to modern man, Homo Sapiens. The other belongs to a kind of small-brained ape-man called Australopithecus, which became extinct about a million years ago. On the Homo line, the brain got bigger and skills evolved with each successive species. Habilis, 'handy-man,' earliest **Homo**, made stone tools. **Erectus was the first to go out of Africa and colonize Eurasia."**

John Noble Wilford's front page special to the **New York Times** (Oct. 19, 1984) entitled, " 'Strapping' Youth of Eons Ago" revealed that:

"The skull and bones of a 'strapping' young male who lived 1.6 million years ago, described as the most complete skeleton of an early human ancestor ever found, have been discovered by fossil hunters in Kenya."

The skeleton was found by the paleoanthropologists Dr. Alan Walker, Professor of Cell Biology and Anatomy at John Hopkins University, and the world renowned anthropologist, Richard Leakey.

J. Wilford of the *New York Times* quotes Professor Walker regarding the importance of the discovery:

> "We've never seen anything like this before... Here, you can see the whole thing ... We've looked like humans for 1.6 million years."

Leakey adds:

> "It was clearly a strapping youth, and quite different to what we might have envisaged for a 1.6 million-year-old ancestor."

Wilford reports:

> "At a news conference here, Alan Walker of John Hopkins University ... said the new skeleton was extraordinary not only because it was the oldest known HOMO ERECTUS, but also because it was so complete...
>
> The paleontologists said the similarities between the bones of the skeleton and those of modern man appeared to confirm the widely held belief that these species, which lived from 1.6 million to 400,000 years ago, was a **direct ancestor of modern man, HOMO SAPIENS.**"

The "expedition was supported by the National Geographic Society and the National Museum of Kenya."

From the booklet published by the american museum itself we have:
American Museum Of Natural History
April 13 - September 9, 1984

ANCESTORS
four million years of humanity

This exhibition of original fossils documenting the long course of human evolution

The booklet begins with the section heading:

"The Earliest Human Beings

The **oldest forms** that can clearly be admitted to the **human lineage** on the grounds already mentioned belong to the species grouped into the genus *Australopithecus*.

The first specimens of this kind were found in **South Africa** in the 1920s and 1930s by Raymond Dart and Robert Broom; the Leakeys began finding others at **Olduvai Gorge, Tanzania**, in 1959, and numerous subsequent discoveries have been made in **Kenya** and **Ethiopia** as well.

The **earliest** of these **species**, and thus the first certain hominid known, is *Australopithecus afarensis* (item 46) from **eastern African** deposits between 4 and 3 Myr.

The largest collection of such fossils comes from the Hadar area of **Ethiopia** and includes the famous skeleton Lucy."

Next, they had a section on the *"Early Advanced Humans And Their Lifeways"*:

"All members of the human family subsequent to Australopithecus are nowadays assigned to our own genus: Homo. The earlier of the two extinct species of our genus normally recognized is homo habilis.

It first appeared in the fossil record at about 2 Myr and seems to have persisted for under half a million years. Found first at Olduvai Gorge and now known from **South Africa, Kenya**, and **Ethiopia**."

And, finally a section entitled,

"The Origin Of Modern Humans"

"The first hints of transition from earlier forms come from **sub-Saharan Africa**.

Fragmentary or poorly dated remains from Ethiopia may be as old as 125,000 years: the anatomically modern Border Cave (item 36) skull from **South Africa** is claimed to be over 50,000 and perhaps as much as 90,000 years old.

Further some possibly 'transitional' forms (e.g., items 16, 47) are known in sub-Saharan Africa.

The second ancient Homo species, the long-lasting H. erectus, also turns up first in **East Africa** (e.g. item 45), where it appears from about 1.7 Myr, and is found in sites from Algeria (item 28) to South Africa until about 0.5 Myr. Apparently widespread in the Old World although its physical remains are known only from Africa. "

Thus, the **Museum of Natural History** clearly confirms that the ancestral home of the first man and woman is... **Africa**.

As B. Rensberger says, "we may look into the faces of the old bones and, like orphans searching for **biological parents**, perceive resemblances that make them part of our family." **The Family of Man in Africa.**

A fact that leads others such as Dr. Kamuti Kiteme, Associate Professor of Black Studies at City College, to entitle a lecture sponsored by New York Telephone as,

"Africa: The Origin of Mankind and
The Mother of Civilization."

Which is why Prof. Van Sertima in the preface to his book, *Blacks in Science* speaks of

"man's earliest beginnings in the land called
Af-rui-ka (birthplace)."

It seems that a seventeenth century writer had it right more than three centuries ago when the respected English physician and author, Sir Thomas Browne (1605-1682 A. D.), wrote the following:

"There is africa and her Prodigies in us"

In the prestigious scientific magazine Cell, the findings of a team of researchers headed by Dr. Svante Paabo:

" 'supports a scenario in which

modern humans **arose recently** *in* **Africa**

as a distinct species and replaced Neanderthals with little or no inbreeding,' the researchers conclude."

"DNA Suggests Neanderthal Not Ancestor," *Washington Post*, July 11, 1997

According to the *Washington Post* (July 11, 1997):

He [Christopher Stringer] and other out-of-Africa proponents believe that early forms of primitive humans, such as *Homo erectus* (the presumptive ancestor of both Neanderthal and modern man) made their way **out of**

Africa hundreds of thousands of years ago, leaving fossils around the Earth. But

all present-day *people*, they believe, are directly descended *from* the anatomically *modern humans* that developed *in Africa*

and migrated in one or more waves over the past 75,000 years or so, supplanting all other populations including Neanderthals.

On the front page of the *New York Times* on Friday, July 11, 1997 Nicholas Wade startled the world in an article entitled, "Neanderthal DNA Sheds New Light On Human Origins." He reported on:

> "The finding, made by a team of scientists led by Dr. Svante Paabo of the University of Munich in Germany...reported in today's issue of the journal *Cell* , comes down firmly on the side

of **Neanderthal** having been distinct species that

contributed nothing to the modern human gene pool..."

Christopher Stringer of the Natural History Museum, London hails their discovery with this affirming proclamation:

" In terms of our knowledge of human origins, it's as big as the Mars landing. "

The Washington Post in an equally revealing article entitled, "DNA Suggests Neanderthal Not Ancestor," reported that:

> ...if Neanderthals—who generally inhabited the region from Wales to Moscow and south to the Mediterranean— were the evolutionary precursors of modern humans, their DNA sequence should be more prevalent in contemporary European populations than in, for example, Asians or Africans.

> Yet Paabo's group found that the Neanderthal DNA differed by exactly the same amount from human samples taken around the world.

Those numbers 'do *not* indicate that [Neanderthal are] more closely related to modern Europeans than any other population of contemporary humans...' "

African Exodus, The Origins of Modern Humanity (1997) is a recent book by Christopher Stringer and Robin McKie that was reviewed by Robert J. Richards, a professor of history and the philosophy of science at the University of Chicago, who stated that:

> Christopher Stringer...with the help of Robin McKie, a science writer argues for a theory that has come to be called "Out of Africa"... Stringer marshals considerable paleontological, anthropological and genetic evidence for his position - for instance, the genetic difference within each race are much larger than the average differences among the races, suggesting very close biological relationship...

And **out of Africa**, they **came**, as the final colonizing wave of hominids, **our ancestors**.

New York Times Book Review, "Neanderthals Need Not Apply," August 17, 1997

Along the same line of coverage, *The Washington Post* disclosed that:

> "The report in today's issue of the journal *Cell* strongly supports the recent **out-of-Africa** position by showing that one sequence of Neanderthal DNA differs drastically from the same stretch of modern human DNA— about half as much as today's humans differ from chimps."

The Washington Post confirms the fact that:

...the recent out-of-Africa hypothesis is now the predominant theory among experts...

"DNA Suggests Neanderthal Not Ancestor," July 11, 1997

John Noble Wilford, a well-known science reporter, declared that:

An African origin of modern human

is supported by recent studies of mitochondrial DNA, genetic material that is passed only through females. Measuring variations on mitochondrial DNA in different populations today, scientists have concluded that

all humans are descended from one common female ancestor who lived **in Africa**

between 100,000 and 200,00 years ago - the hypothetical "Eve."

New York Times, "Humans' Earliest Footprints Discovered," August 15, 1997

Chris Stringer, an highly —regarded authority on paleoanthropology at London's Natural History Museum and Robin McKie, a science editor of *The Observer* explained in an article for the *New York Times* that this new evidence shows, "Neanderthals on the Run":

... Europe's most famous cavemen, the Neanderthals...

were *not* our ancestors...

Skull shapes, measurements of leg and arm bones, and the dating of fossil finds all indicate

that Europeans did *not* evolve

from Neanderthals,

but from the *people* who replaced the Neanderthals...

we all have a recent African origin...

Our DNA lineage points unmistakably to a

common ancestor whose offspring evolved into

Homo sapiens

shortly before the African exodus.

Though modern humans may not look exactly alike,

we are indeed all Africans

under the skin."

Creators Of Civilization

All the elements of civilization were created by Black People in Africa.

"A scholar of no less distinction than the late Sir Richard Burton wrote the other day of Egypt as "the inventor of the alphabet, the cradle of letters...and generally,

the source of all human civilization.

Amelia B. Edwards, Pharoahs, Fellahs and Explorers, Harper & Bros., New York, 1891, p. 158-159

The author of *The Wisdom of the Egyptians* clearly declared that:

"Egypt has been called

the 'Father of History and

the Mother of Civilization'

Brian Brown, Brentano, New York, 1923, p. 1

" 'Egypt, the mother of men civilized,' has

always fascinated the kinds of the successive generation of mankind by her immemorial antiquity."

Robert De Rustafjaell, *The Light Of Egypt*, London, 1909

As Professor Margaret A. Murray notes:

"For every student of our modern civilization **Egypt** is the great storehouse from which to obtain information, for within the narrow limits of

that country are preserved the origins of most (perhaps all) of our knowledge.

In *Egypt* are found

the first beginnings of ...culture—building, agriculture, horticulture, clothing (even cooking as an art);

the beginnings of the sciences— physics, astronomy, medicine, engineering;

the beginnings of...law, government, religion."

Margaret A. Murray, *The Splendour That Was Egypt*. Philosophical Library, New York, 1957, p. xvii

Count Volney adds:

"...This Race Of Blacks ...

Is The Very One To Which

We Owe Our Arts, Our Sciences,

And Even The Use Of The Spoken Word ..."

(*Voyages en Syrie et en Egypte*, Paris, 1787, Vol. I pp. 74-75)

Ian McMahan, a faculty member at Brooklyn College, City University of New York, begins his book *Secrets of the Pharaohs* with these words:

When Julius Caesar went to **Egypt** in 48 B. C., he was the leader of a military expedition against one of his rivals for power. He was also a pilgrim, paying his respects

to the world's oldest civilization.

For the Romans, as for the Greeks before them, Egypt was the land where humans had first learned the names of the gods.

Here people had invented

the alphabet,

learned to do complex calculations, domesticated wild animals, developed irrigation, and constructed the first buildings in stone. And what buildings—temples, tombs, colossal statues and obelisks so huge and elaborate that the gods themselves must have helped put them up!

Avon Books Inc., New York, 1998, p. 6

"The valley of the Nile was for many centuries

the storehouse of civilization.

The most impressive thing about Egypt is its imposing grandeur, overwhelming even in ruin and desolation."

Willis N. Huggins & John G. Jackson, *Introduction to African Civilizations*, Imprint Editions, Black Classic Press, Baltimore, 1937, p. 28

William H. Peck, Senior Curator and curator of ancient art at the Detroit Institute of Art, asserts that:

> Egypt's complex social structure produces pyramids...but those are only the best known of the culture's accomplishments, which included inspiring works of architecture and art in many different media and a heritage of sophisticated literature and poetry. It is no wonder that the ancient Greeks and Romans believed that

Egypt, one of the great civilizations of Africa,

was the originator of many of the arts and sciences.

Splendors of Egypt, Abbeville Press Publisher, New York, London, Paris, 1997, introduction

Penelope Lively, author and winner of the prestigious Booker Prize in 1987, wrote the following essay in the book *Egypt, Antiquities From Above*:

> Who would not be affected by the revelations of that extraordinary place? For the Victorian visitor, there was the unsettling reflection that here was the record of an ancient civilization whose technical achievement and spiritual complexity cast a shadow over the intellectual and scientific exuberance of their own time. This evidence of past sophistication threw doubts on the idea of history as a system of continuous progress. The monuments of European prehistory were primitive by comparison with the constructions of the Nile valley. A blow had been dealt to Eurocentrism. The tombs, the temples, all the evi-

dence of that way of life and of the knowledge and abilities of those people made it clear that

what we think of our civilization had its origins here and not in France or Italy or Germany or along the banks of the Thames.

Marilyn Bridges, Little Brown and Company, Boston, 1996, p. 11

"It is very interesting to note," says Professor Martin Bernal of Cornell University, "that European culture did not begin in Germany or Sweden."

Professor M. Bernal of Cornell stressed the fact that:

"Greece is extremely important because it is the greatest single source of European culture." (Debate on "African Roots," March 3, 1996, attended by Mary Lefkowitz and John Rodgers of Wellesley College, Martin Bernal of Cornell University and Professor Emeritus the late John Henrik Clarke):

Which explains why "Modern scholars working in an intensively racist nineteenth and twentieth centuries...wanted Greece to be pure, White and European," according to Bernal.

Yet, in the words of Professor Emeritus John Henrik Clarke:

"Rome and Greece were *not* European creations...because at the time

there was *NO EUROPE!"*

(Debate on "African Roots," March 26th, 1996)

According to Sir Grafton Elliot Smith in his work *Ancient Egyptians*, he suggested that:

"Not a few writers, like the traveler Volney, in the Eighteenth Century, have expressed the belief that

the Ancient Egyptians were Negroes,

or at any rate strongly Negroid."

Willis N. Huggins & John G. Jackson, *Introduction to African Civilizations*, Imprint Editions, Black Classic Press, Baltimore, 1937, pp. 29-30

Giovanni Caselli, a Fellow of the Royal Anthropological Institute of Great Britain, compares ancient Egypt this way:

> "The products of thousands of years of human labor during the age of the pharaohs still outnumber the products of human activity since that time...In reality, Egypt goes beyond any imagination or preconceived idea..." (*Egypt*, Flint River Press Ltd., London, 1992, p. 23)

Who were these great builders?

> "Even Petrie admits the African origin of the great monument builders of the Third and Fourth Dynasties. This culture which Petrie calls the fifth civilization of Egypt, 'was due to an invasion from the south; a conqueror, of Sudani features founded the Third Dynasty...'"

Willis N. Huggins & John G. Jackson, *Introduction to African Civilizations*, Imprint Editions, Black Classic Press, Baltimore, 1937, p. 28

> The obvious African connection of the Ancient Egyptians is explained in plain terms by Professor Clarke who cited Herodotus as observing :
>
> "...that the tint of the complexion of the Ethiopians and the Egyptians seem to be the same...so, let us at least concede that Herodotus had good eyesight."

(Debate on "African Roots," March 26th, 1996)

Professors Willis N. Huggins and John G. Jackson fifty years ago noted the fact that:

> "The Edfu Text is an important source document on the early history of the Nile valley. This famous inscription found in a temple at Edfu gives an account of the origin of Egyptian civilization. According to this account, civilization was brought to Egypt *from the south* by a band of invaders under the leadership of King Horus...this ruler, Horus, was in later days deified, and became the untimely Egyptian Christ."

Introduction to African Civilizations, Imprint Editions, Black Classic Press, Baltimore, 1937, p. 28

> Jeremy Naydler, a philosopher and cultural historian who lectures at universities such as Oxford, Reading and

Southampton, England, made this piercing observation in his book *Temple of the Cosmos, the ancient Egyptian experience of the Sacred*:

Today, we are all brought up to believe that our own era began with the Greeks, on the one hand, and the Israelites on the other. The Greeks gave us science and reason; the Israelites gave us monotheism. Thus the soul of the West was forged by the means of a heroic antipathy toward a previous epoch of irrational superstition and rampant paganism. This is, however, a picture of our cultural identity that carries less and less conviction with the passage of time.

> *The Greeks did **not** so much inaugurate a new epoch of science and rationalism* as let slip from their grasp an older
>
> dispensation. It was a dispensation of which

the Egyptians were the chief guardians

in the ancient world

> , and according to which knowledge of the spiritual powers that pervade the cosmos was assiduously cultivated.
>
> As the Greeks slackened their grip upon this older, more attuned mode of consciousness, they had increasingly to orient themselves by reference to the narrower human faculties of logic and sense perception.
>
> Similarly, the Israelites did not found their monotheistic religion in a spiritual vacuum, but in the teeth of the ancient polytheistic consensus...The traditional biography of the Western mind that sees our roots in Greece and Israel does not give us the complete picture.

Inner Traditions, Rochester, Vermont, 1996, p. viii-ix

We learn from the Old Testament that, **while the Jews,** the earliest nation that has handed down to us the history of its rise and civilization, **were yet a tribe of wandering shepherds, under Abraham,** depending solely upon the unbought gifts of nature, who, when they had exhausted a district, instead of cultivating it, [they] drove off their flocks in search of another,

the Egyptians were acquainted with agriculture, and all those arts of civilization and government, and notions of property, which usually belong to nations which have been long settled and civilized.

This we find confirmed in a striking manner by the architectural remains that have survived the ravages of above thirty centuries; for, while the Jews, under the immediate successors of Joshua, were still warring with the Canaanites for the possession of the country, Egypt itself possessed palaces, temples, porticoes, obelisks, statues, and canals, which are even now the admiration of the world.

J. G. Wilkenson, *Manners and Customs of The Ancient Egyptians*, John Murray, London, 1887, p. 4

In Volumes I and 2 of the *Book of the Beginnings*, Gerald Massey launches forth his position on where we may find the origin of civilization:

"...has now to be sought for in **Africa** the birthplace of the Black race, **the land of the oldest known human types**, and of those which preceded and most nearly approached the human...

Aethiopia And Egypt Produced

The Earliest Civilization In The World

and it was indigenous. So far as the records of language and mythology can offer us guidance, there is nothing beyond Egypt and Aethiopia but Africa..."

"...the sands have destroyed only the body of ancient Egypt," writes Professor Durant, "its spirit survives in the lore and memory of our race. The improvement of agriculture, metallurgy, industry and engineering; the apparent invention of glass and linen, of paper and ink, of the calendar and the clock, of geometry and *the alphabet*; the refinement of dress and ornament, of furniture and dwellings, of society and life;

the remarkable development of orderly and peaceful government, of census and post, of primary and secondary education, even of technical training for office and administration; *the advancement of writing and literature, of science and medicine; the first clear formulation known to us of individual and public conscience,*

the first cry for social justice, the first widespread monogamy, *the first monotheism, the first essays in moral philosophy, the elevation of architecture,* sculpture and the minor arts to a degree of excellence and power never (so far as we know) reached before, and seldom equaled since: these contributions were not lost, even when their finest exemplars were buried under the desert, or overthrown by some convulsion of the globe. (Thebes was finally destroyed by an earthquake in 27 B. C.)

Through the Phoenicians, the Syrians and the Jews, through the Cretans, the Greeks and the Romans, the civilization of Egypt passed down to become part of the cultural heritage of mankind.

The effect or remembrance of what Egypt accomplished at the very dawn of history has influence in every nation and every age. "It is even possible," as Faure has said, "that Egypt, through the solidarity, the unity, and the disciplined variety of its artistic products, through the enormous duration and the sustained power of its effort, offers the spectacle of the greatest civilization that has yet appeared on the earth. We shall do well to equal it."

The Story of Civilization, Part I, Simon and Schuster, New York, 1954.

Dr. Cheikh Anta Diop, the leading cultural historian on Africa and Director of the radiocarbon laboratory at the University of Dakar, illustrates through historical, archaeological and anthropological evidence that Black Africans created all the elements of civilization.

Dr. Diop does so in both of his thought provoking books, *The African Origin Of Civilization: Myth Or Reality and Barbarism Or Civilization*

Professor of European History, (Washington University) Henry S.

Dr. Diop illustrates through historical, archaeological and anthropological evidence that Black Africans created all the elements of civilization

Lucas, is in line with the rest of his fellow colleagues when he reveals that:

> "...The skill of Egyptian handicraftsman, engineers, and artists is justly admired; and their creative ingenuity is shown in pyramids, spacious temples, panoramic pictures on temple walls, and statues of Pharaohs and other great personages...
>
> ## It may truly be said that Egypt led in the development of the sciences of mathematics, chemistry, medicine, and astronomy.
>
> 'The high attainments, the permanence, and continuity of Egyptian life, with a fuller record than that of any other country,' according to Flinders Petrie, 'will always render it the most important human growth for study, whether socially, politically, or in the history of invention which is the life blood of civilization....
>
> Egypt's influence upon the civilization of neighboring lands during Fifty Centuries or more has been incalculable." p. 63

Elsewhere, Professor Lucas writes: "...Egypt therefore, was by far the most populous land in antiquity, exceedingly rich, and **a leader in all phases of culture**. " (p. 46)

> "It is the Pharaohs' peculiar sovereignty that emerges as the most impressive theme of **ancient Egypt - by their individual genius they guided the world's first great civilization.** That human story, now that it can be told with greater realism and accuracy, may outlast any of the towering structures that were once erected against the wind and sands of time."

Jacquetta Hawkes, *Pharaohs of Egypt*, American Heritage Publishing Co., Inc., New York, 1965, p. 7

"The oldest monuments hitherto known

scarcely transport us further than

six thousand years,

> yet they are of an art so fine, so well determined in its main outlines, and reveal so ingeniously combined a sys-

tem of administration, government, and religion, that we infer a long past of accumulated centuries behind them.

It must always be difficult to estimate exactly the length of time needful for

a race as gifted as were the Ancient Egyptians

to rise from barbarism into a high degree of culture.

Nevertheless, I do not think that we shall be misled in granting them forty or fifty centuries wherein to bring so complicated an achievement to a successful issue, and in

placing their first appearance at eight or ten

thousand years *before* our era."

Gaston Maspero, *History of Egypt,* Charles Scribner's Sons, 1912, p. 55

"...Viscount E. Melchoir de Vogue who, after visiting the Egyptian monuments under the guidance of the two great masters, Mariette and Maspero, wrote:

'At the beginning of everything, in the confused darkness of what, given the present condition of our historical knowledge, are for us the first day of humanity, we find here the spirit, that is to say a civilization learned, powerful, coming we know not whence, born we know not of whom,

the MOTHER OF ALL THE OTHERS.

Two thousand years before Jewish thought
had agitated the questions of origin, these people lived, thought, wrote in full development.

At the hour when Abraham is seen at the summit of history, when the Empires of Chaldea and Assyria appear confusedly, when

we were accustomed to see in the patriarchal life the first attempt at human society this Egyptian race has already grown old...

or twenty centuries its cities have been prospering in the shade of pyramids...' "

Jean Capart and Marcelle Werbrouck, *Thebes*, The Dial Press, New York, 1926, p. 352

William H. Peck of *The National Geographic Society* gives us an indication of why Egypt has held the attention of the world for such a long time by citing the words of two well-known travelers:

> "Concerning Egypt itself I shall extend my remarks to a great length, because there is no country that possesses so many wonders. *Herodotus*

> I had seen a hundred things, while a thousand others had escaped me; and had, for **the first time, found access to the archives of the arts and sciences.** *Vivant Denon*

> Two travelers separated in time by 2,250 years - one from the fifth century B. C., the other from the 19th century A. D. - sound a common chord. Egypt is a land of so many wonderful things the mind can hardly encompass them.

On *Arts & Entertainment* cable television (1986) Professor Basil Davidson, a widely recognized British authority on Africa, boldly proclaimed:

"Egypt of the Pharaohs was the greatest and the oldest and the most inventive of all the high civilizations of antiquity and it flourished for 3,000 years. It set a pattern, an example, for people near and far."

An eighteenth century French academician of the highest esteem in European academic circles once wrote:

"There A People

Now Forgotten

Discovered While Others Were Yet Barbarians, The Elements Of

The Arts And Sciences.

A Race Of Men Now Rejected
For Their Black Skin And Woolly Hair
Founded On The Study Of
The Laws Of Nature,

Those Civil And Religious Systems
Which *Still* Govern The Universe."

Count C. F. Volney, *Ruins of Empire* 1789, (Preface of 1st Edition)

"Another Alexandrian deity linked with Thoth...said at the beginning of a prophecy :

'Do you know, O Asclepius, that
Egypt is the copy of Heaven,

or rather, the place where here below are mediated and projected

all operations which govern and actuate the
heavenly forces?

Even more than that, if the whole truth is to be told, our land is the temple of the entire World.' "

John Romer, *People of the Nile*, Crow Publishers, Inc., New York, 1982, p. 214

"In the Cairo museum, an inscription on a relief of Rameses II's temple can be read as follows:

'This temple is like the sky
in all its proportions.'

Theophile Obenga, *Ancient Egypt & Black Africa*, Karnak House, London, 1992, p. 98

As Benot de Maillet puts it:

"Think of the immense power and great art
that made such a country
into the wonder of the Universe."

Discourse on Universal History, Monseigneur Dauphin, Lyon, 1697, PART II, pp. 249-50)

"When the history of Negroland comes to be written in detail, it may be found that the kingdoms lying towards the eastern end of the Sudan were the home of races who inspired, rather than of races who received, the traditions of civilization associated for us with the name of ancient Egypt.

For they cover on either side of the Upper Nile, between the latitudes of ten and seventeen degrees, territories in which are found monuments more ancient than the oldest Egyptian monuments. If this should prove to be the case, and

the civilized world be forced to recognize in a

black people the fount of its

original enlightenment,

it may happen that

we shall have to revise entirely

our view of the Black races,

and regard those who now exist as the decadent representatives of an almost forgotten era, rather than as the embryonic possibility of an era yet to come."

Lady Lugard, *A Tropical Dependency,* (originally published in 1832, by James Nisbet & Co., Ltd., in 1906), ECA Associates, Chesapeake, New York, 1992.

Dr. Diop, the foremost contemporary authority on African history and culture concludes:

"Universal knowledge runs **from** the **Nile Valley**

toward the rest of the world, in particular toward Greece which served as an intermediary.

As a result, **no thought, no ideology** is **foreign** to **Africa** which was the land of **their birth**."

In fact, he notes:

"Egypt Was The Cradle Of Civilization For 10,000 Years

While The Rest Of The World

Was Steeped In Barbarism."

Dr. Diop uses:

> Anthropology, iconography, melanin dosage tests, osteo-logical measurements, blood groupings, the testimony of classical writers, selfdescriptive Egyptian hieroglyphs, divine epithets, Biblical eyewitnesses, linguistics and various cultural data to support the fact that ...

The Egyptians Were Black.

Dr. Albert Churchward cites several scholars in affirming the seemingly spontaneous development of Egyptian civilization:

> "Donnelly quoted Renan to the effect that Egyptian civilization had no archaic epoch. This assertion is confirmed by Osborn and by Dr. Reis, the latter of whom Donnelly quoted as saying as to *Egypt*, that,
>
> > 'It suddenly takes its place in the world in all its magnificence, without father, without mother, and as clean apart from all evolution as if it had dropped from the heavens...' "

The Origin and Evolution of the Human Race., George Allen & Unwin, London, 1921, p. 34

The distinguished British historian Basil Davidson hosted the television series "Africa" on *Arts and Entertainment* Network (March 26, 1986) and advanced this view about ancient Egypt:

"...5,000 years ago, this homeland had already become the scene of a civilization

> in many ways unmatched anywhere else in the ancient world. This is where we have to begin in the Egypt of the Pharaohs, in the *African land* that was the gift of the god of the Nile.

It is easy enough to believe within these corridors built to a gigantic scale and yet wonderfully proportioned, that you have

entered a world sprung complete from the lap of the gods..."

"The Old Kingdom reached its high point at the time of the construction of the great pyramids of Snofru, Khufu (Cheops), Khephren, and Menkaure (Mycerinus) during the Fourth Dynasty. Previously, King Djoser had set an example with the oldest pyramid of the world, in Saqqara.

Nothing so powerful had been built by men before that time, and this is also amazing in Egyptian history. Suddenly, 5,000 years ago, humankind made a major step forward.

Without preparation, advanced civilization developed with breathtaking technical highpoints. A civilization was able to move in all directions. Certainly, the pyramid construction was a milestone in the history of humankind, since, for the first time, a form of technology of major breadth was utilized and problems that resulted from this were resolved."

Cornelius Stetter, *The Secret Medicine of the Pharoahs*, Edition Q, Chicago, 1993

"In Europe, during the second half of the eighteenth century, there was a great deal of discussion on the origins and evolution of architectural styles, and the influence of one culture on another.

By the mid-nineteenth century, it was widely held that **the Egyptians, at that time considered the world's oldest civilization**, were *the ultimate progenitors of many, if not all, major civilizations.*

It was even proposed that the Gothic style was initiated in Northern Europe on the basis of the pyramid, and that the Chinese culture, in addition to the Greek and the Roman, had its origins in Egypt.

Barbara Blowmink, "Introduction," *The Sphinx and The Lotus: The Egyptian Movement in American Decorative Arts*, 1865-1935

Professor James Breasted reminds us that:

It is to **Egypt** that we must look as

the dominant power in the Mediterranean

basin, whether by force of arms or

by sheer weight of *superior* civilization

throughout the earliest career of man in southern Europe, and for long after the archaic age had been superseded by higher culture, is of vital interest to raise the curtain and peek beyond into the ages which

bequeathed our forefathers so precious

a legacy...

The Conquest of Civilization, Harper & Bros., New York and London, 1946, preface

The ancient Egyptians were a people

of *superior* attainments.

The conditions in the Nile valley being favorable to life and conducive to prosperity, the people utilized their advantages, developed their resources, and were...

pioneers and leaders in the

arts of civilization."

Walter Addison Jayne, M. D., *The Healing Gods of Ancient Civilizations*, Yale University, New Haven, 1925, p. 4

Drawing from the work of J. Leibovitch we find an important statement about Egypt: "...this country was the natural chief cultural center of three great continents,

Egypt was, so to say,
the foremost of all the lands
of the ancient Mediterranean world..."

Ancient Egypt, Imprimerie De L'Institut Francais D'Archeologie Orientale, Cairo, 1938, p. 2

"Historians will see in the most ancient times of Egypt a state of things that the course of generations has not perfected, because that could not be:

Egypt is always herself, at all her epochs,

always great and powerful

in art and enlightenment.

Going back up the centuries, we see her always shining with the same brilliance..."

Leslie Greener, *The Discovery of Egypt*, Dorset Press, New York, 1966, p. 154

"After the time of Abraham the history may be traced with certainty through the reigns of Amunothph, Thothmosis, Rameses, and the other great Coptic kings, who for upwards of five hundred years made Thebes their capital, and usually held Lower Egypt as a province. It was during these reigns that

Egypt surpassed every country of

the known world in wealth and power,

and

was foremost in all the arts of civilization,

of commerce, and of agriculture.

Moses was then educated in all the learning of the Egyptians; and though Upper Egypt was at that time little known to the Greeks,

Homer speaks of

the armies and wealth of Egyptian Thebes as proverbial.

No Theban historians, it is true, have recorded their great deeds; but the buildings are themselves the deeds and the sculptures on the walls show that the nation was conscious of their greatness while performing them."

Samuel Sharpe, *The History of Egypt*, vol. I & II, (6th ed.), George Bell & Sons, London, 1876, p. i v-v

The author of *The History of Egypt* continues:

"The massive temples and obelisks covered with hieroglyphics, and the colossal statues, which have already outlived three thousand years, prove the high civilization of the kingdom, even *before* the Jews had become a people, *before* the Greeks had got an Alphabet...

They marked these buildings with a serious gravity wholly their own.

We have ourselves *no* national style in architecture..."

To understand better the immense sweep of time that ancient Egypt covered consider the following graph, which shows the life span of ancient Egypt compared to those of some other world powers across history.

McMahan, *Secrets of the Pharaohs*, Avon Books Inc., New York, 1998, p. 131

Israel could *not* become a nation without Egypt.

The first and greatest of Israel's prophets was rescued from a watery grave, nurtured, schooled, and outwardly fitted for his sublime legation by the daughter of Egypt's king. Abraham himself, though from quite another section of the world, was ministered unto by Egypt.

Joseph became the illustrious type of Christ by connection with Egypt. Humanly speaking, Jacob and his house would have come to a sad end had it not been for Egypt, which furnished him with bread, welcomed him to its richest lands, and gave his body a royal burial when he died. To Egypt's sovereign God sent that double dream of the kine and ears of corn, which proved the means of Joseph's exaltation and of the salvation of so many peoples.

Even when the blessed Jesus was born into our world Egypt was his asylum from the bloody sword of Herod, and once more and most literally of all were those words of Jehovah fulfilled, "Out of Egypt have I called my son." It was Egypt that gave to mankind the first translation of the Hebrew Scriptures. It was Egypt that proved the stronghold of Christianity after Jerusalem fell.

It is from Egypt that we have the noblest and greatest fathers of the Christian Church.

And however ignoble now may be the land or its population, we may rest assured that God has something further to accomplish by means of a country of which he has thus availed himself in the past, and that out of it will yet come some of the greatest of sacred marvels which are to mark the closing periods of time.

Joseph A. Seiss, *The Great Pyramid: A Miracle in Stone,* Harper & Row Publishers, San Francisco, New York, London, 1973

It would be very surprising if it had *not* taken a long time; **for whatever the achievements of the Greeks, they certainly did *not* create ancient civilization,** and as comparatively late arrivals on the ancient scene they did not lack respect for what they found already there. Karl Marx, a lifelong devotee of the Classics, once wrote about the Greeks: "Why shouldn't the childhood of human society - the stage at which it attained its most attractive development - exercise an eternal charm, as an age that will never return?"

In 1857, when he wrote those words, good progress had been made for some time with the decipherment of Egyptian hieroglyphic inscriptions and papyri, and the decisive steps in the decipherment of Babylonian inscriptions had just been taken, but **when people thought of** "the ancient world" they had in mind the Greeks, Romans and Hebrews, not the Egyptians and Babylonians.

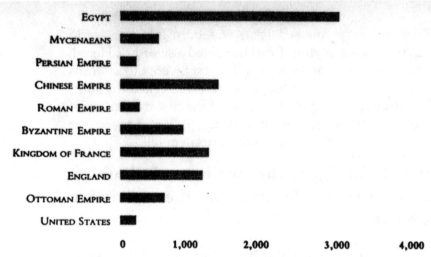

THE SURVIVAL (IN YEARS) OF SOME MAJOR POWERS

Nowadays it would seem odd to assign Socrates and Parthenon to "the childhood of human society." Seen against a background of the whole history of human-like creatures living in groups and using tools, fire, color and language, Socrates was around only yesterday; he is virtually our contemporary.

Placed in the context of the history of the eastern Mediterranean and the Near East, he stands no nearer to the beginnings of civilization than he does to us. **Two and a half thousand years** *before* **Socrates was born the inhabitants of ancient Egypt... had evolved systems of writing and the distinctive styles of art, work and life which generated ancient civilization.**

Kenneth Dover, *The Greeks*, (from the BBC television series by Christopher Burstall and Kenneth Dover) British Broadcasting Corporation, London, 1980, p. viii.

"That **Egypt was the most ancient of nations,**

and that the civilization of mankind had been at very remote periods materially advanced by the inhabitants of the valley of the Nile, are positions elementary to all that has been written by the Greek and Roman authors regarding this country."

William Osburn, *Egypt*, Trübner and Co., London, 1954

The scientific students of our day, who trace back the history of mankind to the times when the races of men still lived in the condition of savages,

have arranged in order the three ages of stone, or bronze, and of iron, in order to fill up by this regular series the void which exists in all the records of history.

Although we will not dispute that history may regard everything as an object for its consideration, yet we must openly acknowledge the fact, that, up to this time at least,

Egypt throws scorn upon these assumed periods.

So far as the historical record on the surviving monuments of Egypt reaches back

the history of Egypt must appear to us in light of the first human civilization.

Henry Brugsch-Bey, *The History of Egypt*, Trans. D. Seymour, John Murray, London, 1879

"To this nation which first translated sounds into signs, and the memory of its deeds to future generations, we naturally turn for

the **earliest information of other races,**

nor do we so turn in vain. And in these inscriptions, graven on storied walls of temples and pylons

older by a thousand years **than**

the opening chapters of

classical history,

we also find

the first – *the very first* –

mention of

the people of Greece and Italy."

Amelia B. Edwards, *Pharaohs, Fellahs and Explorers*, Harper & Bros., New York, 1891, p. 158-159

> "It is accordingly to **Egypt** that we look for all our earliest information concerning **the Land of Blacks**, and
>
> **it is to Egypt,** and through Egypt to Asia Minor and Arabia, **that the Blacks themselves trace their oldest traditions.**"

Lady Lugard, *A Tropical Dependency*, (originally published in 1832, by James Nisbet & Co., Ltd., in 1906), ECA Associates, Chesapeake, New York, 1992, p. 9

The Ancient Egyptians gave the world the first major civilization in history. Like the Nile which cradled its growth, the surprising ideas of these remarkable people flowed out to the world around them.

In this early period, some 6,000 years ago, two other civilizations were stirring: the Sumerian in the valleys of the Tigris and Euphrates, and the Chinese on the yellow river.

Of these, now only the Chinese remains but in antiquity neither the Chinese nor the Sumerians reached the level achieved by the people of the Nile Valley or affected western civilization so much.

William Macquitty, *The Wisdom of the Ancient Egyptians*, (New York: New Direction Books, 1978), p. 3

The historian Bothwell A. Gosse compares the West with ancient Egypt and concludes:

> The most striking characteristic of the civilizations of the world, especially of the West, is their evanescent nature. A state, to some extent primitive, comes to the front, evolves rapidly, reaches its zenith and then declines.
>
> A few hundred years covers the whole process. Carthage,

Greece and Rome 'have their day and cease to be.' There is no stability; no permanence. On the contrary, however, the most notable quality of the Egyptian civilization is its permanent character.

Instead of lasting only a few hundred years, it endures for thousands; and whereas in other countries the entire evolution of the civilization can be traced from its primitive beginnings, through infancy, maturity, old age and death, in **Egypt there appears to be no beginning, the civilization apparently starts mature."**

(*The Civilization of the Ancient Egyptians*, T. C. E. C. Jack Ltd., London, 1916, p. 1)

The distinguished British historian Basil Davidson hosted the television series "Africa" on *Arts and Entertainment* Network (March 26, 1986) made the following disclosure:

"The Greeks *knew* well and firmly believed that

the original Egyptians were Black people

who had come from the south

to settle the land of the Nile."

Even Aristotle says that **the Egyptians** were **"very Black"** and **the Ethiopians "woolly haired"** (See Physiognomy, Chap. VI).

The French archaeologist, Abbe Breuil, who is an authority on the Paleolithic age writes:

'**Africa** not only knew stages of primitive **civilization** comparable to those of *Europe* and *Asia Minor*, but was perhaps

the source of several such civilizations,

whose swarms conquered those classic lands toward the North.' "

('L'Afrique Du Sud,' Les Nouvelles, Literaries, April 5, 1951).

Drawing from one of the great figures in Egyptology, John D. Baldwin quotes Professor Lepsius who said:

"Under the fourth dynasty, when the two great pyramids were built, the nation seems to have approached

the highest glory of that wonderful

development of intelligence and power

to which after **the flight of nearly 6000 years, the ruins still bear witness,** and to which they will continue to bear witness for ages to come."

Pre-Historic Nations, Harper & Brothers, New York, 1898, p. 29

"Thus Egypt was able to bring her influence to bear upon the springs of European civilization in two distinct ways. There was the community of early customs which was brought about by movements of the population, so that

Egypt as the inventor of civilization exercised a predominant part in molding the beliefs, the habits, and the arts of the rest.

Thus the outstanding achievements in culture and the arts on the part of one nation helped to raise the whole family group; and, as the individual people of this group which earliest attained position of pre-eminence, **the Egyptians, by the force of their achievements, were able to lead their European relations out of the wilderness of the Stone Age into the promised land of the higher stage of civilization..."**

G. Elliot Smith, *The Ancient Egyptians and the Origin of Civilization*, Harper & Brothers, London & New York, 1923, p. 28-9

"Old Egypt, 'Mother of Nations,'

requires no formal introduction to civilized man, nor he to her... Once the Pharaohs that built pyramids, knew Joseph...greeted the great men of youthful Greece...it is possible to know much of a civilization—stable, industrious, high-minded, virtuous, religious—that flourished

for 5000 years *before* Christ, or from the morning

of known history."

Charles H. S. Davis, Camden M. Cobern, *Ancient Egypt in Light of Modern Discoveries*, Introduction by Rev. C. Winslow, of the Egypt Exploration Foundation, Biblia Publishing Co., Meridian, Conn., 1892, introduction

"Egypt was the supreme power in the

Mediterranean area

during the whole of the Bronze Age and a great part of the Iron Age; and as our present culture is directly due to the Mediterranean civilization of the Bronze Age it follows that it has its roots in ancient Egypt."

Margaret A. Murray, *The Splendour That Was Egypt*, Philosophical Library, New York, 1957, p. xviii

Professor Carter G. Woodson in his classic *The Mis-Education of the Negro* indicated that:

"Thinkers are now saying that **the early culture of the Mediterranean was chiefly African."**
(African World Press, New Jersey, 1990, p. 137)

"Egypt is the oldest country in the world;

so old that we, brought up on the History of England, can scarcely realize her age. The dawn of history in these islands took place at a time when in Egypt it was forgotten that

she once had been

Empress of the known world.

Mere comparison of dates scarcely helps us"

Lawrence W. Balls, *Egypt of the Egyptians*, Sir Isaac Pitman & Sons, Ltd., New York and Melbourne: 1915, p. 1

Professor Capart reasoned that:

"It is only by an attentive study of details, sometimes infinitesimal, that one arrives at showing clearly the ties which unite us to **these old Egyptians who were probably the first to cause man to pass from barbarism to civilization.** The universities, the great American museums, have happily recognized this..."

Lectures on Egyptian Art, The University of North Carolina Press, Chapel Hill, 1928, p. 204-5

"Even if one limits the fullest expression of the Egyptian culture to the period from 2650 to 1450 B. C., one must admit that twelve hundred years of stability constitute a very weighty achievement.

Toynbee speaks respectfully of 'the immortality' which Egyptian culture sought and found in stone. It seems probable that the Pyramids, which have already borne inanimate witness to the existence of their creators for nearly five thousand years, will survive for hundreds of thousands of years to come.

It is not inconceivable that they may outlast man himself and that, in a world where there are no longer human minds to read their message, they will continue to testify;

' Before Abraham was, I am.'

(Of what importance to us is such a civilization, which was so long-lived and so immortal in its physical expression? [A Study of History, Oxford Press, 1947 p. 30]) "

John A. Wilson, *The Culture of Ancient Egypt,* The University of Chicago Press, Chicago and London, 1951, p. 310

The author of *"The Living Pageant of the Nile* indicates that:

...in Egyptian history we find a fixed and acknowledged date that fell more than two centuries

earlier than the Biblical date of the Creation."

Robert Forrest Wilson, The Bobbs-Merrill Company, Indianapolis, 1924, p. 13-4

And, the late great Senegalese intellectual giant Cheikh Anta Diop chronicles the early advancement of Egyptian civilization:

"...the myth of Isis and Osiris...dates from the origin of Egyptian history. From this distant period...to the end of Egyptian history...During this lengthy period, unique in history by its duration,

Egypt must have known

all the refinements of civilization

and

must have instructed *all* the younger peoples

of the Mediterranean..."

The Cultural Unity of Black Africa, (Trans. 1963), Third World Press, Chicago, 1963, p. 58

A late nineteenth-century historian wrote that:

"Architecture and sculpture, the art of writing and the use of paper, mathematics, chemistry, medicine,

indeed we might add legislation, and almost every art which flourishes under a settled form of government,

either took its rise in Egypt or

reached Europe through that country."

Samuel Sharpe, *The History of Egypt,* vol. I, (6th Ed.), George Bell & Sons, London, 1876, preface

"The first pages in the annals of

human history

tell us of its great works and its glory.

Its physical makeup was characterized by very special phenomena, and scientific progress has not at all weakened even today the powerful interest that these have always excited."

Jacques Champollion, *The World of the Egyptians*, Minerva

As one writer puts it,

...we cannot escape a strong feeling that

our existence really begins

in the shadow of the pyramids.

Jacquetta Hawkes, Pharaohs of Egypt, *American Heritage Publishing Co., Inc., New York, 1965*

"Egypt had evidently a great charm for the penetrating genius of Plato... He seems to have believed in

the 10,000 years of antiquity,

claimed by the Egyptians

for certain of their monuments...

(*Plato*, Legg II 567.—already mentioned in the section—comp. With *Timeus* p. 23)."

Christian Bunsen, *Egypt's Place in Universal History*, vol. I (trans. Charles Cottrell), Longmans, Green & Co., 1867, p. 122

The New York Times (February 8, 1992) reported on Dr. R.M. Schoch, "a geologist whose research findings suggest that the Great Sphinx of

Egypt is *thousands of years older* than

scholars generally believe...

at the convention of the American Association for the Advancement of Science...the geologist, **Dr. Robert M. Schoch of Boston University**, *using sound waves*, suggested that it was carved sometime between **7000 and 5000 B. C.**"

"...for at the time when the heroes of Homer were fighting before Troy, ancient Egypt had already passed her zenith and had reached her period of decadence...In Egypt the number of monuments which have come down to us seems inexhaustible."

Adolph Erman, *Life in Ancient Egypt,* H.M. Tirard, trans., Benjamin Blomdale, New York, 1969, p. 3

Even Professor C. Seignobos of the University of Paris in his book, **History of Civilization** traces civilization back to Africa:

"It is within the limits of Asia and **Africa** that the **first civilized peoples** had their development;

the Egyptians in the Nile Valley, the Chaldeans in the plains of the Euphrates.

Their **skin** was **dark,** the hair short and thick, the lips strong (some terming them Cushites, others Hamites)."

"The existence of Thebes was prior to that of the other cities. The testimony of writers is very positive in this respect.

'**The Thebans'** says Diodorus, 'considered themselves as the **most ancient people** of the earth, and assert, that with them **originated philosophy** and the **science** of the stars.

Their situations, it is true, is infinitely favorable to astronomical observation, and they have a more accurate division of time into months and years than other nations,' " etc.

Count Volney, *The Ruins of Empire* p. 16

On the same page, Volney continues:

"What Diodorus says of the Thebans, every author, and himself elsewhere, repeat of the Ethiopians, which tends more firmly to establish the identity of this place of which I have spoken.

'The **Ethiopians** conceive themselves,' says he, lib. iii, **to be of greater antiquity than any other nation** and it is probable that, born under the sun's path, its warmth may have ripened them earlier than other men.

They suppose themselves also to be the **inventors** of **divine worship**, of festivals, of solemn assemblies, of sacrifices, and every other religious practices."

The *Pyramids and Sphinx* is a book by Desmond Stewart and the editors of the *Newsweek* Book Division (1971). In it, the editors made the following statement:

"Out of the mists nearly five thousand years ago appeared the **world's first civilizations** - that of Mesopotamia and the splendid edifice of ancient **Egypt**.

With its art, architecture, religion, political organization and given its cryptic hieroglyphic system of writing, the **culture** that **developed along the Nile took man forward** from his prehistoric past in truly giant steps."

Continuing:

"...the developments in this favored land during the thousand or more years before the pyramid age represent a series of

creative advances unrivaled in human experience ...

the fourth millennium *before* **Christ** is like some talented, unnamed ancestor in a family tree whose genes send valuable but unacknowledged donations to descendants now alive."

Cheikh Anta Diop *The African Origin Of Civilization* clearly shows that:

"Ethnically homogenous, the

Negro peoples created all the elements of civilization

by adapting to the favorable geographical conditions of their early homelands."

To which he adds: "**Africa's civilizing role**, even in prehistoric times, is increasingly affirmed by the most distinguished scholars."

"What we can infer from untidy graves and abandoned feint tools, from mace heads and statuettes, is an accelerating growth of village communities along the Nile and its delta branches.

The men who peopled them were '**Africans**' related to their Libyan neighbors to the west and **the Nubians to the south. Their small communities are**

the remote ancestors of modern towns."

Desmond Stewart, *The Pyramids and Sphinx* Newsweek, Inc., 1971
p. 20

The opinion of all the ancient writers on the Egyptian race is
more or less summed up by Gaston Maspero (1846-1916):

"By the almost unanimous testimony of ancient historians, they belonged to an African race (read: Negro) which first settled in Ethiopia, on the Middle Nile;

following the course of the river, they gradually reached
the sea ... Moreover, the Bible states that Mesraim, son of
Ham, brother of Chus (Kush) the Ethiopian, and of
Canaan, came from Mesopotamia to settle with his children on the banks of the Nile."

The Dawn Of Civilization, London, 1894

In the book **Origin of Civilized Societies**, there is a chapter entitled, 'Civilized Man and His History,' where the
historian Ruston Coulborn asserts that:

"The earliest civilized societies were the Egyptians and
Mesopotamian societies, which arose in the valleys
respectively of the Nile and of the Tigris and Euphrates,
probably in the fifth millennium B. C."

The history text known as *A Short History of Western Civilization*
by Professors Harrison, Sullivan and Sherman published by
Alfred A. Knopf, New York points to the consensus;

"It is now generally agreed that a great leap forward in
human history occurred shortly after 4000 B. C., allowing
people occupying the Tigris-Euphrates Valley in
Mesopotamia and the Nile Valley in Egypt to make a
SPECTACULAR ADVANCE from primitive agricultural
life to complex urban civilization."

The authors Edward Burns and Philip Ralph in their well-known
work, *World Civilizations*, 5th ed. further remarked that:

"**...progress in the arts and sciences had reached unpar-
alleled heights** in both of these areas as early as 3000 B.
C., when most of the rest of the world was steeped in
ignorance."

"In all, the belief of the nation attributes to itself the immemorial possession of its own soil; and to its progenitors or to the gods the invention of the arts and sciences. Whether these have really had a single origin, and what has been their primitive seat, is a question which the present state of historical knowledge does not enable us to answer. But there is no difficulty in fixing on the country from which Ancient History must begin.

The monuments of Egypt, its records and its literature, surpass those of India and China in antiquity by many centuries."

John, M. A. Kenrick, *Ancient Egypt Under the Pharaohs*, Vol. I, Charles Edwin Wilbour, London, 1850, p .2

"THE MESOPOTAMIAN AND PERSIAN CIVILIZATIONS" is a chapter heading from the history textbook, **World Civilizations** by Burns and Ralph. These historians declare that:

"The other of the most ancient civilizations was that which began in the Tigris-Euphrates valley at least as early as 4000 B. C. This civilization was formerly called the Babylonian civilization. It is now known, however, that the civilization was not founded by either the Babylonians or the Assyrians but by an earlier people called the Sumerians. It seems better, therefore, to use the name Mesopotamian to cover the whole civilization."

In the same chapter, they added:

"More than to any other people, the Mesopotamian civilization owed its character to the Sumerians."

Thus "the pioneers in the development of the Mesopotamian civilization were the people known as Sumerians, who settled in the lower Tigris-Euphrates valley between 5000 and 4000 B. C."

Edward McNall Burns and Philip Lee Ralph World *Civilizations*, 5th Ed. W. W. Norton, New York, p. 149

"The myths, legends, and traditions of the Sumerians definitely point to **AFRICA** as the **ORIGINAL HOME OF**

THE SUMERIANS. The first Sumerian remains were unearthed in the middle of the nineteenth century by Hincks, Oppert, and Rawlinson. Sir Henry Rawlinson called these people Kushites ... Rawlinson anticipated Perry by tracing **the Sumerians back to Ethiopia."**

(John G. Jackson, *Man, God and Civilization*)

> "Modern archeological investigations have discovered the remains of numerous flourishing Neolithic villages in the Tigris-Euphrates basin, which seem to have been becoming more populous and complex around 4000 B. C. The first city builders in Mesopotamia were the Sumerians, invaders who settled in the extreme southern area of the Tigris-Euphrates Valley in a land named Sumer after the new settlers."

The Western Experience, Professors: Chambers, Green, Herlihy, Rabb and Woloch Alfred A. Knopf, N. Y., p. 8

Likewise:

> "Far to the east, in modern Iraq (ancient Mesopotamia, between the rivers' Tigris and Euphrates)... at Uruk on the banks of the Euphrates River, farmers were using the plow to scratch the soil before sowing their seeds, and were already keeping the business accounts of their temple in simple picture writing.

> ## This was the great leap forward that took human beings out of prehistory and into history.

> Similar advances are also found in Egypt at roughly the same time."

A History of Civilization, Vol. I, Brinton, Christopher, Wolff, Prentice-Hall Inc., New Jersey, p. 10

The Western Experience is a well-known history text by Professors M. Chambers (University of California); R. Green (University of Michigan); D. Herlihy (Harvard University); T. Rabb (Princeton University) and I. Woloch (Columbia University).

The introduction to the content of their textbook begins:

"By Western experience we mean the history of European civilization and its remoter origins in earlier civilizations located in Mesopotamia and around the Mediterranean. Man began to abandon a nomadic existence and live in settled agricultural communities only about 10,000 years ago.

Some 5,000 years later, settlements grew up along the banks of the **Tigris**, **Euphrates**, **Nile** and **Indus**."

"For Well Over A Thousand Years After Their First Flourishing, The Peoples Of The Valley Civilizations Held The Stage Virtually Alone....

About 3,000 B. C., at approximately the time that the Sumerian civilization emerged in Mesopotamia, the Egyptians had reached a comparable state of development. Much better known to us than Mesopotamia, Egypt was another ancient valley civilization that made major contributions to our own."

A History of Civilization, Vol. I, Brinton, Christopher, Wolff. Prentice-Hall Inc., New Jersey p. 16, 20

Thus,

"...the emergence of civilization in the Near East, unfolded in two river valley systems in the Near East: the Tigris-Euphrates in Mesopotamia and the **Nile in Egypt**.

For it was in the challenging environment of these river valleys that human communities developed the first complex patterns of institutions, techniques, and ideas that can be called **'civilization.'**

What was achieved in this setting established the foundations upon which Western civilization was to grow.

Beyond characterizing the main features of the early civilizations of Mesopotamia and *Egypt*, we must consider the beginnings of a process as important to the history of the Western world as was *the original creation of civilized life* namely, the beginning of the expansion of the river valley civilizations into a large area of northeast Africa and southwest Asia.

Not only did this process permit new peoples to raise the level of their existence, but it also created a stream of civilization.

Until at least 500 B. C. the peoples of the Near East were on the forefront of the civilized world.

This creative population fashioned a priceless heritage that was later exploited by other peoples participating in the shaping of Western civilization."

A Short History of Western Civilization Professors: John B. Harrison, Richard E. Sullivan (Michigan State University) Dennis Sherman (John Jay College of Criminal Justice City University of N. Y.), Alfred A. Knopf, N. Y.

"THE ORIGINAL HERITAGE OF THE NEAR EAST," is a chapter authored by Hayes (Columbia University), Baldwin (New York University) and Cole (Rockefeller Center). They maintained that:

"The origins of what we understand as European civilization are to be found, not in Europe itself, but in the eastern Mediterranean basin... in either northeastern AFRICA or southwestern Asia, the achievements of its inhabitants in ancient times constitute the first important heritage of Mediterranean and hence of European civilization.

Long before Europeans as such had emerged from barbarism, men had reached a relatively high degree of civilization in the lands bordering the eastern Mediterranean...that region includes two vast river basins, the NILE and the Tigris- Euphrates..."

History of Western Civilization, Macmillan Co., N. Y., 1964

The History of the Ancient World, Vol. I is a book authored by the former Professor of Ancient History at Yale University, M. Rostoutzeff who defined it in these words:

"Ancient history is the history of man's development in the earliest period of his existence: it tells how at that period he created and developed the **civilization** from which the **culture of all nations now** existing is **derived**. This ancient civilization, which spread by degrees over the world, was **first developed** in the Near East, and chiefly **in Egypt**, Mesopotamia...

In this civilization there were successive epochs of high development ... a series of creative periods which produced inestimable treasures not only of a material kind but also in the intellectual region of culture ...

The zenith of cultural creation was attained by Egypt and Babylon in the third millennium B. C.; by Egypt again in the second millennium..."

However, Dr. Albert Churchward in his book, *Signs & Symbols Of Primordial Man* makes it clear that:

The Babylonians copied and obtained all their knowledge from the Egyptians (p. 213)

Quoting Baldwin's *Pre-Historic Nation*:

"the Cushite race appeared first in the work of civilization....

The Hebrews saw nothing geographical

more ancient

than this land of Cush..."

"The German historian Professor A. H. L. Heeren, also speculated on the place of the origin of the world's earliest civilization, and he had no hesitation in locating it among the African Ethiopians:

"In Nubia and Ethiopia, stupendous, numerous and primeval monuments proclaim so loudly a civilization contemporary to, aye, earlier than that of Egypt,

that it may be conjectured with the greatest confidence that

the arts, sciences and religion descended from Nubia

to the lower country of Mizraim; that civilization descended the Nile ... (*Historical Researches: African Nations* by Arnold Hermann Ludwig Heeren, cited by Lady Lugard, p. 220-21.)"

John Jackson, *Man, God and Civilization*

The German scholar of history, Herr Eugen Georg declared:

"A splendid era of Black seems to have preceded all the later races!

There must once have been a tremendous *negro* expansion, since the *original masters of all* the lands

> between Iberia and the Cape of Good Hope and East India were primitive and probably dwarfed **Black men**.

We have long had proof that a primitive Negroid race of pigmies once lived around the Mediterranean.

Blacks were the first to plow the mud of the Nile."

The Adventure Of Mankind, E. P. Dutton & Co., 1931

> "Since **Egypt**" lies "on the Mediterranean Sea, its ancient wonders have always been known and marveled at ... From the days of Greece and Rome on down to modern times the civilization of the land of the

NILE has exercised an influence directly upon western civilization."

Chester G. Starr, *A History of the Ancient World*, 2nd Ed., Oxford University Press, N. Y., 1974

"History begins on the banks of the Nile.

When the curtain first rises upon civilization we find here a great empire. After an unbroken silence of over fifteen centuries **this *eldest child of the Race* is now whispering into the ear of its youngest sister the...facts of human history.**

When Abraham visited Egypt he saw a great monarchy, the inhabitants of which had already been long enjoying all the advantages of a settled government and established laws."

Charles H. S. Davis, Camden M Cobern, *Ancient Egypt in Light of Modern Discoveries*, Introduction by Rev. C. Winslow, of the Egypt Exploration Foundation, Biblia Publishing Co., Meridian, Conn., 1892, p. 1

Here is how one great historian, John Henrik Clarke, quotes another great historian W. E. B. Dubois:

"Always Africa is giving us something new...

On its Black boson arose one of the earliest, if not the earliest, of self-protecting civilizations, and

grew so mighty that it still furnishes superlatives to thinking and speaking men.

Out of its darker and more remote forest...came, if we may credit many recent scientists, the first welding of iron, and

we know that agriculture and trade flourished there when Europe was a wilderness."

The Foundations of White Supremacy

(How White Supremacy is *"proven"* and *"justified"*)

Pillar # 1

Greece [And Rome]

Founded Civilization

Translation:

White people are *the* major contributors to mankind and world progress. The natural conclusion therefore is that Europeans/Caucasians are generally the smartest human beings in the world because they were the first to develop civilization —- a superior intellectual trait. Thus, the Greeks gave the world logic and reason in place of superstition and instinct. The Romans gave us law in place of emotionalism.

The White man is the most intelligent man on earth because if it were not for him the rest of the non-Whites would still be primitive barbarians and savages —- an inferior intellectual trait.

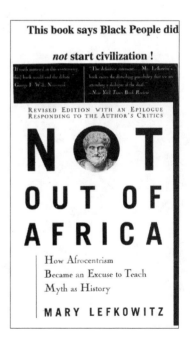

This book says Black People did *not* start civilization !

If truth mattered in this controversy [this] book would end the debate."
George F. Will, *Newsweek*

"The definitive statement... Ms. Lefkowitz's book meets the disturbing possibility that we are attending a dialogue of the deaf."
—*New York Times Book Review*

REVISED EDITION WITH AN EPILOGUE
RESPONDING TO THE AUTHOR'S CRITICS

NOT
OUT OF
AFRICA

How Afrocentrism
Became an Excuse to Teach
Myth as History

MARY LEFKOWITZ

The White man saved them with his superior intelligence and civilizing ways. White people were the first in science, mathematics, medicine, philosophy and all other disciplines that require intellectual maturity and "brain power".

Humanity would still be in the Stone Age if it weren't for the innate superiority of the White race.

Conclusion to the subconscious: If they are smarter and more intelligent, then they must also be superior or better.

Creators Of "Greek Philosophy"

[The African Origins of "Western Intelligence"]

The famous English writer, Percy Bysshe Shelly, declared:

"We are all Greeks; our laws, our literature, our religion, our arts have their roots in Greece. But for Greece...we might still have been savages..."

Even so, "Shelley's exclamation," says Sheldon Cheney, "still rings down the corridors of our universities..."

A World History of Art, New York, 1952, p. 138

In commenting on Western civilization, Professors Chambers, Herlihy, Rabb, et. al. are of the opinion that:

"Greek Civilization influenced our own in a far more direct way than did that of the ancient Near East."

The Western Experience vol. I, 3rd Ed.   Alfred A. Knopf, New York

In the book *The Origin of Greek Civilization 1100 - 650 B. C.*, (1961), the historian Chester G. Starr states that:

"The **pattern of civilization**, however, which we call **"Greek"** and which has directly **influenced all subsequent Western history**, was evolved only in the centuries between 1100 and 650 B. C." (p. 5)

J. M. Roberts, a contemporary modern historian and author of *A History of Europe*, provides an explanation in one of his chapters entitled, "The Earliest European":

"...Europe...long remained profoundly conscious of its classical roots...Yet when all this has been said and allowed for, and when skeptical modern scholars have done their spectacular best to qualify and explain the limits of civilization in the Greek and Roman World, we are left with a huge mass of cultural fact which down to this day have helped **to determine the way in which Europe and the minds of Europeans took shape in history. To understand that, we have to start with the Greeks."**

Allen Lane, The Penguin Press, New York, New York, 1996, p. 22

"The first Indo-Europeans to emerge into the clear light of history, in what is now Europe, were the Greeks...The newcomers consisted of separate *barbaric tribes* and their coming ushered in several centuries of chaos and unrest before a gradual stabilization and revival began in the ninth century. The *Iliad* and the *Odyssey*, written down about 800 B. C...probably refer to wars between the Greeks and other centers of civilization, of which one was at Troy in Asia Minor..."

R. R. Palmer and J. Colton, *A History of the Modern World*, (3rd ed.). Alfred A. Knopf, New York, p. 4

"The Modern Western world, it is often said, was born in the Greek cities of Ionia toward the close of the eighth century B. C..."

And yet, 'J. Brunet' as quoted by Herbert Muller 'wrote in his Early Greek Philosophy' that Ionia was a country without a past..." there was no traditional background there at all."

Herbert J. Muller, *The Loom of History*, Harper and Bros., N. Y., 1958

"Our classical studies start from texts: theirs did not, and we exaggerate their literacy

(There are more outward signs of literacy in the Indian subcontinent today than there were in ancient Greece, yet well over 70 % of the population cannot read or write)."

John Boardman, Ed., Jasper Griffin, Oswyn Murray, *The Oxford History of the Classical World*, Oxford University Press, Oxford, 1987, p. 300

"According to tradition, about 1200 B. C. the cities were attacked by an invading horde of more primitive Greeks known as Dorians.

They were ***illiterate,*** and though they possessed weapons of iron, their knowledge of the arts and crafts was no more than ***rudimentary***.

They burned the palace at Mycenae and sacked a number of the others."

Edward Burns and Philip Ralph, *World Civilizations*, W. W. Norton & Co., New York, p. 177

"By that time, however, signs of internal decay were evident and the process was hastened by the invasion of the Dorians, a people who were Greek but who were

culturally impoverished and

unacquainted with the art of writing."

Jean Hatzfeld, *History of Ancient Greece*, E. H. Goddard Trans., W. W. Norton & Company, New York, p. 27

"The archaeological remains from the late twelfth century give the impression that a giant hand had suddenly swept away the splendid Mycenaean civilization.

Leaving in its wake only *isolation and poverty...*

For the next 450 years...

the art of writing was forgotten

and would not return until the 6th century."

Sarah B. Pomeroy, Stanley M. Burstein, Walter Donlan, and Jennifer T. Robert, *Ancient Greece, A Political, Social and Cultural History*, Oxford University Press, New York, Oxford, 1999, p. 41

"The culture of many of the Greeks had always been *rudimentary*.

That of the Mycenaeans rapidly deteriorated following the destruction of Mycenae. We can therefore conclude that

cultural achievement in most of Greece remained at a low ebb throughout the period from 1000 to 800 B. C... essentially the period was a long night."

Edward Burns and Philip Ralph, *World Civilizations*, W. W. Norton & Co., New York, p. 177

A Professor at Corpus Christi College, Oxford, Robin Osborne points out that:

In Greece fewer places have revealed material signs of human presence in 1000 B. C...Indeed, the picture we get from material evidence for the two centuries after 1050 B. C. is one of successive failures to establish any extensive political, economic, or social organization.

Greece In The Making 1200 - 479 B. C., Routledge, London and New York, 1996, p. 41

"And, Greece settles down into a Dark Age of 300 years, dark both because its history is wrapped in obscurity and because **no light of art or culture seems to have shone upon it."**

Cyril E. Robinson, *A History of Greece,* Methuen Educational, 9th Edition, London, New York, 1983,

A similar point is made in the book, *The Rise of the West* by William H. McNeil:

"The Greeks of the Dark Age were **rude** and **barbarous**."

Professor at the University of Chicago, James H. Breasted says the same:

"Long after 1000 B. C. the life of the Greeks continued to be **rude** and even **barbarous..."**

The Conquest of Civilization, Harper & Bros., New York and London, 1946, p. 276

"It is known that these **Indo-Europeans** from the grasslands spread over Europe some time after 2000 B. C., and that they spread their language far and wide over the Continent. But there may not have been great numbers of them.

They may have been hardly more than a sprinkling of... barbarian conquerors....

These invaders were *barbarians* and remained barbarians save as Mediterranean civilization taught them better things.

Geoffrey Parsons, *The Stream of History,* vol. II, Charles Scribner's Sons, New York, 1929, p. 36

"Greece in ancient times was never a nation; it never had a capital, a government

or a single ruling element.

The typical Greek-speaking sovereign state was a tribe cultivating an area of land separated from the next cultivable area by a range of rocky hills or mountains."

Kenneth Dover, *The Greeks*, (from the BBC television series by Christopher Burstall and Kenneth Dover) British Broadcasting Corporation, London, 1980, p. viii

"The Greeks were not...a deeply religious race."

Cyril E. Robinson, *A History of Greece*, Methuen Educational, 9th Edition, London, New York, 1983, p. 160

As Geoffrey Parsons, author of *The Stream of History*, vol. II demonstrates:

"...the morality of the Greeks in the Dark Ages had only the vaguest connection with their religion....**The gods...did not consider it their duty to combat evil and make righteousness prevail.**"
(Charles Scribner's Sons, New York, 1929, p. 36)

"*Long after* they had taken possession of the Aegean world

the Greeks remained a barbarous people

of flocks and herds, without any commerce by sea."

James Breasted, *The Conquest of Civilization*, Harper & Bros., New York and London, 1946, p. 276

"The Greeks, unlike the Hebrews,

had no sacred book

that chronicled their past. Instead they had the Iliad and the Odyssey to describe a time when gods still walked the earth. And they learned the origin and descent of the gods from the Theogony, an epic poem by Hesiod (ca 700 B. C.). For all their importance to Greek thought and literature, Homer and Hesiod were shadowy figures. Later Greeks knew little about them and were not even certain when they had lived. This uncertainty underscores the fact that *the Greeks remembered very little of their own past, especially the time before they entered Greece.* They had also forgotten a great deal about the Bronze and Dark ages."

John P. Mc Kay , Bennett D. Hill, John Buckler, *A History of World Societies, volume I: to 1715*, Houghton Mifflin Company, Boston, 1987

Nevertheless, **"GREECE has traditionally been looked upon as the CRADLE of WESTERN CIVILIZATION."**

Michael Carter, *Archaeology*, Brandford Press Ltd.

In the book *Ancient Greece, The Dawn of the Western World*, by Furio Durando, it declares that:

The civilization of ancient Greece is the root, essence, and inexhaustible **core of western thinking**

as well as, variously, the source, tributary, or delta of the numerous cultures in the Mediterranean bases. Over the centuries its power to fascinate each new generation has never waned. (Stewart, Tabori & Chang, New York, foreword)

The historian, of course, will inform us that **all Western civilization has Greece for its mother and nurse**, and that unless we know something about her our knowledge of the past must be built upon sand...

Lastly, there are a few elderly people who have survived the atmosphere of "the classics," and yet cherish the idea of Greece as something almost holy in its tremendous power of inspiration...They talk of Greece as if it were in the same latitude as Heaven, not Naples.

J. C. Stobart, *The Glory That Was Greece*, 3rd ed, Grove Press, Inc. New York, 1962, p. 2

"In other fields, **Greece has left a unique legacy to the world. Nearly all the great achievements of western civilization**, in politics and philosophy, in art and architecture, in literature and science, have either drawn their inspiration from ancient Greece or at least owed much to her example.

The Greeks were "a race accustomed to take little and give much." **They have given a treasure to the world that is not exhausted...they carried human nature almost to the limit of its glorious power.**

Their call to the eternal ideals of Truth and Beauty, Political Freedom and Justice still echoes clearly down the centuries from that distant time when the world still seemed lit with morning glory..."

W. N. Weech (ed.) *History of the World*, Odhams Press Limited, London, p. 172

...Nearly four thousand years ago the Greeks descended into the peninsula at the southeastern extremity of Europe that still bears their name. With them the history of Europe and of western civilization begins...the rocky peninsula of **Greece was the home of the civilization that fundamentally shaped Western civilization...**

John P. McKay, Bennett D. Hill, John Buckler, *A History of World Societies*, volume I: to 1715, Houghton Mifflin Company, Boston, 1987, p. 45

"...With the Greeks, there emerged what might be called the specifically 'Western intelligence.' ..."

Helen Gardner, *Art Through The Ages*, 3rd Edition, Harcourt, Brace and Company, New York, 1948.

"...we idealize the Greeks as the originators of western civilization..."

Jasper Griffin, Oswyn Murray, *The Oxford History of the Classical World*, Oxford University Press, John Boardman, Ed., Oxford University Press, Oxford, 1987

In a chapter entitled, "The Cradle of Western Thought: Ionia" from the book *A History of Philosophy*, vol. 1, by Frederick Copleston S. J, he declares that:

"The Greeks, then, stand as the uncontested original thinkers and scientists of Europe."

Robert Payne makes a similar claim:

" We owe to the Greeks

the **beginning of science**

and

the **beginning of thought**..."

The Splendor of Greece, Harper and Row, New York, 1960, p. 75

To cite noted historians R. R. Palmer and J. Colton:

The Greeks proved to be as gifted a people as mankind has ever produced, achieving supreme heights in thought and letters.

A History of the Modern World, (3rd ed.), Alfred A. Knopf, New York, p. 4

Speaking of the Greeks themselves, the learned scholar Charles Rollins had this to say in his book *The Ancient History*:

"Who would imagine that the people, to whom **the world is indebted for all her knowledge in literature and the sciences,** should be

descended from mere savages,

who knew no other law than force, were ignorant even of agriculture, and *fed on herbs and roots like the brute beast* and yet this appears plainly to be the case."

"And indeed for nearly all of us there was a time in our most impressionable years when we were taught to accept **"the Greek miracle"** and "Athenian perfection" as ideas beyond challenge or comparison. Classical education bathed Hellas and the Greek Isles in a golden haze. We were expected to believe uncritically in the legend of a people gifted and inspired above all others. We were accustomed and content to see the Parthenon, the Venus of Milo, and the figured vases with a glamorous light upon them: as of an eminence unquestioned and unquestionable."

Sheldon Cheney, *A World History of Art*, The Viking Press, New York, 1952

"Among all the peoples of ancient world, the one whose culture most clearly exemplified the spirit of the Western man was the Hellenic or Greek ..."

Edward McNall Burns and Philip Lee Ralph, *World Civilizations*, 5th Ed., W. W. Norton & Co., N. Y., p. 175

"Never in all the world's history was there such a leap of civilization as in Greece of the fifth century."

J. C. Stobart, *The Glory That Was Greece*, 3rd ed., Grove Press, Inc., New York, 1962

As the author of *The Stream of History*, vol. II would have us believe:

"...the growth of the Greek genius seemed a *miracle*.

So far as was known barbarians descending from the north suddenly became the greatest race the world had seen. Without training or precedent they flowered into the wisest and most artistic of peoples." (Geoffrey Parsons, Charles Scribner's Sons, New York, 1929, p. 121)

"Almost every phase of modern or Western civilization has been molded by the thought of Ancient Greece.

Greek influence in art, education, literature, philosophy, politics, science, and medicine has been so great and all-pervading that, especially during the end of the last and the beginning of the present century, scholars deeply imbued with the Hellenic tradition too often came to look upon Greece so exclusively as their spiritual home that

they referred to

these origins as

the 'Greek Miracle'."

J. B. deC. M. Saunders, M. D., *The Transitions from Ancient Egyptian to Greek Medicine*, University of Kansas Press, Lawrence, 1963, p. 1

The African Origins of the "Greek Miracle"

We quote the respected scholar Professor George Sarton of Harvard University:

"It is childish to assume that science

began in Greece.

The 'Greek miracle' was prepared

by millennia of work

in Egypt."

A History of Science, Harvard University Press, N. Y., 1953

"The 'Aryans' did not establish civilization—they took it from ...Egypt.

Greece did *not* begin civilization

—it inherited far more civilization than it began;

it was the spoiled heir of

three millenniums of

arts and sciences..."

Will Durant, *The Story of Civilization*, Part I, Simon and Schuster, New York, 1954, p. 116

Like Professor Sauneron and Professor Davidson, Dr. Diop tellingly illustrates how the Greeks themselves testified to having been taught by the ancient Egyptians:

"...*All* the statements, unanimously, from the pen of *the greatest Greek* scholars, philosophers, and writers, *glorify* the theoretical sciences of *the Egyptians*

—a fact all the more important because these Greek scholars are contemporaries of the ancient Egyptians. One might expect that the Greeks, who had just succeeded the Persians on the throne of Egypt, through national pride, have tried to misrepresent the facts on the fundamental point of the origin of theoretical science and particularly of mathematics; the idea could not occur to them, because their emergence was too recent and the reputation of Egyptian science too ancient!

Also *Egypt* even conquered, remained

The Venerable Home of The Sciences

that

She Had Kept Secret For Millennia.

Now, the barbarian had broken through the doors of her sanctuaries; she is conquered and will become by force the teacher of young nations, of the Greeks in particular: the 'Greek miracle' will begin, as a consequence of the occupation of Egypt by the foreigner, Greek in particular, and therefore of the forced access to the scientific treasures of Egypt, of the plundering of the temple libraries and of the submission of the priests.

It must be strongly emphasized that the Greeks never said that they were the students of the Babylonians or of the Chaldeans; their most reputable scholars will always boast about having been the pupils of the Egyptians, as the writings of their biographers reveal: Thales, the semi-legendary father of Greek mathematics, Pythagoras of Samos, Eudoxus, etc."

Cheikh Anta Diop, *Civilization or Barbarism*, Lawrence Hill Books, New York, 1981, p. 256

The Legacy of Egypt edited by Dr. S. Granville of the University of Cambridge points out the intellectual abilities of the Egyptians:

"...a nation which had evolved sufficient knowledge and skill

to plan and accomplish feats of architecture and engineering

as early as the fourth millennium *before* Christ,

and whose mathematical knowledge...involved the principles of cubic capacity, angles fractional notation, and the square-root,

must clearly have been *far ahead* of its contemporaries in
intellectual capacity."

Oxford University Press, London, 1942, p.179

**"Intellectually, the Egyptians must take rank
among the foremost nations
of remote antiquity."**

George Rawlinson, *History of Ancient History*, vol. II, Dodd, Mead
& Co., New York, 1918, p.106

**Under the Old Kingdom, Egypt realized her
highest material and intellectual powers.**

She was a new culture, with all the excitement of working
out her form of national expression.

**In future ages she would have very great
achievements to her credit,**

but her subsequent endeavors never had the same self-
assured composure.

The Old Kingdom had vigor, savoir faire, and confidence.
In terms of what the ancients seemed to be trying to estab-
lish as a way of life, the Old Kingdom appeals as the most
Egyptian of periods...

John A Wilson, *The Culture of Ancient Egypt*, The University of
Chicago Press, Chicago and London, 1951, p.104

As the Prussian scholar Professor Baron von Bunsen noted in his
Egypt's Place in Universal History, (vol. I) about the so-called
"father of botany," (p.122):

"We have seen...that Theophrastus quoted 'Egyptian
Annals.' Porphyry mentions his having described

the Egyptians as the most learned people,

and

the deepest antiquarians in the world."

To quote two twentieth century scholars of philosophy, Professors R. Solomon and K. Higgins from the University of Texas at Austin:

The Greeks traded throughout the Mediterranean, borrowing freely from other cultures...

From Egypt they obtained the ideas that defined what we call Greek architecture, the basics of geometry, and much else besides...

Greece was not a 'miracle' it was a lucky accident of history and the product of many unattributed lessons from neighbors and predecessors...

As part of this process, the Egyptian god Osiris became the Greek demigod Dionysus and a powerful cult of Dionysus spread across Greece in the sixth century B. C. E."

Robert C. Solomon and Kathleen M. Higgins, *A Short History of Philosophy*, Oxford University Press, New York, Oxford, 1996, p. 7

Later on, they continue:

Many of the leading ideas of Greek philosophy, including the all-important interest in geometry and the concept of the soul, were imported from Egypt.

Indeed, it might be more enlightening to view the 'miracle' in Greece not as a remarkable beginning but as a culmination, the climax of a long story the beginnings and the middle of which we no longer recognize." (p. 9)

Before Greece and Rome

To quote National Geographic's, *The Mysteries of the Ancient World*:

"They have stood for almost 5,000 years these man-made mountains we call pyramids. *Five Thousand Years*—**time enough for the Roman Empire to rise and fall a dozen times over. Time, indeed, for all of Western civilization to run its course.**

Long before Caesar or Pericles

or even Hammurabi;

before Moses and the Exodus,

before Tutankhamun;

before Egypt's Valley of the Kings sheltering a single royal tomb or Mesopotamia's ancient city of Nineveh...

the pyramids already were old.

Yet they stand tall relatively intact despite nearly fifty centuries of earthquakes, wars, tourists, tomb robbers, neglect, and natural decay. Little wonder that they have come to symbolize eternity itself.

ALL THINGS DREAD TIME,

BUT TIME DREADS THE PYRAMIDS."

(Arab Proverb)

Tom Melham, *Egypt's Pyramids: Monuments of the Pharaohs*, p. 56

Missing Pages of History, Indus Khamit-Kush, 1994

Willis N. Huggins in his book *Introduction to African Civilization*, wrote these words in the 1930's:

"...before there was any 'Glory that was Greece' or 'Grandeur that was Rome,' the Monarchs of Egypt were creating Empires,

building pyramids, fashioning colossi, using measurements to the billionth of an inch, devising chemicals and arraying themselves in all combinations of the spectrum..."

"The splendour of Egypt was not a mere mushroom growth lasting but a few hundred years.

Where *Greece and Rome* can count their supremacy by the *century*

Egypt counts hers

by the *millennium*,

and the remains of that splendour can even now eclipse the remains of any other country in the world..."

Margaret A. Murray, *The Splendour That Was Egypt*, Philosophical Library, New York, 1957, p. xviii

New York University's Professor of Classics, Lionel Casson in his book *Ancient Egypt* (1965) gives an impressive portrayal of this fabled land:

"Antiquity, vast and richly textured, cloaks the land of Egypt. In the dimness of prehistory, more than **10,000 years ago**, man began to settle in the long valley ribboned by the Nile.

Sustained by the life-giving river, the land prospered and, in the **Fourth Millennium** *before* **Christ**, burst into splendor under the first of the Pharaohs. And in splendor outstanding in the ancient world, it flourished for 27 centuries.

Egypt was ancient even to the ancients.

It was a great nation a thousand years ago before the Minoans of Crete...It flourished when tribesmen still dwelt in huts above the Tiber. **It was viewed by Greeks and Romans of 2,000 years ago in some what the same way the ruins of Greece and Rome are viewed by modern man.**" (Time-Life Books, Inc., Virginia, p. 10)

Auguste Mariette, a recognized titanic figure in Egyptology, pays tribute to ancient Egypt in a similar way:

"It was **Egypt** who in the very earliest times appeared under the Pharaohs, as

the ancestor of all nations.

At the time *when history was not*, Cheops was raising monuments which modern art can never hope to surpass."

Outlines of Ancient Egyptian History, Trans. & ed., Mary Brodrick, Charles Scribner's Sons, New York, 1892, p. xxx-xxxi

"For she was already *old*

before

history turned the page

from 'ancient' to 'classical.'"

William A. Ward, *The Spirit of Ancient Egypt,* Khayats, Beirut, p. xvii

The French historian, Jacques Weulersse in his work, *L'Afrigue Noire* (Paris, Ed. Artheme Fayard, 1934, p. 11) offers this view:

"Africa long remained a mystery and, yet ... was it not one of the **cradles of history? An African country, Egypt,** thousands of years old, still presents, practically intact today, the most venerable monuments of Antiquity.

At a time when all Europe was only savagery, when Paris and London were swamps, and Rome and Athens uninhabited sites,

Africa already possessed an antique civilization in the valley of the Nile;

it had populous cities, . . . great public works, sciences, and arts; it had already produced gods."

A very influential scholar by the name of Sir Gardner Wilkinson concluded: "It may be inferred, from their *great advancement* in the *arts and sciences* at this early period, that *many ages of civilization* had *preceded* the accession of *their first monarch.*"

John Baldwin, *Pre-Historic Nations,* Harper & Brothers, New York, 1898, p. 271

"We are accustomed to think of **the days of Plato and Pericles, of Horace and the Caesars, as "ancient times."**

But *Egypt was old* and outworn *when Athens and Rome were founded;*

the great Assyrian Empire was a creation of yesterday

as compared with

that of the Pharaohs;

the middle point of Egyptian history was long past when Moses received this education at the court of Rameses II.; and

the Pyramids were already hoary

with antiquity

when Abraham journeyed into the land of Egypt..."

Amelia B. Edwards, *Egypt and Its Monuments*, Harper & Bros., New York, New York, 1891

Geoffrey Parsons, author of *The Stream of History*, cautions us that:

"It has been custom to class Greece and Rome as ancient history; but the phrase is misleading in so far as it tends to class these civilizations with Egypt... "

Charles Scribner's Sons, New York, 1929, p. 36

To appreciate Egypt's great antiquity one has only to read the words of W. Lawrence Balls:

"To carry our imagination back through two thousand years in England is a long stretch. In Egypt we must go back that much, and then twice as far again. On the most conservative estimate the actual History of Egypt begins 3400 B. C., and one date can be fixed definitely before this at 4241 B. C...

When the Romans came to Egypt the Pyramids of Giza had been standing for nearly thirty centuries,

and Caesar borrowed the Egyptian calendar—spoiling it in the process—which was thirteen centuries older than the Pyramids."

Egypt of the Egyptians, Sir Isaac Pitman & Sons, Ltd., New York and Melbourne: 1915, p. 2

Drawing from one of the great figures in Egyptology, John D. Baldwin quotes Professor Lepsius who said:

"Under the fourth dynasty, when the two great pyramids were built, **the nation** seems to have **approached the highest glory of that wonderful development of intelligence and power to which after the flight of nearly 6000 years, the ruins still bear witness**, and to which they will continue to bear witness for ages to come."

Pre-Historic Nations, Harper & Brothers, New York, 1898, p. 29

"What is most characteristic about Egypt is its enduringness. Here the continuous record of man spans three times the age of the Christian civilization...the pyramids...reveal...art as living as compelling, as it was forty-five centuries ago."

Sheldon Cheney, *A World History of Art,* The Viking Press, New York, 1952, p. 65

"The Nile has become for us a great historical volume disclosing stage by stage the first advance of man from bestial savagery to civilization.

On the other hand, as we look forward, we should remember also that the three great chapters of civilization which terminated with the Empire did not end the story; for Egyptian institutions and civilization continued far down into the Christian Age and greatly influenced later history..."

James Breasted, *The Conquest of Civilization,* Harper & Bros., New York and London, 1946, p. 418

"The tremendous significance of Champollion's encipherment of Egyptian writing was not confined to Egypt. It changed the whole concept of historical science. The reading of the hieroglyph alone tripled the number of centuries in which history could be founded on written documents.

The story of mankind was thrust back...eighteenth-century scholars, who believed that beyond Homeric Greece there had been nothing but primitive barbarism. Now it was revealed that

the heroic days of Greece were lived at a time when great empires of the more ancient world were declining after millennia of splendor..."

Leslie Greener, *The Discovery of Egypt*, Dorset Press, New York, 1966

The American Egyptologist George R. Gliddon proclaimed that:

"The 'veil' of obscurity was...with the force of an earthquake...ceased to be mysteries! The 'Veil of Isis'—"the curtain that no mortal hand could raise"—which for 2000 years, had baffled the attempts of Greeks and Romans with the still more vigorous efforts of modern Egyptologists—was lifted by Champollion Le Jeune: and

the glories of Pharonic epochs—the deeds of the noblest, the most learned, pious...

and civilized race of ancient days—-whose monarchy has exceeded by 1000 years the duration of any of our modern nations

—whose words surpass in magnitude, in boldness of conception, accuracy of executive, and splendor of achievement the mightiest labors of any other people."

Ancient Egypt, The New World, Nos. 68-69, Park Benjamin, Ed., J. Winchester, New York, April, 1843, p. 62

"...Osler emphasized...

'Out of the ocean of oblivion,

man emerges in history in a highly civilized state on the banks of the Nile, some sixty centuries ago.' "

He refers, of course, to the early Egyptian people...

M. G. Seelig, M. D., *Medicine, A Historical Outline*, Williams I. Wilkins Company, Baltimore, 1925.

"How ancient this was,

will appear from the fact that tombs of Egypt are now recognized by Egyptologists as dating, perhaps,

4,500 *before* Christ!

Over six thousand years

since, and, very probably, a thousand years or more before that epoch, the mummy system was in existence. Whatever originated it therefore, must have been a principle of extreme antiquity."

James Bonwick, F. R. G. S., *Egyptian Belief and Modern Thought*, ECA Associates, Chesapeake, New York, 1990

In the words taken from the book *Ancient History* :

Twenty-six known dynasties of native kings had come and gone before Plato visited Egypt. Alexander and the Romans were episodes in a following lesser age, still before Christ was born in near-by Palestine.

The Cross came, and centuries later gave way to the Crescent; but the Nile endured and the ancient Egyptian art endured, for the river and the desert, obscuring men and institutions, find their counterpart only in Egyptian art.

The rock-cut tombs, the pyramids and the basalt statues, outlast empires. The sun still shines on pyramid, temple, domed mosque, and minaret, and the opened tombs reveal art as living, as compelling, as it was forty-five centuries ago

Edward Farr, Ed., Hurst & Co., New York

Professor A. H. L. Heeren explains:

> ... that no one has yet been able to count them, much less to copy them. "No description," says an eyewitness, "can adequately express the sensations inspired by this astonishing sight, in which

the magnificence and might of the ancient rulers of Egypt are made perceptible to the eye.

> Of what deeds, of what events, now lost to the history of the world, of what scenes have these columns formerly been the witness!

Can it be doubted that this was the spot, where those rulers of the world, of the nations of the east and of the west, exhibited themselves in their glory and power?

> That this was the spot to which those nations brought their presents and their tribute?"

Historical Researches into the Politics, Intercourse, and Trade of the Carthaginians, Ethiopians, and Egyptians, vol. II. (originally published in 1832)

> "The things which surround the monarch in death are doubtless those in which he took most delight in life; and so we learn **that**

Pharaoh of 6000 years ago was no rude barbarian,

but

a man of refined and cultured taste..."

Rev. James Baikie, F. R. A. S., *The Life of the Ancient East*, (originally published in 1923), ECA Associates, Chesapeake, New York, 1992, p. 42

Emeritus Professor of Semitic languages, H. W. F. Saggs wrote a book whose title speaks for itself, *Civilization Before Greece and Rome*:

'The grand object of traveling,' pronounced Doctor Samuel Johnson in the eighteenth century, 'is to see the shores of the Mediterranean. On those shores were the four great Empires of the world; the Assyrian, the Persian, the Grecian, and the Roman. **All our religion, almost all our law, almost all our arts, all that set us above savages, has come to us from the shores of the Mediterranean.**

The beginnings of civilization are indeed linked with the shores of the Mediterranean, since those shores were the bounds of all the peoples who contributed to it; but the peoples he [Johnson] credits with these achievements all came late in the rise from savagery which we call civilization.

Yale University Press, New Haven, 1989, p. 1

Cornelius Stetter had this to say about the following historical figures:

> **...Siculus, Herodotus of Halikarnassos, and Homer.** They probably wondered, above all, about the significant level of specialization that had already been attained in "the most ancient times." These knowledge-thirsty "reporters" of ancient times carried the writings (which we could not read for so long) to Hellas and ladled information from these ancient sources of knowledge.
>
> **They did not recognize a western world without Egypt, knowing well also, that** *the cradle of Mediterranean culture lies in the Nile.* At the time when the oak woods of central Europe were still healthy, sick people died "because of the will of Odin."

The Secret Medicine of the Pharaohs, Edition Q, Chicago, 1993

According to the Keeper of Egyptian Antiquities at the British Museum in London, V. Davies and the director of the American expedition to Hierakonpolis:

When the Greek historian **Herodotus visited Egypt four and a half centuries** *before* **the**

birth of Christ, he was awestruck. The wonders were greater than those of any other land, he observed. There were pyramids taller than any man-made structures on earth, avenues of sphinxes ...colossal statues of long-dead pharaohs...

Here along the banks of the Nile was a civilization that had flourished since time immemorial...

to the ancients,

Egypt was already *ancient*

It was a culture so old that its origins remained shrouded in mystery...

Vivian Davies and Renee Friedman, *Egypt Uncovered*, Stewart, Tabori, and Chang, New York, 1998, p. 11

Professor Richard Wilkinson of the University of Arizona reminds us that:

Long *before* the rise of classical Greece,

Egypt had already **enjoyed at least three long periods of prosperity and centralized power."**

Reading Egyptian Art, Thames Hudson, Ltd., New York, 1992, p. 12

"The Egyptians attained a high degree of refinement and luxury

at a time

when *the whole western world* was involved

in barbarism,

when the history of Europe, including Greece, was not yet unfolded,

and *ages before* Carthage, Athens, and Rome *were founded.*

They were indeed, *the first people* **who rightly understood the rules of government,** who perceived that the just design of politics is to make life easy and a people happy. This high state of civilization was attained under a system of institutions..."

Edward Farr, Editor, *Ancient History: From Rollin and Other Authentic Sources, Both Ancient and Modern,* vol. I., Hurst & Co., New York, p. 60

However, historians Terne L. Plunkettt and R. B. Mowat in their book *A History of Europe* offer this view:

Although a number of grand civilizations have existed in various stages **it is the civilization of Europe which has made the deepest and widest impression**, and which now (as developed on both sides of the Atlantic) sets the standard for all peoples of the earth. p. vii

But, Ruth D. Benedict and Gene Weltfish remind us that:

"If you had to Depend on

the Inventive Genius

of the Ancient Europeans,

you'd be living on

crab apples and hazel nuts..."

"The Races of Mankind" (Public Affairs Pamphlet #85) Produced by the Public Affairs Committee Inc., 381 Park Ave., New York, N. Y.

"It is hard for you to imagine

that *there was a time* when

not only did *Europeans not exist,*

there was a time when *the word did not exist.*"

Dr. Yosef A. ben-Jochannan and Dr. John Henrik Clarke, *New Dimensions in African History*, African World Press, Inc., New Jersey, 1991, p. 9

"The earth, indeed, might have remained savage, if some other race, lacking the mental power of the Egyptians, had occupied the Nile Valley."

Robert Forrest Wilson, *The Living Pageant of the Nile*, The Bobbs-Merrill Company, Indianapolis, 1924, p. 13

As one writer puts it: *"The pharaohs of ancient Egypt were the first real kings in the world.* That is, they ruled over a complete country rather than a town or a tribe."

"The Egyptians were probably *the most* industrious people the world has ever known.

Their extraordinary talent for organization produced monument after monument; their spiritual insight coupled with their manual skill created some of the world's finest art. **Their system of government ran smoothly...for 2500 years."**

Janet Van Duyn, *The Egyptians*, Cassell, London, 197439-40), pp. 39-40

Professor Martin Bernal of Cornell University suggested that:

...most Renaissance thinkers believed that

Egypt was the original and creative source and Greece the later transmitter of Egyptian ... wisdom...

Black Athena, vol. I, Rutgers University Press, New Brunswick, New Jersey, 1987, p. 19

Professor Obenga in *Egypt Revisited* (1989, p. 289) quotes a key statement made by Frederic Tomlin [*Great Philosophers of the East*, Paris, Payot trans., 1952, p. 19]:

"Egypt was the cradle of philosophical

speculation as we know it."

The African Origins of "Greek Philosophy"

[The Black Egyptians were *the* first Teachers of the Ancient Greeks]

Serge Sauneron, the former Director of the French Oriental Archaeological Institute in Cairo, in his book *The Priests of Ancient Egypt*. [Grove Press: Distributed by Random House] puts it this way:

"In going through the **ancient Greek** texts, one cannot escape the idea that in the eyes of these old authors,

Egypt was The Cradle Of All Knowledge And All Wisdom.

The most celebrated among the Hellenic wise men or philosophers crossed the sea to seek, with the priests, initiation into new knowledge.

And, Sauneron tells us who some of these men were:

What were these celebrated voyagers. First the great ancestors, **Orpheus**, who took part, in Egypt, in the feasts of the Dionysian mysteries

Diodorus I, 23, 2

And **Homer** himself, who visited the country.

Diodorus I, 69

The Greeks' dependence on Egypt for instruction in the arts and sciences was a historical truth reported by a contemporary British historian and one which:

"...**the historians of Classical Greece** had themselves accepted as fact.

Without exception,

so far as surviving texts can show,
***every Greek thinker* of the Classical Age**
looked to *Egypt*
for inspiration and guidance,
and accepted the cultural primacy of
Egypt."

Basil Davidson, *Race & Class*, vol. XXIX, p. 4

Charles Freeman and the Herbert Thompson Reader in Egyptology, and a Fellow of Selwyn College at the University of Cambridge, Professor John D. Ray once wrote that:

"Egypt was more than 2000 years old when the Greeks – the first Westerners- began to arrive.

They marveled at the already ancient pyramids, at the wealth, and at the massive temples where Egyptians priests were willing to share their knowledge with outsiders. From the Greek, the Egyptians acquired a reputation as the guardians of superior wisdom."

The Legacy of Egypt, Fact on File, Inc., New York, 1997, p. 6

"In every aspect of life Egypt has influenced Europe, and though the centuries may have modified the custom or idea, the origin is clearly visible. Centuries *before* Ptolemy Philadelphus founded his great temple of the Muses at Alexandria,

Egypt was to the Greek

the embodiment of

all wisdom and knowledge.

In their generous enthusiasm the Greeks continually recorded that opinion; and by their writings they passed on to later generations that wisdom of the Egyptians which they had learnt orally from the learned men of the Nile Valley."

Margaret A. Murray, *The Splendour That Was Egypt*, Philosophical Library, New York, 1957, p. xvcc

According to Egyptologist John Anthony West:

> ...Jomard was...the first modern scholar to suggest that the long sloping inner corridors originally served some astronomical function, and that the builders of the pyramid had advanced knowledge of geometry, geography, and geodesy.

> But the rough approximations that he used to support his ideas did not convince his fellow savants, all of them loath to abandon the idea that true civilization began with the Greeks.

> Nor did it help when Jomard pointed out that **the Greeks themselves, almost *without exception*, hailed Egypt as the source of knowledge and wisdom.**

The Traveler's Key to Ancient Egypt, Alfred A. Knopf, New York, 1985

The founder of the Egypt Exploration Society in England, A. B. Edwards once remarked:

> "I am drawing no imaginary picture. The sites of Daphnae and Naukratis have been excavated within the last four years by Mr. Flinders Petrie, and it is not too much to say that the direct and indirect results of these explorations have completely settled that interesting question which has been so often debated and so long unanswered - namely, the question of the nature and extent of the aesthetic debt of Greece to Egypt. That debt, in so far as it was in their power to estimate it, was freely admitted by the later Greeks themselves.

> **Solon, Thales, Pythagoras, Eudoxus, Erastosthenes, Plato, and a host of others, were *proud to sit at the feet* of the most ancient of nations...**

> they owed the **first elements** of civilization and those greatest of all gifts, the alphabet and the art of writing, **to the wisdom of the Egyptians."**

Amelia B. Edwards, *Pharaohs, Fellahs and Explorers,* Harper &

Bros., New York, 1891, p. 167

> "He [Heordotus] was the representative of a people still in the full ferment of youthful development, and so Egypt, with its age-long civilization, and its by that time stereotyped culture,

created in him the impression that here was the original home of all, even of the Greek, civilization."

Wilhelm Spiegelberg, *The Credibility of Herodotus' Account of Egypt in the Light of the Egyptian Monuments,* (originally published, 1927, Basil Blackwell, Oxford), ECA Associates, Chesapeake, New York, 1990, p. 38

"Greece seems to have been the natural successor

and continuator of Egypt,

> to which country she was tied by important currents even in the legendary times when gods lived on Earth. This age-old tradition was never interrupted until the Islamic conquest.."

Paul Ghalioungui, *Magic and Medical Science in Ancient Egypt,* Hodder and Stoughton, Ltd., London, 1963.

As Professor Bernal maintains

"...Egypt was seen as the fount of all 'Gentile' philosophy and learning, including that of the Greeks;

> and that the Greeks had managed to preserve only some part of these..."

Black Athena, vol. I, Rutgers University Press, New Brunswick, New Jersey, 1987

Edward Said commented that:

> "As early as 1804 Benjamin Constant noted in his *Journal in Time* that...

the French...had decided

after Napoleon and Champollion that

everything originated

in Egypt."

Orientalism, Vintage, New York, 1979, p. 137

"If this theory is to prevail, then

we shall owe the Egyptians

a great deal more than admiration. Our debt to them must be one of eternal gratitude as the due of

the chief benefactors of humanity

except for whom we should all

be still engaged in the jungle

struggle for survival."

Robert Forrest Wilson, *The Living Pageant of the Nile*, The Bobbs-Merrill Company, Indianapolis, 1924, p. 13

The *Legacy* television series hosted by Michael Wood (1991) observed that:

"In upper Egypt the monuments were covered with graffiti by awestruck Greek tourists. ' To think,' fumed an Egyptian priest,

' we taught these upstarts all they know.' "

By the same token, Professor Bernal explains a major premise of his classic *Black Athena* concerning Egypt's early relationship with the ancient Greeks:

"The main body of the book began with a description of the ways in which Classical, Hellenistic and later pagan Greeks from the 5th century BC to the 5th century AD saw their distant past. I attempted **to trace their own vision of their ancestors' having been civilized by Egyptian...colonization** and the later influence of Greek study in Egypt..."

Similarly, Professor Heeren asserts that:

"According to their own traditions, Egyptian colonies were founded in the most opposite regions of the world: in Greece, Colchis, Babylon, and even India.

But, in the foundation of *these colonies* out of Egypt, there was always a view to the *extension of* Egyptian civilization.

Even the whole mythus of the expedition of *Osiris*, as found in Diodorus, is nothing more than a figurative representation of

the spread of Egyptian religion and civilization, by the planting of colonies... "

Historical Researches into the Politics, Intercourse, and Trade of the Carthaginians, Ethiopians, and Egyptians, vol. II.

"...the Greeks did not begin without foundations. It is necessary to remember that the groundwork for many of their achievements had already been laid by certain . . . peoples.

The rudiments of their

Philosophy* and *Science

had been prepared by the Egyptians."

Edward Burns and Philip Lee Ralph *World Civilizations*, 5th Ed. W. W. Norton & Co., N. Y., p. 175

"[Egypt]...soon flowered into civilization specifically and uniquely its own; one of the richest and greatest, one of the most powerful and yet one of the most graceful, culture in history. **By its side Sumeria was but a crude beginning; and not even Greece or Rome would surpass it.**

Will Durant, *The Story of Civilization*, Part I, Simon and Schuster, New York, 1954

In the book *The Discovery of Egypt* the author, Leslie Greener says that:

The *Greeks* and the *Phoenicians*...drew
the first inspiration
of their arts and science
from the well of Egyptian culture..."

(Dorset Press, New York, 1966, p. 2)

According to Charles Freeman and Professor John D. Ray:

The reputation of ancient Egypt is itself a legacy handed from the Greeks and the Romans to Renaissance Europe and onto the modern world...

it was the arrival of Napoleon's invading army in 1798 that opened Egypt once again to the West. Like the Greeks and Romans before them, Europeans were stunned by the overwhelming scale of the buildings.

The Legacy of Egypt, Fact on File, Inc., New York, 1997,

It was during **the Renaissance** that European scholars rediscovered the accounts of ancient Egypt in the texts of the classical authors of Greece and Rome. The rebuilding of Rome also revealed **a number of Egyptian monuments** that had been brought there by the Roman emperors. These discoveries stimulated an interest in Egyptian hieroglyphs, which **were seen as the product of an advanced civilization.**

Jamomir Malek, ed., *Cradles of Civilization Egypt*, University of Oklahoma Press, Oklahoma, 1993, p. 39

"For Egypt was old, older than any other culture known at the time.

It was already old when the political policy of the future Roman Empire was being framed...

It was already old...when the Germans and Celts of the north European forest were still hunting bears.

When the first Dynasty came into power, about *five thousand years ago*...

marvelous cultural forms had already been evolved in the land of the Nile...common were Egyptian scarabs representations of the dung beetle held sacred by the people of the Nile.

These scarabs were at one time used throughout Europe as amulets, later as ornaments and ring seals."

C. W. Ceram, *Gods, Graves, and Scholars*, (trans. E. B. Garside) Alfred A. Knopf, New York, 1975, p. 79-80

In a similar vein, Professor A. H. L. Heeren mentioned that:

"Can we then be surprised to see in Egypt, thus united, the same principal form continued, and the kingdom in its most flourishing period assume the appearance of a vast hierarchy?

This brilliant period began, according to the most probable settlement of the chronology, between the years of 1600 and 1500 B. C.; at a time when we have as yet heard of *no* great empire in Asia; when, as yet, Phoenicia possessed *no* Tyre, nor the commerce of the world; when the Jews, after the death of Joshua, remained without a leader, weak and inconsiderable; and when **the obscure traditions of the Greeks represent that nation as but little removed from barbarism.**

There can be *no doubt* therefore, but *EGYPT* ranked at this time, *as THE MOST CIVILIZED COUNTRY OF THE KNOWN WORLD,*

at least as far as the Indus; and for succeeding centuries no one could enter the lists with her, or cause her any dread; and thus through a long period of tranquillity, she continually increased and prospered, till she attained that pitch of greatness, which is not only set forth in the narratives of antiquity, but displayed in her own monuments.

The first symptoms of decay are discernible towards the beginning of the eighth century before the Christian era, the period at which a little light breaks into her history; and we therefore may conclude, with much probability, that this golden period lasted from seven to eight centuries."

Historical Researches into the Politics, Intercourse, and Trade of the Carthaginians, Ethiopians, and Egyptians, vol. II. (originally published in 1832, by D. A. Talboys, Oxford), rep., ECA Associates, Chesapeake, New York. 1991

The scholar Robert De Rustafjaell in his book *The Light of Egypt,* [London 1909] agrees:

"It was some 5000 Years ago that the Egyptians had brought their civilization to so high a pitch. At this time Europe was still living in the twilight of the Neolithic age.

At the time when the inhabitants of the

Nile Valley were raising

these mighty pyramids,

and engraving on the walls of their tombs the sculptures which have preserved the records of their religion and their life, the thoughts which animated their living brains, and the hopes which they held for their heads,

the men of Great Britain were

still **in a state of** *semi-savagery*
still **dwelling** *in caves*
from which they had driven out animals only wilder than themselves,

still roughly scratching on bone with sharp flints those rude figures which were all of art they knew."

The words of the legendary Auguste Mariette flowed along a similar current of thought:

"While as yet the world in general was plunged in the depths of barbarism; and the nations that later on were to play so important a part in the world's history were *still savages,* *the banks of the Nile* were nurturing *a people both cultivated and civilized*; and a powerful monarchy, aided by a complete organization of court functionaries and civil servants, was already ruling the fate of the nation.

However far into the dim past we gaze,

we are everywhere met by

a fully developed civilization

to which the succeeding centuries,
numerous as they are, have added nothing."

Outlines of Ancient Egyptian History, Trans. & ed. Mary Brodrick, Charles Scribner's Sons, New York, 1892, p. 10-11

The distinguished Egyptologist Dr. Margaret A. Murray had this to say about ancient Egypt:

"Within the narrow bands of that little country, enclosed as it was to east and west by waterless deserts, there was **evolved a civilization which was the foundation of Greece, of Rome, and finally of our own.**"

The Splendour That Was Egypt, Philosophical Library, New York, 1957

Physics Professor, J. Pappademos (University of Chicago at Illinois) declared that:

"The **most brilliant** of the Greek students of science, such as Thales of Miletos (c.600 B. C.), Democritos, Pythagoras, and Eudoxos (408-355 B. C.) **traveled to Egypt to study.**

Seneca tells us that Eudoxos had to go to Egypt to study planetary motion; and at that time Egypt must have been the world's leading center of astronomy. Pythagoras (c. 6th century B. C.) spent no less than 22 years in Egypt studying astronomy, geometry, and the mysteries."

Blacks in Science, Edited by Ivan Van Sertima

In addition, Professor Serge Sauneron writes that:

In less mythical times, **Solon**, in his turn, crossed the sea; Plato has described his voyage:

But the oldest one among the priests exclaimed:

'Solon, Solon you Greeks are always children; there are no old men in Greece!'

'What are you trying to say?' asked Solon.

'You are young in spirit,' replied the Egyptian priest, 'for you possess no truly antique tradition, no notion gray with time...'

... in Egypt ... it is said that here are preserved the oldest traditions ... Thus there is nothing beautiful nor great nor remarkable done, be it in your country, or here, or in another country known to us, which has not long since been consigned to writing and preserved in our temples.'

Plato, *Timeus* 22-23

As we can see, the **BLACK EGYPTIANS** taught the best minds of Europe such as Plato, Aristotle, Pythagoras, Thales, Solon, Archimedes, Democritos, Eudoxos, et al.

Sir Gaston Maspero, who held the premier place in Egyptology in his generation, indicates that the Egyptians were also quite aware of their vast antiquity:

"When questioned as to the remote past of their race, they proclaimed themselves

the most ancient of mankind,

in comparison with whom

all other races were but a mob of young children."

History of Egypt, Charles Scribner's Sons, 1912, p. 221

The author of *The History of Egypt* commented that:

"They called

the Greeks mere children

of yesterday,

and professed to have a knowledge of the events of the last nine thousand years."

Samuel Sharpe, 2 vols., (6th Ed.), George Bell & Sons, London, 1876

Dr. Albert Churchward in his *The Origin and Evolution of the Human Race* underlines this fact:

[Professor]..."W. J. Perry regarded

Egypt as the fountainhead of

religion and civilization.

Ignatius Donnelly, like Perry, traced all cultures back to Egypt, but he did not stop there.

He wrote:

'Egypt was the magnificent,

the Golden Bridge, ten thousand years

long,

glorious with pyramids and temples,

illuminated and illustrated by the most complete and continuous records of human history...

in a great procession of kings and priests, philosophers and astronomers, artists and artisans, who streamed from Egypt to Greece, to Rome and to Europe.' " (London, 1921, p. 33)

However, To quote the famous German philosopher Hegel:

The name of Greece strikes home to the hearts of men of education in Europe.

Two professors of philosophy at the University of Texas at Austin, Robert C. Solomon and Kathleen M. Higgins, also remind us of the direct connection between Greek philosophy and Western science:

To be sure, the origins of philosophy in Greece were also the origins of Western science.

A Short History of Philosophy, Oxford University Press, New York, Oxford, 1996, p. 12

And yet, a pair of modern scholars G. S. Kirk and J. E. Raven are cited by the author of *The African Origin of Greek Philosophy* in which these researchers testified in their massive work *The Presocratic Philosophers* that:

"It was the custom to credit the sixth-century sages with visits to

Egypt, the traditional fountainhead

of

Greek science.

Thales, as the earliest known Greek geometer had a special reason for being associated with the home of land-measurement."

(Cambridge University Press, Cambridge, 1957, p. 79)

Innocent C. Onyewuenyi, University of Nigeria Press, Nsukka, Nigeria, 1993, p. 120

The Ancient Historian Plutarch says:

"Witness to this also that the wisest of the Greeks: Solon, Thales, Plato, Eudoxus, Pythagoras who came to Egypt and consorted with the priests, and in this number some would include Lycurgus also.

Eudoxus, they say, received instruction from Chonuphis of Memphis, Solon from Sonchis of Sais, and Pythagoras from Oenuphis of Heliopolis.

Pythagoras, as it seems, was greatly admired, and he also greatly admired the Egyptian priests and copying their symbolism and occult teachings incorporated his doctrines in enigmas. As a matter of fact, most of the Pythagorean precepts do not at all fall short of the writings that are called Hieroglyphics...

Frank C. Babbitt, Translator, 1969 PLUTARCH'S MORALIA, VOL. #5, Cambridge, Harvard University Press

"The role of Egypt in civilizing the Greeks has been vividly depicted by the English historian, Winwood Reade:

Egypt from the earliest times had been the university of Greece.

It had been visited, according to tradition, by Orpheus and Homer . . . And now

every intellectual Greek made the voyage to that country;

it was regarded as a part of education, as a pilgrimage to the cradle land of their mythology. " (*Martyrdom of Man*, Watts & Co., London, 1934)

John G. Jackson, *Man, God and Civilization*

On *ABC* television network's show *Like It Is* hosted by Gil Noble (October 30, 1988) a professor at Cornell University, M. Bernal unmasked the fact that:

"...the ancient Greeks

when they told the history of their

own distant past, said that they

had been civilized by Egyptians."

Bernard Roman, author of *Life in Egypt in Ancient Times*, traces even the practice of circumcision to its ancient roots in Egypt:

"The antiquity of its institution [circumcision] in Egypt is fully established by the monuments of the Upper and Lower Country,

long before the Exodus and

the arrival of Joseph;

and Strabo tells us that

'a similar rite was practiced in Egypt ...'

Though very generally adopted, no one was compelled to conform to this ordinance unless initiated into the mysteries or belonging to the priestly order; and it is said that:

Pythagoras submitted to it **in order to obtain the privileges it conferred,**

by entitling him to a greater participation

in the mysteries *he sought to study."*

Minerva, S. A. Genàve, 1978/1981, p. 18

"Accordingly to his biographers (*Olympiodorus, Life of Plato* and anonymous author, the Life), *Plato* went to Egypt precisely in order to be initiated in theology and geometry. Here are the terms in which *Strabo*, one of the greatest Greek scholars of his time (58 B. C. to A. D. 25), confirms Plato's and Eudoxus's voyage to Helipolis, in Egypt:

We saw over there (in Heliopolis) the hallowed, halls that were used in the past for the lodging of the priests: but that is not all; we were also shown Plato's and Eudoxus's dwelling,

for *Eudoxus* had accompanied *Plato* here; after arriving at Heliopolis, they stayed there for thirteen years among the priests; this fact is affirmed by several authors.

These priests, so profoundly knowledge-able about celestial phenomena,

were at the same time mysterious people, who did not talk much, and it is only after a long time and with skillful maneuvering that Eudoxus and Plato were able to be initiated into some of their theoretical speculations...[the priests] kept the best part to themselves.

And if today the world owes them the knowledge of what fraction of a day (of a whole day) has to be added to 365 whole days in order to have a complete year,

the Greeks did not know the true duration of the year and many other facts of the same nature until translators of the Egyptian priests' papers into the Greek language

popularized these notions among modern astronomers...

(Strabo, *Geographie*, Book xvii,1, 29)"

Cheikh Anta Diop, *Civilization or Barbarism*, Lawrence Hill Books, New York, 1981. p. 346

A similar view is taken by Herbert Wendt's *In Search of Man*:

"So great was the achievement of the Africans in the Nile Valley that all the great men of ancient Europe journeyed there - -

the philosophers Thales and Anaximander, the mathematician Pythagoras, the statesman Solon and an endless stream of historians and geographers whose works are all based on Herodotus,' outstanding description of Egypt, to which the second volume of his history entirely was devoted."

The book *The Egyptian Mysteries*, (Arkana, London, 1988) authored by Arthur Versluis also credits the ancient Egyptians as being the original tutors of the Greeks (p. 94):

"...our debt to Egypt is incalculable...

Consider, for instance, that virtually *EVERY GREAT GREEK PHILOSOPHER*

was said to have traveled to Egypt,

or

to have been Egyptian himself. "

Writes Dr. A. Churchward from his *The Signs and Symbols of Primordial Man*:

"Professor G. Sergi, in his *Anthropological Studies*, proves more conclusively than anything else - outside our statement of the facts which we have brought forward - that

we are correct in placing EGYPT and the Nile valley as
THE BIRTHPLACE
AND CENTER OF CIVILIZATION..."

George Allen & Company Ltd., London, 1913, p. 282

"This affectation of extreme antiquity is strongly put by Plato in his Tinnaeus (p. 22 B), where

the *Greek nation* is taxed by the Egyptians with being in its *infancy* as compared with them.

The Egyptian claims to a high relative antiquity had, no doubt, a solid basis of truth." [See Rawlinson's footnote]

Herodotus, *Histories Book II*, Loeb Classical Library, p. 110

To quote the American Egyptologist George R. Gliddon: "...we may make due allowance for...**the antiquity of a country, which was already ancient long before the fathers of the Greeks were known in history**."

Ancient Egypt, The New World, Nos. 68-69, Park Benjamin, Ed., J. Winchester, Pub., New York, April, 1843, p. 38

As *The Story of Philosophy* (Simon and Schuster, New York, 1953) by Dr. Will Durant points out (p. 14):

"He (Plato) seems to have gone first to Egypt; and was somewhat shocked to hear from the priestly class...

that *Greece* was an *infant state*,

without stabilizing traditions

or

profound culture,

not yet therefore to be taken seriously..."

"Plato relates that when Solon visited Egypt, the priests of Sais said to him, *'O Solon, Solon! you Greeks, you are nothing but children* ; there is not one old man among you in all Greece!' To have opened the way along which for 2500 years so many nations have followed in her train is for all time Egypt's crowning glory."

Auguste Mariette, *Outlines of Ancient Egyptian History*, Trans. & ed. Mary Brodrick. Charles Scribner's Sons, New York, 1892, p. xxxi

As the eminent German Professor Adolph Erman points out:

> "The Greeks, who from the seventh century B. C. were frequent visitors to the Nile Valley... saw to their astonishment powerful populous towns, strange gigantic temples, and a people who in no [way] resembled the inhabitants of Ionia and the Greek islands."

Life in Ancient Egypt, H.M. Tirard, trans., Benjamin Blomdale, New York, 1969, introduction

Egyptian "Genesis" of Greek Civilization & Philosophy

"The majesty of ancient Egypt dazzled all the peoples

who came within its radiance.

Even the Greeks, who saw the country only in its far decline, had no difficulty **in recognizing its greatness and accepting it as**, in more ways than one,

the mother of their own civilization..."

Basil Davidson, "Civilization of the Nile," *The Ages of Man*, p. 33

> "Indeed, belief in Egyptian ingenuity has known few bounds, and it is no exaggeration to say that the antique conception of Egypt" was

"as a storied wonderland of learning,

the *fons et origo* (source and origin) of all wisdom..."

John R. Harris, (ed.), *The Legacy of Egypt*, 2nd ed., Oxford University Press, London, 1971, p. 83

> According to the author of *The African Origin of Greek Philosophy*, Professor Innocent C. Onyewuenyi, historians "were conversant with the writings of Plato, Aristotle, Plutarch, Herodotus,

all of whom record that

the Egyptians were the originators of philosophy…"

University of Nigeria Press, Nsukka, Nigeria, 1993, p. 121)

"Greek authors point to

EGYPT as *THE SOURCE*

of *their* philosophy.

Thales, Solon, Pythagoras, Democritus of Abdera, and Plato are all asserted to have visited Egypt and to have

sat at the feet of Egyptian priests…

Of Pythagoras it is even related that he had been initiated into ancient Egyptian literature by the high priest Sonchis. "

S. R. K. Granville, (ed.), *The Legacy of Egypt*, Oxford University Press, London, 1942, p. 64-5

"For many centuries the Egyptians alone held the scepter of the sciences and arts.

When Classical Greece and Rome began to come out of barbarism Egypt had already traversed successive periods of greatness and decadence…

the Greeks themselves regarded

Egypt *as*

THE ANCIENT SOURCE OF ART

AND KNOWLEDGE."

Charles Greene Cumston, M. D., *An Introduction to the History of Medicine*, Dorser Press, New York, 1987, p. 35

And yet, a scholar of the stature of Professor Will Durant helps to bring out the fact that:

"Historians of philosophy have been wont to begin their story with the Greeks. The Hindus, who believe that they invented philosophy, and the Chinese, who believe that they perfected it, smile at our provincialism. It may be that we are all mistaken;

for among the most ancient fragments left to us by Egyptians are writings that belong under the rubric of moral philosophy. **The wisdom of the Egyptians was a proverb with the Greeks, who felt themselves children beside this ancient race.**

The *oldest work of philosophy* known to us is the '*Instructions of Ptah-hotep,*'

which apparently goes back to 2800 B. C. - 2300 years

***before* Confucius, Socrates and Buddha.**

Ptah-hotep was Governor of Memphis, and Prime Minister to the King, under the Fifth Dynasty."

The Story of Civilization, Part I, Simon and Schuster, New York, 1954, p. 193

"The Greeks themselves always spoke with respect of the Egyptian progress in the sciences, and Greeks of high culture constantly visited Egypt with a view of improving themselves.

It has been questioned whether the Egyptians had much to teach them...

but

the Greeks themselves were probably the best judges on such a point.

Among those who sought improvement in Egypt are said to have been Hecateaus, Thales, Solon, Pythagoras, Herodotus, Enopides, Democritus, Plato, and Eudoxus."

George Rawlinson, *History of Ancient History*, vol. II, Dodd, Mead & Co., New York, 1918, p. 62

The same fact is recorded by Professor Alan Gardiner:

"Credence was still given to the late tradition according to which

early Greek philosophers like Thales and Pythagoras had

sat as pupils *at the feet*

of the Egyptian priests."

(Th. Hopner, Orient und griechishe Philosophie Leipzig, 1925)"

Egypt of the Pharaohs, Clarendon Press, Oxford, 1961, p. 9

The ancient historian Diodorus Siculus helps to identify all the important men of classical Greece who came to ancient Egypt to learn and study:

...we must recount the number of those who, celebrated among the Greeks for intelligence and learning, ventured to Egypt **in olden times, that they might partake of the customs and sample the teaching there.**

For the priests of the Egyptians cite from the records in their holy books, that in former times they were visited by Orpheus and Musaeus, Melampos and Daedalos, besides the poet Homer, Lycurgos the Spartan, Solon the Athenian, and Plato the philosopher. Pythagoras of Samos and the mathematician Eudoxos, as well as Democritos of Abdera and Oenopides of Chios, also came there.

Diodorus on Egypt, Book I of Diodorus Siculus, Historical Library trans. Edwin Murphy), McFarland & Company, Inc., North Carolina, 1985, p. 125

"Mr. Petrie discovered at least as many papyri of later dynasties, besides hundreds of fragments of Greek papyri of Ptolemaic and Roman times. These consist chiefly of accounts, deeds, royal edicts, and the like, not forgetting a magnificent fragment containing nearly the whole of the Second Book of the *Illiad.*

Nor is this the first time that *Homer* has been found in

Egypt. The **three oldest Homeric texts** previously known come from the land of the Pharaohs. To those three Mr. Petrie has now added a fourth. Other papyri found within the present century contain fragments of *Sappho, Anacreon, Thespis, Pindar, Alcaeus, and Timotheus*."

Amelia B. Edwards, *Egypt and Its Monuments*, Harper & Bros., New York, New York, 1891, p. 196

"It was in Egypt that the greatest of the Greeks got their education.

Of these, some assert that Pythagoras was the leader. He studied under the Egyptian Masters for fifteen years...Perhaps few people ever received more from other countries than the Greeks received from Egypt."

Albert Churchward, M. D., *The Origin and Evolution of the Human Race*, George Allen & Unwin, London, 1921, p. 76

The German Egyptologist Professor Adolph Erman, one of the most prominent names in the field, talks about the attitude the Greeks had towards the ancient Egyptians:

"...they had a feeling of respect for this people, **who with their ancient civilization looked upon the Greeks as children**; there might be a deep hidden meaning in those strange deities and temples, and it was possible that those...priests possessed a secret wisdom unknown to the ordinary human understanding."

Life in Ancient Egypt, H. M. Tirard, trans., Benjamin Blomdale, New York, 1969, p. 2

At the Sorbonne University in Paris Professor of Egyptology Nicolas Sir Alan Gardiner in his *Egypt of the Pharaohs* brings out the fact that:

"The multitude of the wonders to be seen in Egypt, and their indisputable antiquity, cannot have failed to strike awe into the hearts of those travelers from across the Mediterranean; and thus was sown the seed of

that *legendary Wisdom of the Egyptians*, belief in which remained almost *uncontested for* the next 2,000 years."

(Claredon Press, Oxford, 1961, p. 2)

Grimal informs us that:

"Pharaonic culture has always been a source of fascination, even to those unable to understand the profundity of
a system in which everything gives an impression of permanence and unchanging wisdom.

The Greek travelers...presented it as an impressive...

fountainhead of human thought,

where a remarkable advanced level of civilization had
been achieved...

Their description of Egyptian culture were characterized...by unbridled enthusiasm...

Egypt was regarded as a place of great scholarly achievement..."

A History of Ancient Egypt, trans. Ian Shaw, Basil Blackwell, Ltd.,
Cambridge, Mass., 1992, p. 14

In a 1991 issue of *Archaeology* (Sept./Oct., vol.39, No.5) a contemporary perspective is voiced by Frank L. Holt (p. 60):

"The Greeks, too, were great admirers of ancient
Egypt...Back in the fifth century B. C., Herodotus
expressed the 'modern' awe felt by his age for the ancient
mysteries of Egypt.

'No other place,' he wrote, 'possesses so many wonders
impossible to describe'...To this inquisitive Greek,

Egypt was an ancient land of wonder...

In a world 25 centuries more modern, we are wide-eyed
with wonder in ways that Herodotus could never understand."

Professor of Greek and Latin at the Collège de France Jean
Terrasson

"insisted on

the great superiority of Egypt over Greece...

giving details of

all the arts and sciences

in which the

Egyptians excelled the Greeks.

Using Classical quotations, he demonstrated that the founders of Greek politics, astronomy, engineering and mathematics had all studied in Egypt." (*Séthos*, 1731)

Martin Bernal, *Black Athena*, p. 18

In the *Legacy* series, "Barbarian West," (Maryland Public Television, 1991) the host, Michael Wood, admitted that:

"...for all their brilliant qualities of mind,

the Greeks had to *borrow from Africa*...

to create their civilization."

"Through Pharaonic Egypt, **Africa lays claims to being the cradle of one of the earliest**

and most spectacular civilizations of antiquity."

B. G. Trigger, B. J. Kemp, D. O'Connor, and A. B. Lloyd, *Ancient Egypt*, Cambridge University, Cambridge, 1990, p. 1

Thus, **"...Plato says the Egyptians looked upon the *Greeks* as *children*, too young and innocent**

to be the creators of great things.

The Greeks had *no* pyramids, *no* kings

as splendid as the Pharaohs..."

Robert Payne, *The Splendor of Greece,* Harper and Row, New York, 1960, p. 9

Professor Bernal in *Black Athena* (p. 389) quotes Victor Bérard (*On the Origin of the Arkadian Cults*, Paris, 1894, p. 10) who wrote:

"We see...from their material and tangible monuments that

the Greeks...were the pupils of...Egypt..."

"The Greeks acknowledged rather simply that they had learned a great deal from Egypt and that this had been formative in their own lives.

> The Hebrews were both resentful of and allured by the sophistication of Egypt...They also wrote about 'all the wise men' of Pharaoh and how Moses had learned 'all the wisdom of the Egyptians.' "

Will Durant, *The Story of Civilization,* Part I. Simon and Schuster, New York, 1954, pp. 31617

As the American Orientalist J. Baldwin noted:

> "Herodotus showed that religion, letters, and civilization came to the Greeks from the...Egyptians..." (*Pre-Historic Nations*, Harper & Brothers, New York, 1898, p. 45)

> "To begin with, there is the evidence of what the Greeks themselves thought...

The Greeks all agreed upon the cultural supremacy of Pharaonic civilization, and the ways in which they wrote about this clearly show that they would have **thought it absurd to advance a contrary opinion...**

And they thought this, one may remark in passing, for the most persuasive reason that Egyptian civilization enjoyed a towering prestige and influence, and seemed of immemorial weight and value. Their grasp of exact historical chronology could not be as good as ours, but they were perfectly alive to Egypt's immense time dimension...**For the Greeks of the Classical Age, Egypt was where one went to learn history."**

"The Ancient World and Africa: whose roots?" *Race and Class*, vol. XXIX, Autumn 1987, Number 2, p. 5-6)

And, he cites George Sarton's *A History of Science* and a quotation referred to by G. T. Allman's *Greek Geometry* as his sources.

"So, the most ancient representative of Greek philosophy and science (Aristotle affirms that Thales is the founder of natural philosophy: Metaphysics, Book 1, chap. III) is a former pupil of the Egyptians. Thales brought back from Egypt numerous cosmological, philosophical, mathematical, astronomical knowledge. The influence of Egypt upon Greece with the intermediary of Thales, is consequently real since

Thales had no other masters

but Egyptian ones."

Theophile Obenga, *Ancient Egypt & Black Africa*, Karnak House, London, 1992, p. 84

"They called the Greeks

mere children of yesterday,

and professed to have a knowledge of the events of the last nine thousand years."

Samuel Sharpe, *The History of Egypt*, vol. I & II, (6th Ed.), George Bell & Sons, London, 1876

In fact, Professor Bernal goes so far as to title one of his chapters

"EGYPTIAN WISDOM AND GREEK TRANSMISSION FROM THE DARK AGES TO THE RENAISSANCE..."

Black Athena, vol. I, Rutgers University Press, New Brunswick, New Jersey, 1987

Clearly, Egypt became the place to be if one sought a "higher" education. Which explains why so many of the well-known Greeks went there to study as pointed out in the book *The Priests of Ancient Egypt*:

" '. . . Thales of Milet made voyage to the priests and the astronomers of Egypt, and according to his biographers, he seems to have learned geometry from the Egyptians...'

Diogenes Laerce, *Thales*, 43 and 24

Pythagoras ... on the advice of Thales ... came to seek revelations of knowledge and faith among them. Porphyrius (233-304 A. D.) recounts the voyage of Pythagoras in these terms:

'Having been received by Amasis the king of Egypt 568-525 B. C., he obtained from them letters of recommendation from the priests of Heliopolis, . . .'

Porphyrius, *Life of Pythagoras*, 3

Another biographer Jamblicus, shows us **Pythagoras**

'... frequenting all the sanctuaries of Egypt with great ardor ... he met all the priests, learning from each what he knew. And it is in these conditions that

he passed twenty-two years

in the temples of Egypt.' "

Jamblicus, *Life of Pythagoras*, 4, 18-19

"Isocrates mentions **Pythagoras** and his study in Egypt:

'On a visit to Egypt he (Pythagoras) became a student of the religion of the people, and was the first to bring to the Greeks all philosophy.'

Isocrates, Van Hook (Trans.) vol. 3

PYTHAGORAS returned to Greece to teach 'in a way perfectly similar to the documents by which he had been instructed in Egypt.'

Jamblicus: *Life Of Pythagorus*, T. Taylor (Trans.)

'Most of the precepts which he taught he copied from Egyptian hieroglyphic texts.' "

Plutarch, *Moralis*, Babbitt, F. C. (Trans.)

[Source: Serge Sauneron, Grove Press, Random House]

Professor Sauneron continues his list of famous Greek intellectuals who came to Egypt to be educated:

'Still other wise men, other Greek philosophers, came to learn in the Egyptian temples. **Onenopidus,** for example, learned several secrets from the priests and astronomers.'

Diodorus, 1, 98

'**Democritus**, on his part, visited the priest five years to learn things related to astronomy.' " 11

Diogenes Laerce, *Democritus*, 3

"As for **Plato**, he seems to have sought in Egypt to learn both geometry and theology (Anonymous, *Life*), and of the priestly knowledge in general.

Olympiodorus, *Life of Plato*

'... the geographer Strabo, in his description of Egypt (XVII, 1,29) in fact speaks in these terms of his (Plato's) voyage to Heliopolis:. . . for **Eudoxus** accompanied **Plato** this far: arrived at Heliopolis, they established themselves here and

both resided there *thirteen years* in the society of the priests:

the fact is affirmed by several authors...' "

As we can clearly see, the authors of "Greek Philosophy" were not the Greeks but Black Africans known to the Greeks as the Egyptians.

Therefore, it should come as no surprise that a noted scholar such as Gerald Massey would be inspired to entitle his other book —

EGYPT, the LIGHT of the WORLD.

Our Western civilization originated *in*

Mediterranean **Africa,**

along the banks of the Nile River...Thus **the ancient Egyptians** were...to establish an orderly government, and to make notable progress in the arts, sciences, and technology. Just as important, the Egyptians **developed a moral code, involving standards of right and wrong, and ideas of man's obligation to his fellow man.**"

Emil Lengyel, *Africa: Past, Present, and Future*, Oxford Book Company, New York, 1967, p. 16

"For **in Egypt,** . . . traditions, skills, and values were evolved which *are* **the very roots of Western civilization.**

The light of the Occident was received from . . . the Nile Valley. Europe herself is of Oriental lineage..."

Leo Deuel, *The Treasures of Time*, Avon Books, New York, p. 12

Massey in the book *Ancient Egypt* said it all simply and eloquently:

"THE WISDOM OF THE ANCIENTS WAS THE WISDOM OF EGYPT."

Dr. Cheikh Anta Diop sums up the evidence in the introduction to his book *The African Origin of Civilization Myth or Reality*, page xiv:

"The ancient Egyptians were Negroes...

that BLACK WORLD is

the very INITIATOR

OF... 'WESTERN' CIVILIZATION...

Pythagorean mathematics, the theory of the four elements of Thales of Miletus, Epicurean materialism, Platonic idealism, Judaism, Islam, modern science are **rooted in Egyptian Cosmogony and science**.

One needs only to meditate on Osiris, the redeemer-god, who sacrifices himself, dies, and is resurrected to save mankind, a figure essentially identifiable with Christ.

A visitor to Thebes in the Valley of the Kings can view the Moslem inferno in detail (in the tomb of Seti I, of the Nineteenth Dynasty), 1700 years *before* the Koran.

Osiris at the tribunal of the dead is indeed the 'lord' of revealed religions, sitting enthroned on Judgment Day, and we know that certain

Biblical Passages are practically copies of

Egyptian moral texts."

"Let's take the first thousand years for granted and begin at 2000 B. C.

At that time Egypt was one of the two great centres of power, wealth and culture...

Greece and the Aegean are *off the edge*

of

THE WORLD DOMINATED BY EGYPT..."

Kenneth Dover, *The Greeks*, (from the BBC television series by Christopher Burstall and Kenneth Dover) British Broadcasting Corporation, London, 1980, p. 5

Professor at the University of Strasbourg Pierre Montet makes the following observation:

"...the store of Egyptian knowledge

was sufficiently impressive

to inspire the Greeks

to imitation and

emulation."

Eternal Egypt, Trans. Doreen Weightman, The New American Library, New York, 1964, p. 230

Not out of Europe

[Civilization did not begin in Europe]

While the Greeks (and Romans) were being civilized in Egypt by Africans, most of what we now know as "Europe" was still barbaric and unheard of.

The historians R. R. Palmer and Joel Colton in their massive book, *A History of the Modern World* wrote:

"THERE WAS REALLY NO EUROPE

IN ANCIENT TIMES...

and Europe as we know it was divided by the Rhine-Danube frontier, south and west of which lay the civilized provinces of the empire, and north and east the 'barbarians' of whom the civilized world knew almost nothing."

"The Dawn of History" is a chapter heading taken from the history book, *World Civilizations* by Professors Edward McNall Burns and Philip Lee Ralph. In this chapter, they point out the fact that:

"In other parts of the world the beginnings of civilization were retarded.

There was nothing that could be called civilized life in China until about 2000 B. C. And, except on the island of Crete,

there was *no civilization*

in Europe until more than

1000 years later." (1000 B. C.)

"Europeans were by *no* means the pioneers

of human civilization.

HALF OF RECORDED HISTORY HAD PASSED *BEFORE* ANYONE IN EUROPE COULD READ OR WRITE.

The priests of Egypt began to keep written records between 4000 and 3000 B. C...Shortly after 3000 B. C., while the pharaohs were building the first pyramids,

Europeans were creating nothing more distinguished

than huge garbage heaps."

R. R. Palmer and J. Colton, *A History of the Modern World*, (3rd ed.), Alfred A. Knopf, New York, p. 3

In contrast, in the book *The Legacy of Egypt* edited by the eminent Professor S. R. K. Granville, it states that:

They [the Egyptians] were pioneers...

It is now recognized that the contribution of the Greeks to world knowledge was not entirely original. Greek colonists settled in Asia Minor, traveled widely. Thales and others full of enterprises and love of adventure, and a thirst for wonders in strange lands came to Egypt. There they saw the Egyptians at work and marveled.

There they found the beginnings of mathematics and science...

Through the Greeks, the legacy of Egypt was transmitted to the rest of the world.

(Oxford University Press, London, 1942, p. 177178)

One of the greatest historians of the twentieth century, the late Dr. John Henrik Clarke made this declaration at a "lecture"/debate (3/29/96) attended by opposing scholars, Mary Lefkowitz and John Rodgers of Wellesley University:

"... [the Europeans] were *the last* branch of the human race to enter that arena marked, CIVILIZATION!"

IN ALL EUROPE THERE WAS

NO WRITING, nor

did the continent of Europe

ever devise a system of writing...

The men of Stone Age Europe were still (about 3000 B. C.) without writing,

for making the records of business, government, and tradition; they were still without metals with which to make tools and to develop industries and manufactures; and they had no sailing ships in which to carry on commerce. Without these things they could go no farther."

Geoffrey Parsons, *The Stream of History*, vol. II, Charles Scribner's Sons, New York, 1929, p. 36

"No less paradoxical is the fact that

the Indo-Europeans *never* created a civilization in their own native lands: the Eurasian plains."

Cheikh Anta Diop, *The African Origin of Civilization, Myth or Reality*, Mercer Cook, trans., Lawrence Hill Books, Chicago Illinois, 1967, p. 151

Likewise, Professor Breasted drew this related conclusion:

...the possession of metal did not enable the peoples of Europe to advance to a high type of civilization (3000-2000 B. C.).

They still remained *without writing,*

without architecture in hewn-stone masonry,

and *without* large sailing ships for *commerce.*

The failure to make progress in architecture beyond such rough stone structures as Stonehenge is an illustration of this backwardness of western and northern Europe.

It clearly proves the failure of Bronze Age Europe to bring forth a high civilization, such as we have found in the Orient. It was naturally in that portion of Europe nearest Egypt that civilization developed most rapidly; namely, around the Aegean Sea.

Breasted, James, *The Conquest of Civilization*, Harper & Bros., New York and London, 1946, p. 240

"How low the savage European must have looked to the Nile Valley African looking north from his pyramid of Cheops? "

Professor Dorsey in his book *Why We Behave Like Human Beings*

Dr. Yosef A. ben-Jochannan and Dr. John Henrik Clarke provide this insightful, historical observation:

If you look at the map you see that Greece was one of the nations that was closest to Africa. This proximity put them closest to the intellectual mainstream of the Mediterranean.

When the *intellectual miracle of Egypt* existed (...it existed thousands of years *before* anybody knew that there was a Europe)...

New Dimensions in African History, African World Press, Inc., Trenton, New Jersey, 1991, p. 99

A History of Europe by Professor J. M. Roberts informs us that:

In early *Europe*...bands of a few families could get along, scratching a living from hunting, fishing and primitive agriculture, with no need for complex government or social arrangements to regulate their small numbers. They hardly inhabited a rustic paradise, but they got by, even if

it meant *later arrival at civilization* than elsewhere.

Allen Lane, The Penguin Press, New York, New York, 1996, p. 8

The "Founding Fathers" of Europe were 'savages' during the Ancient History of Man

Professor Cheikh Anta Diop supplies a revealing examination of the first contact the Egyptians had with the inhabitants of Europe:

"...about the year 1500 B. C., the Western region of the Nile delta was

invaded by *Indo-Europeans*, tall, blond, blue-eyed, their *bodies covered by tattoos* and *clothed in animal skins*.

This is how they are described in documents found by Champollion at Biban-el-Molouk.

'...lastly (and I am *ashamed* to say so, since *our own race* is *the last and*

most savage of the series)...

It must be understood that reference here is made to the people of the **blond race with White skins**, living not only in Europe, but in Asia...

I certainly did not expect, on arriving at Biban-el-Molouk, to find sculptures which would serve as vignettes of the history of

the *primitive inhabitants of Europe,*

should one ever have the courage to undertake this.

The sight of these has however, something flattering and consoling, since **it does make us appreciate the long way we have traveled since that time.'** " [Champollion le Jeune, Lettres, (Coll. l'Univers, 1839), pp. 30-31]

The Cultural Unity of Black Africa, (Trans. 1963), Third World Press, Chicago, 1963, p. 62-63

To cite the author of *Arts, Sciences, and Civilization Anterior to Greece and Rome,* R. W. Haskins:

"Here is antiquity not dreamed of by our classics, when such barbarians were Europe's only representative at the learned and refined court of the Pharaohs." (p. 21)

"In the days when there was famine in Canaan, and Jacob—who was called no more Jacob, but Israel—sent his sons to Pharaoh to buy corn,

Egypt **was even then a** *Land of Antiquities.*

At the time that the Britons were staining their bodies with ochre and woad,

the Great Pyramid **was** *already an ancient monument.*

Egypt sculptors...depicted *skin-clad savages—* **these were** *Europeans.*

Centuries passed, and *sunburnt barbarians*,

blue-eyed and red of hair, peered

into the valley of the Nile..."

Victor Robinson M. D., *The Story of Medicine,* Albert & Charles Boni, New York , 1936, p. 28

According to the historian, Joseph McCabe:

"...our ancestors remained...

pure barbarians,

during the two thousand years

when the dark men...were constructing civilization...

Until about 700 B. C. the philosophers of the world would have said that White men seeme*d incapable of civilization..."*

(*The New Science and the Story of Evolution,* P. 292-98)

John Jackson, *Introduction to African Civilization,* Citadel Press, 1990, p. 78-9

"Fabre d'Olivet says:

The Black Race more ancient than the White, was dominant upon the earth and

held the scepter of science and power...

The White Race was still weak,

savage and without laws, without

cultivation of any sort,

destitute of memories and too devoid of understanding even to conceive hope."

(G. K. Osei, *The African,* The African Publication Society, London, 1971, p. 46)

"*Greek history begins* with the Trojan war, when Egyptian Thebes was already falling from its high rank among cities.

Jewish history begins a little earlier...when

the Egyptian kings already boasted of a

long line of ancestors.

And **even when the first faint Jewish tradition brings Abraham from Chaldea and makes this father of the Hebrew nation** lead his herds to drink of the waters of the Nile**,**

Egypt was then a

highly civilized country,

the pyramids had

been built near

Memphis...

and the obelisk of Heliopolis, with the other sculptured monuments which he must have seen as he passed,

still prove the high state

of the arts at that time."

Samuel Sharpe, *The History of Egypt,* vol. I & II, (6th ed.), George Bell & Sons, London, 1876, p. iv

As H. G. Wells in his *Outline of History* explained:

HOW THE ICEMAN MIGHT HAVE LOOKED

This rendering is based on artifacts found near the frozen body, but many facts are unknown.

"But after about 1200 BC and perhaps earlier, a set of names would come into the map of the ancient world from the north-east and from the north-west. These would be the names of certain **barbarian tribes**, armed with iron weapons and using horse chariots, who were becoming a great affliction to the Aegean and Semitic civilizations on northern borders. They all spoke variants of what once must have been the same language, Aryan.

Round the northeast of the Black and Caspian Seas were coming the Medes and Persians. Confused with these in the records of the time were Scythians and Sarmatians. From northeast or northwest came the Armenians, from the north-west of the sea-barrier through the Balkan peninsula came Cimmerians, Phrygians, and the Hellenic tribes whom now we call the Greeks.

They were raiders and robbers and plunderers of cities, these Aryans,

east and west alike. They were all kindred and similar peoples, hardy herdsmen who had taken to plunder. In the east they were still only

borderers and raiders,

but in the west they were taking cities and driving out the civilized Aegean population…

Of these Aryans who came thus rudely upon the scene of the ancient civilizations we will tell more fully in a later section. Here we note simply all this stir and emigration amidst the area of the ancient civilizations, that was set up by the swirl of the gradual and continuous advances of

these Aryan barbarians

out of the northern *forests* and *wildernesses* between 1600 and 600 B. C."

Wells stated that:

"In…Egypt **the coming of the Aryans** did not cause fundamental changes until after 600 B. C…

Dynasties came and went...In Egypt the accumulated monuments of more ancient times –

the pyramids were already in their third thousand of years

and a show for visitors just as they are today - were supplemented by fresh and splendid buildings, more particularly in the time of the Seventeenth and Nineteenth Dynasties. The great temples Karnak and Luxor from this time date from this time."

Later he adds:

"We know that life, for prosperous and influential people in such cities as...the Egyptian Thebes, was already almost

as refined and as luxurious as that of comfortable and prosperous people today.

Such people lived an orderly and

ceremonious life in beautiful and beautifully furnished and decorated houses, wore richly decorated clothing and lovely jewels;

they had feasts and festivals, entertained one another with music and dancing, **were waited upon by highly trained servants, were cared for by doctors and dentists."**

A more recent writer, Elizabeth Payne, in the book *The Pharaohs of Ancient Egypt* (Random House), makes a similar case:

"In Napoleon's day historians knew almost nothing about Egypt past or present. It was a land the world had all but forgotten. And yet once,

long before the birth of Christ,

Egypt had been the most famous and powerful country in the world.

At a time in history when the ancestors of

Western man still lived as semi-savages in the dense forests of England and Europe,

a great civilization had existed along the banks of the river Nile. Ruled over by awesome god-kings called Pharaohs.

Egypt had been a land of bustling cities, golden palaces, huge stone temples, busy dock sides and luxurious country estates. Her people had been fun-loving and light-hearted, her nobles elegant and worldly and her **gods the most powerful in all the world.**"

"Thus at the dawn of history barbarian Europe

looked across the Mediterranean

to

the great civilization of the Nile."

James Breasted, *The Conquest of Civilization*, Harper & Bros., New York and London, 1946, p. 239

And, according to the scholar Morris:

"Were the White an inherently superior race

we should not have found it

at the beginning of authentic history

almost lost in the sea of under-life,

but its superior qualities would have told at a far remote epoch; the Negro and the Mongolian expansion would have been checked long before, and history opened up with the Caucasian as the dominant element."

J. A. Rogers *Sex and Race*, vol. I

Adds Lord Raglan:

"**Civilization** is often thought of as **associated with** the possession of a White skin..." But, he continues,

"...The Whites were,

it seems,

incapable of civilizing themselves..."

"Anthropology and the Future of Civilization," *The Rationalist Annual*, 1946, p. 39-40

However, in the book *Race Life of the Aryans* (1917), J. P. Widney maintained that there was:

"...a widespread...civilization ruling the world from its seats of power

in the Valley of the Ganges, the Euphrates and the Nile and it **was of** *Black races*...

The earliest Egyptian civilization seems to have been Negroid. It was in the days *before the Semite* was known in either land..."

This same English scholar, McCabe, goes on to say that:

"Four thousand years ago, when civilization was already one or two thousand years old, White men were just a bunch of semi-savages on the outskirts of the civilized world.

If there had been anthropologists in Crete, Egypt, and Babylonia, they would have pronounced the White race obviously inferior, and might have discoursed learnedly on the superior germ-plasma or glands of colored folk."

Professor Breasted reminds us:

"On the borders of this earliest civilized world of Egypt and Western Asia lay **for some two thousand years the wilderness of savage Europe** stretching far westward to the Atlantic, **untouched by civilization**, except at its south-eastern corner, where the Greek Islands looked south-eastward to the mouths of the Nile and eastward toward Hittite Asia Minor."

American Historical Review, January, 1929

According to the authors of *Ancient Greece, A Political, Social and Cultural History:*

When the Greek attained a high civilization

(around 1500 B. C.), the civilized cultures of...**Egypt**...[was] **already 1500 years old**. (Sarah B. Pomeroy, Stanley M. Burstein, Walter Donlan, and Jennifer T. Robert, Oxford University Press, New York, Oxford, 1999, p. 6)

From the pen of Bishop William Montgomery Brown:

"For the first two or three thousand years civilization, there was

not a civilized White man on the earth. Civilization was founded and developed by the swarthy races of Mesopotamia, Syria and Egypt,

the White race remained so barbaric that in those days an Egyptian or a Babylonian priest would have said that the riffraff of White tribes a few hundred miles to the north of their civilization were hopelessly incapable of acquiring the knowledge requisite to progress.

It was southern colored people everywhere, in China, in Central America, in India, Mesopotamia, Syria, Egypt and Crete, who gave the northern White people civilization."

The Bankruptcy Of Christian Supernaturalism, vol. II, p. 192

In fact, John Romer suggests that even in later times "civilization" was somewhat of a distant goal for Europeans:

...by the thirteenth century the fully amalgamated peoples of **the West had created a society**. *It was still quite crude and ignorant* and new, a pioneer society just struggling out of a long past of bitter toil for a bare subsistence, both physical and spiritual. **If we take the eleventh century as marking the end of those "Dark Ages"** in which the Western peoples were fighting to assure themselves of the physical basis of life, we must recognize that

Western Europe was still an outpost of human life.

In the primeval forests of France there dwelt a few million hardy tillers of the soil, in the clearings of England barely a million. ***Wild beasts still roamed the streets of the few tiny hamlets and market towns.*** Art there was, to be sure, of a rather "primitive" and wholly delightful type, but learning and the refinements of urban existence were about as remote as they were from the frontier settlements of the Mississippi Valley in the days of Washington.

People of the Nile, Crow Publishers, Inc., New York, 1982

According to Norman Davies, author of *The History of Europe*:

"Europe" is a relatively modern idea. It gradually replaced the earlier concept of 'Christendom' in a complex intellectual process lasting from the fourteenth to the eighteenth century."(Harper Perennial, New York, 1996, p. 97)

Later, he adds that:

There is a quality of excellence about Ancient Greece that brooks few comparisons...**The rise of Ancient Greece often strikes its many awestruck admirers as miraculous...** (p. 95)

"Indeed, in the twentieth century, the philosopher and mathematician Alfred North Whitehead claimed that 'the European philosophical tradition...consists of a series of footnotes to Plato.' "

Richard D. Goff, George H. Cassar, Anthony Esler, James P. Holoka and James C. Waltz, *A Survey of Western Civilization*, vol. 1, West Publishing Company, New York, 1987

"From the Greeks later Europeans were to inherit an immense and indissoluble residue of mental achievement

from which our ancestors copied and learnt for centuries, and of which our ancestors copied and learnt for centuries, and of which we still use. Vigorous and restless - even to the point of self-destructiveness

- the Greeks passed to the future modes of thought, ideas, ideals and institutions, which take us out of the mysterious uncertainties of the first civilizations and into,

as an Oxford scholar once put it,

'a world whose air we can breathe.'

A. Andrews, *Greek Society*, Hammondsworth, 1971. p. 294

J. M. Roberts, *A History of Europe*, Allen Lane, The Penguin Press, New York, New York, 1996, p. 22

Continuing, Roberts writes:

> Yet philosophic thought itself, the business of reflecting systematically (even on thought itself), was invented by the Greeks, who left us not only specific ideas, but also frameworks within which philosophers can still work.

One even in this century described **the whole European philosophical tradition as a series of footnotes to the work of the Athenian Plato.**

A. N. Whitehead, Process and Reality, Cambridge, 1929, p .53

As for Aristotle:

> "Dante rightly called Aristotle 'the master of those who know.' "

Richard D. Goff, George H. Cassar, Anthony Esler, James P. Holoka and James C. Waltz, *A Survey of Western Civilization*, vol. 1 West Publishing Company, New York, 1987

These same scholars authors credit him with the following:

Aristotle's systematizing of the departments of human knowledge was the most influential and enduring in the intellectual history of the West.

Likewise, Professors Palmer and Colton hailed him as:

The great codifier of Greek thought on almost all subjects in the classical period was Aristotle, who lived in Athens from 384 to 322 B. C.

R. R. Palmer, Joel Colton, *A History of the Modern World*, Alfred A. Knopf, New York, 1984, p. 15

"STOLEN LEGACY"

However, Professor George G. M. James clearly illustrates in his book:

"STOLEN LEGACY"

That the Greeks were NOT the authors of "Greek philosophy," but the people of North Africa commonly called the Egyptians.

Professor Emile Amelineau, a French philosopher and Egyptologist, expressed a similar view:

"I saw at the time, and very clearly too, that

the most renowned systems of Greece,

namely those of Plato and Aristotle,

have Egypt for their cradle...

I see no reason why *ancient Greece*

would keep the honor of ideas that

she *borrowed from Egypt*."

(Amelineau: *Prolegomenes* Introduction, pp. 8-9)

Cheikh Anta Diop, *Black Nations and Cultures*

For example, the ancient historian Diodorus Siculus offered a revealing description of the Greeks' visitations to Egypt for instruction and tutelage:

Now as evidence of all these visitors, the priests sometimes point out statues, sometimes palaces or building having the same name as one of them; they also offer proof based on the knowledge each one acquired,

since they have established that all the concepts for which these men were noted among the Greeks were transplanted out of Egypt.

Orpheus, for example, brought away from there the greatest part of his mystical rites...and his fables about the souls in Hades. For the ritual of Dionysus is the same as that of Osiris, and the rite of Demeter is very similar to that of Isis, differing only in name.

And Orpheus introduced the notions of the punishment of the wicked in Hades, the fields of the Just, and the other ideas he impressed upon the masses, from his own recollection of the funeral ceremonies in Egypt.

Hermes, for example, the Conductor of Souls, according to the ancient Egyptian custom, leads the body of the Apis up to a certain point and hands it over to the one wearing the mask of Cerberus.

And after Orpheus had made this known among the Greeks, Homer, in conformity with the idea, inserted this in his poem...(Odyssey 24, 1-2)

Diodorus on Egypt, Book I of Diodorus Siculus, Historical Library, (trans. Edwin Murphy), McFarland & Company Inc., North Carolina, 1985, p. 125

The author of *The Civilization of the Ancient Egyptians* Bothwell A. Gosse lists many of the Greeks who came to Egypt to study:

"The Temple courts were crowded with foreigners eagerly seeking the benefits of the magnificent library and the thorough scientific training.

All the master minds of antiquity seem to

have been educated here, and the University rolls present a brilliant galaxy of names.

Moses there became learned 'in all the wisdom of the Egyptians.' *Solon*, the great lawgiver, owed his system to the teaching of the priests. *Plato* followed, and has left the records of his debt for *us* to judge how great indeed was his Alma Mater. Thales of Miletus received his education in science here, and as a result gave to the world the knowledge of electricity. Later on the library and the University were transferred to Alexandria, and then we find Euclid in charge of the mathematical department. Ctesibus who invented the force-pump, and *Hero* the pioneer of the steam-engine, came to Egypt for instruction in mechanics; *Hypatia*, too, who divides with them the renown of introducing the hydrometer, studied there, and afterwards rose to fame as a lecturer.

And who can relate half the wonderful inventions that emanated from the mind of Archimedes, who is considered the greatest mechanical genius of that, or any other, age! He was very young when he arrived at this University, but there he learned the fundamental principles on which his inventions were based. The hydraulic press, cog-wheels, pulleys, etc., are all attributed to him.

Considering the marvels displayed by this race in hydraulic engineering, and in the transport and erection of gigantic masses of stone, we cannot but think that all this mechanical knowledge was in existence, and that these great men only carried the inventions to the outer world...**It is their work at the Courts of other nations, whither they carried the learning of the Egyptians, that has handed down their fame to posterity**..." (T. C . E . C. Jack Ltd., London, 1916, p. 21)

"Ancient Egypt has always been our greatest visible inheritance of antiquity," says J.M. Roberts in his book *A History of the World*.

So, too, with the early Greeks who shared a similar respect for this ancient marvel and traveled afar to be educated by her priests as the following example illustrates:

> "...At Heliopolis near Cairo...Plato allegedly stayed while imbibing ancient wisdom from Egyptian priests..."

Jacob Burckhardt *The Greek and Greek Civilization*, O. Murray, ed., St. Martin Press, New York, 1998, p. 235

As if to compare Egypt's antiquity with that of Greece, Professor Lionel Casson cites a well-known Greek classic:

"In Plato's Timeaus (22B) the aged Egyptian priest said to Solon 'You Hellenes are always children: there is no Hellene who is truly an old man ...you are all young in soul because you have no ancient lore, no old learning, no-age-old knowledge.' "

Travel in the Ancient World, The John Hopkins University Press, Baltimore and London, 1994,

The Conquest of Civilization by J. Breasted provides a supporting illustration regarding one of the "Seven Sages" of Greece, Solon:

"Solon, the Athenian lawgiver came to Naucratis as a merchant, ...while thus carrying on the trade of an oil-merchant, he studied the manner and customs of the country...Solon had been in the highest degree useful to his countrymen in reforming their laws... From the Egyptians he copied the law that every man should be called upon by the magistrate to give an account of how he earned his livelihood. After selling his cargo...he visited Said the capital, where his character secured for him an honorable reception, and where he conversed with the priests of the temple of Neith, and inquired into their accounts of the history of their nation and of the world. Solon's laws were all written, and they formed the first Greek code of laws by which all free men were given equal rights in the courts. Some of these laws have descended to our own time and are still in force. (p.319)

Professor Cheikh A. Diop asserts that:

...the Greeks who were initiated in Egypt appropriate everything they learned once they went back to their country...

like the Greeks (Pythagoras, Plato, Oenopides, etc.), were initiated to different degrees in Egypt, which was then the intellectual center of the world; only this view can explain the above-mentioned numerous encounters, which not only could not stem from chance, but which reestablish clarity and rationality where

Greek plagiarism had created a zone of darkness and obscurity.

Civilization or Barbarism, Lawrence Hill Books, New York, 1981, p. 322

Like Professor Diop and Professor Amelineau, Albert Slosman helps to set the record straight:

> "For let us not forget that it was because of the

rampant use of plagiarism among the Greeks

> that Clement of Alexandria said at the time:

>> **'A one thousand page book will not be long** enough to cite the names of my fellow country-men who have

used and abused the Egyptian science.' "

The Book of the Life Beyond, Boudouin, Paris, 1919

> "They brought philosophy - though originally borrowed from Egypt - and mixed it up with what they gathered from priests."

James Bonwick, *Egyptian Belief and Modern Thought*, New York, 1990

George R. Gliddon, an American Egyptologist, provides the following description of Champollion's monumental contribution to Egyptology and the incredible conclusions his work unveils:

> " A pause followed Champollion's *Precis*. The force of his conclusions laid bare consequences too astounding to be thoroughly estimated, even by the most learned and the most enthusiastic Egyptian students. Like the atmospheric stillness that follows the thunderclap, genius seemed paralyzed by the portentous aspect of the truth.

> On the one hand, the classical scholars, adhering rigidly to the Hebrew, Greek, and Latin authorities, were not willing to cast aside the errors of their masters; and those, whose schools had nailed their colors to the mast, were not prepared

to see Manetho exalted above Herodotus and Diodorus;

to find Hermapion confirmed...

to behold in Plato but the translator,

or in Pythagoras but the adopter of Egyptian mythological doctrine;

still less to consider what amount of instruction accrued to the Hebrew lawgiver from his education in Helipolitan colleges; for 'Moses was learned in all the wisdom of the Egyptians.' Acts vi. 22"

Ancient Egypt, The New World, Nos. 68-69, Park Benjamin, Ed., J. Winchester, Pub., New York, April, 1843, p. 7

As the author of *Black Athena* points out:

> Plato's contemporaries mocked him, saying that he was not the inventor of his republic, but that he had copied Egyptian institutions.

Martin Bernal, vol. I., Rutgers University Press, N. J., 1987, p. 108-9

"Perhaps few people ever receive more from other countries than the Greeks received from Egypt.

> And none appear to have been more tenacious of the pretense that all their attainments originated with themselves in Greece."

Albert Churchward, M. D., *"The Origin and Evolution of Religion,* 1924, p. 76

> Quite naturally, therefore, in the chapter, "Hellenic Thought and Culture," E. Burns and P. Ralph point out:

> "From what has been said in preceding chapters it should be clear that the popular notion

that all philosophy originated with

the Greeks is *fallacious*.

Centuries earlier the EGYPTIANS

had given much thought to

the NATURE OF THE UNIVERSE

and to the **social and ethical problems of man."**

WORLD CIVILIZATIONS

To quote from an ancient source, Diodorus Siculus:

> And Lycurgos also, as well as Solon and Plato, are report-
> ed to have inserted many of the Egyptian customs into
> their own codes of laws, while Pythagoras, they say,
> learned from the Egyptians the doctrine of divine wis-
> dom, the theorems of geometry, the theory of numbers,
> and in addition, the transmigration of the soul into every
> living being

Diodorus on Egypt, Book I of Diodorus Siculus, Historical Library,
(trans. Edwin Murphy), McFarland & Company, Inc., Jefferson,
North Carolina and London, 1985.

> "Between the reign of Psammetichus and the Persian con-
> quest, Thales and Pythagoras visited Egypt, and had been
> initiated into the religion and science of the Egyptians..."

Charles H. S. Davis and Camden M. Cobern, *Ancient Egypt in
Light of Modern Discoveries*, Introduction by Rev. C. Winslow, of
the Egypt Exploration Foundation, Meridian, Conn.: Biblia
Publishing Co., 1892.

> "Nations, like families, have usually been fond of claim-
> ing a long line of ancestors, but none have ever had a bet-
> ter right to that boast than the Egyptians. The Theban
> priest was speaking to Hecataeus in about the fortieth
> reign of this history, while his Greek visitor only pretend-
> ed to be the sixteenth in descent from the gods.
>
> *The Theban could then name with certainty more sovereigns of
> his country in the order of succession than we can kings of
> England.*
>
> He was as far removed from the obscurity of antiquity as
> we English are in the nineteenth century... if he had con-
> fined himself to what we think the truth, his boast would

still have been very remarkable, and

he could probably have pointed to records standing around him which had existed some *centuries before the time of Abraham*."

Samuel Sharpe, *The History of Egypt*, vol. I & II, (6th ed.), George Bell & Sons, London, 1876, p. 161

Jacob Burckhardt, reputed to have been one of the greatest historians of the nineteenth century, a professor of history at the University of Basel, explained that:

In evaluating different civilizations, we tend nowadays to think in terms of "progress" and "inventions," a method of accounting by which the Greeks come off very badly. The Egyptians ...had been an industrious people thousands of years earlier, and had the most remarkable achievements to their credit in technology, engineering and chemistry, before *they* [the Greeks] ever started on their

barefaced borrowing and stealing.

'The Greeks did not leave behind a single practical invention worth speaking of,' say Hellwald, 'and even in the realm of thought and creativity they completely failed to throw off the powerful influence of the…East.' " (Fredrich von Hellwald, p. 277)

The Greek and Greek Civilization, O. Murray, ed., St. Martin Press, New York, 1998, p. 135

The Nigerian Professor Innocent C. Onyewuenyi in his compelling work *The African Origin of Greek Philosophy* drew the following conclusions:

"…some unbiased early Greek philosophers and historians revealed instances of what would amount to *plagiarism* with regard to doctrines and works traditionally credited to some early Greek philosophers. I noted, for example, the revelation by the historian Favorinus (80 B. C. – 50 A. D.) that

Democritus used a strong word 'stolen' to describe Anaxagoras' appropriation of the Egyptian Mystery System doctrine on the

sun and the moon. "

Then he goes on to offer additional references and proofs concerning where the Greeks borrowed their philosophy from. Namely:

> ...the ancient Egyptian cosmogony/cosmology as contained in sources such as the *Pyramid Texts, Coffin Text, Ramesside Stela, The Book of The Dead, Memphite Theology, Leiden Papyrus, Armana Letters* and other relevant texts, encompassing the three major systems of Hermopolis, Heliopolis and Memphis. Every Greek initiate was conversant with these systems.

Lastly, he notes that:

> By comparison of the teachings of ancient Egyptians concerning the creation development of the universe as contained in the hieroglyphic writings of the Mystery System and the doctrine of the pre-socratics as natural philosophers engaged in the study of the nature and origin of the world, it becomes clear that ***the Greeks borrowed heavily from the Egyptians.*** For example taught that water was the source of all things in the universe...Anaximander held that all things originated from primitive matter...the prototypes of these Ionian doctrines are to be found in the Hermopolitan system which introduced Nun, the formless chaos, qualified as primeval waters as Boundless or Unlimited.

The African Origin of Greek Philosophy, University of Nigeria Press, Nsukka, Nigeria, 1993, p. 218

Professor William Sinnegen (Hunter College and Charles Robinson (Brown University) in their book, *Ancient History* said that:

> Hercataeus of Miletus (ca. 500 B. C.), set the stage for Herodotus, founder of the art of history. "Hecataeus," they add, "applied in his Genealogies a free inquiring mind, unwilling to give any greater weight to Greek tradition simply because he was a Greek than to that of another race... (p. 138)

Continuing, he records Hecataeus' belief that:

> "A comparison of Egyptian with Hellenic tradition taught

him the emptiness of the claim of certain Greeks to near descent from a god."(p. 244)

"Another work of Hecataeus called *Geneologies* has often been thought to be the first to exhibit that spirit of critical inquiry which is characteristic of western history writing, for it began:

"Hecataeus the Milesian speaks thus:

I write these things as they seem true to me; for the stories told by the Greeks are various and in my opinion absurd."

Jasper Griffin, Oswyn Murray, *The Oxford History of the Classical World*, Oxford University Press, John Boardman, Ed., Oxford University Press, Oxford, 1987, p. 188

As Clement of Alexandria says:

"The Egyptian neither entrusted their mysteries to everyone, nor degraded the secrets of divine matters by disclosing them to the profane, reserving them for the heir apparent of the throne, and for such of the priests as excelled in virtue and wisdom."

Bernard Roman, *Life in Egypt in Ancient Times*, Minerva, S. A. Genéve, 1978, p. 133-134

Professor Erwin H. Ackerknecht reminds us that:

...until very recent times, men were content to gape and talk mystically about the Greek genius...

A Short History of Medicine, John Hopkins University Press, Baltimore, Maryland, 1982, p. 77

Christopher Burstall of the BBC television series *The Greeks* made the following statement:

"I very much wanted *The Greeks* to be fair, for so much that is vague and high-flown has been said and written about ancient Greek achievements."

Writes J. M. Roberts, author of *A History of Europe*:

"Our picture of **ancient Greece** and its continuing and real influence, came to us mainly through the Greek and Latin writers who provided so much of the syllabus (other than the Bible) which was taken up into later European culture.

What is more, they set what for a long time were unquestioningly **accepted as criteria by which to judge human life.**

This is an implication of the word 'classical':

the classical is *the source* of *standard*

by which subsequent *achievements can be measured.*"

Allen Lane, The Penguin Press, New York, New York, 1996, p. 22

Professor John Williams of Rutgers University has this to say in the *Journal of African Civilizations* (April 1981) about "The Stolen Legacy" in an article by the same name:

> "The late Professor George G. M. James in his work **The Stolen Legacy** dismantles the long-accepted argument that civilization as we know it originated in Greece. **James traces Greek philosophy back to its source in Egypt**, from the Memphite Period until after the invasion by Alexander the Great who, James asserts, was probably accompanied by Aristotle and others who confiscated 5,000 years of knowledge accumulated in the temples and libraries of Egypt."

Dr. Diop records the following incidence:

> "When an eclipse of the sun brought widespread panic in the ranks of the Greek army during Alexander the Great's battle against the Persians, it was not Aristotle, the king's tutor, but a priest, an Egyptian astronomer, who restored calm by giving a scientific explanation of the phenomenon."

"Africa's Contribution To The World Civilization: The Exact Sciences," Nile Valley Civilizations

Professor Williams ("The Stolen Legacy") continues:

> "Professor James is as meticulous about the source of these ideas as he is in citing the Greeks' use of them.

1. The principle of opposites originated from the **Mystery System** whose gods were male and female, and whose temples carried before them two pillars as symbols of the principal opposites.

2. Aristotle's 'Unmoved Mover' is none other than the **Atum of the Memphite Theology** of the **Egyptians**, the Demiurge, through whose command four pairs of Gods were created... **Atum remained unmoved as he embraced Ptah. Thus the family of Nine Gods was created and has been named the Ennead.**

3. The doctrine of the Soul to which Aristotle applies five attributes originated with nine attributes listed in the **Egyptian Book of the Dead** [Budge 1895, 1967].

4. James maintains on the authority of Strabo and Plutarch that after Aristotle and others looted the libraries in concert with the invasion of Egypt by Alexander the Great.

> **'The books fell into the hands of Theophrastus who succeeded him as head of his school. At the death of Theophrastus, they were bequeathed to Neleus of Scepsis.'**

The books were eventually taken to Rome in 84 B. C. 'where Tyrannio, a grammarian, enabled Andronicus of Rhodes to publish them.'

For example, James suggests, if we are told that Socrates taught Plato and Plato taught Aristotle, and there being no evidence that Socrates ever taught Mathematics, Economics or Politics, then something is amiss.

Professor James insists that,

> comparing only two of several lists of Aristotle's works reveals that they differ greatly in number, subject, matter, style and date. The first list, that of Hermippus (200 B. C.), contains 400 books. Ptolemus' list, compiled between the First and Second Centuries A. D., contains 1,000 books.

He asks:

> 'If Aristotle in 200 B. C. had only 400 books, by what miracle did they increase to 1,000 in the Second Century A. D.?'

In each section of his work James lists the doctrines taught together with their Egyptian equivalents, utilizing not only his own considerable skills, but also calling as witnesses in addition to Plutarch and Strabo; Philo, Diodorus, Herodotus and Clement.

Modern classical scholars also take the witness stand; Kendrick, Moret, Davidson, Frankfort, Turner, Vail, Zeller, Budge, Muller, et. al., who in many cases must be considered 'unfriendly witnesses for the prosecution.' "

The significance of the looting of African wisdom and knowledge is expressed by a contemporary scholar of philosophy:

"The looting of Egyptian libraries

occasioned, in modern parlance, the transfer of technology in every field of learning and culture to the Western world. This event

was the genesis of Western scientific, philosophic and technical knowledge."

Innocent C. Onyewuenyi, *The African Origin of Greek Philosophy*, University of Nigeria Press, Nsukka, Nigeria, 1993, p. 157

According to the book, *Stolen Legacy* by Professor James:

"The Memphite Theology offers proof

of the Egyptian Origins

of 'Greek Philosophy.'

For it is an inscription on stone that contains the cosmology, theology and philosophy of the **'Egyptians.'**

For example,

Atom, the Egyptian Sun God *became*

the Logos of Heracleitus;

the Demiurge of Plato

and the Unmoved Mover of Aristotle. Atom, the Sun God is also where they coined the term 'atom.'

Richard Poe, an award–winning and best selling author, makes a similar evaluation of historical reality with these words:

> Yet, improbable as it seems, the Greeks themselves – not George G. M. James – first suggested that philosophy was born on the banks of the Nile. Greek historians recorded that virtually all of their legendary wise men, from Pythagoras to Plato, had studied in the temples of Egypt...if we claim to admire Greek learning, should we not listen more, should we not listen a bit more respectfully to Greek writers?
>
> Should we not, at least, consider the possibility that, when the old philosophers called Egypt their teacher, perhaps they know what they were talking about?

Black Spark, White Fire, Prima Publishers, California, 1997, pp. 93-4

Or, as Professor Bernal puts it to the author of *Not Out of Africa*, when discussing Egypt's massive impact on Greek civilization:

> "Mary Lefkowitz sitting in the twentieth century feels that she knows better than the Greek historians of the fifth, fourth and third centuries when they said that there were significant influences." (Debate on "African Roots," March 3, 1996)
>
> Iamblicus, an ancient philosopher, records an exchange between two well-known Greeks in his *Life of Pythagoras* written in the third century A. D.:
>
> "Thales...advised him [Pythagoras] to go to Egypt to get in touch with the priests of Memphis...Thales confessed that the instruction of these priests was the source of his reputation for wisdom...Thales insisted that, in view of all this, if Pythagoras should study with those priests, he was certain of becoming the wisest and most divine of men." (*The Pythagorean Source Book and Library*, Kenneth Slyvan Guthrie, trans. David Fideler, ed. Planet Press, Grand Michigan, 1987, p. 59)

Richard Poe, *Black Spark, White Fire*, Prima Publishers, California, 1997, pp. 96

"Why Egypt?" asked Poe, "The ancient Greeks looked up to Egypt as an older and wiser culture. They strongly believed that Egyptian priests possessed great stores of ancient wisdom, both mystical and scientific." (p.96-97)

Professor Bernal emphasized the fact that up until the eighteenth century "it was "perfectly orthodox history to the view that Greeks and Romans had of [the] Egyptian sources of their own culture." (Debate on "African Roots," March 3, 1996)

For instance, he repeats a known historical fact that:

"...the Greeks themselves associated the word philosophy with Egypt in their earliest references to it...the Greeks brought up themselves the transmission of mathematical and philosophical ideas..."

At the same meeting Professor John Henrik Clarke compared the intellectual development of Europe to Egypt with these words:

"In the 8th to the 12th century saw the intellectual emergence of Europe at a time

Egypt was in its 23rd dynasty and dying after nearly 10,000 years of some forms of organized society;

Europe intellectually was just being born..."

Continuing he maintained: "that there was **NO EUROPE!** You are giving Europe credit for things that happened

before the first Europeans wore a shoe or lived in a house that had a window."

As Dr. Ivan Van Sertima of Rutgers University, a renowned, internationally acclaimed scholar, said on an *ABC's* television program called *"Like It Is"* (September 23, 1990): "Europe did *not* create ciphers [numbers]; Europe did *not* create algebra; Europe did *not* create geometry. Europe did *not* even create the gun."

According to the book *The African Origin of Greek Philosophy*:

The written testimony of

Greek philosophers, scientist, and historians

all support the claim that

philosophy and the disciplines *originated in Egypt.*

The great role—intellectual, theoretical, practical and material—that Egypt played in shaping the glory that was Greece has been revealed.

The very words of the so-called

pillars of Greek philosophy,

Thales, Plato, Aristotle, Pythagoras, and Hipprocrates

make it clear that they

sought instruction at the feet of Egyptian philosopher-priests.

Innocent C. Onyewuenyi, University of Nigeria Press, Nsukka, Nigeria, 1993, p.56

To which he writes later on that:

This was supported by citing documentary evidence from early Greek writers like Aetius, Plutarch, Herodotus, Plato, Aristotle and modern/contemporary historians such as William Stace, Alfred Benn, Edith Hamilton, James Henry Breasted, etc... (p. 283-4)

Sir Isaac Newton, considered by many to be one of the "greatest European Scientist in history," lends his voice this way:

"That all matter consists of atoms was a very ancient opinion. This was the teaching of a multitude of philosophers who preceded Aristotle, namely Epicurus, Democritus . . . Heraclides . . . Diodorus . . . Pythagoras, and previous to these Moschus the Phoenician, whom Strabo declares to be older than the Trojan War; for I think that the same opinion obtained in that mystic

philosophy which flowed down to the Greeks from Egypt since atoms are some-

times found to be designated by the mystics as monads."

From the work: *Principia*

He goes on to say in the same work that:

"The **Egyptians** were the earliest observers of the heavens and from them, probably, this philosophy was spread abroad.

For **from them** it was that the **Greeks derived their first, as well as their soundest, notions of philosophy**;

and in the Vestal ceremonies we can recognize the spirit of the Egyptian who concealed mysteries that were above the capacity of the common herd under the veil of religious rites and hieroglyphic symbols."

In a similar vein, Dr. Fielding H. Garrison maintained that:

Greek philosophy before the age of Pericles was of Ionian origin and **was derived from Egypt**...

An Introduction to the History of Medicine, W. B. Saunders Company, Philadelphia and London, 1914, p. 59

Professor Theophile Obenga provides a similar historical context of Ionia and its relationship to Greek philosophy:

Miletus, city of Ionia, in the central part of the coastal region of Asia Minor, was, from the eighth century BC a great commercial metropolis and a powerful focus of Greek culture. Miletus was the seat of the very first Greek philosophical school, the "Ionian School." Therefore, philosophy and science appear in the Greek region of Asia Minor around 600 B. C.

'One can see that Greece itself has, at least at the beginning, played no role. The beginnings were in Ionia, particularly in Miletus'

(Moses I. Finley, Les premiers temps de la Grece: L'age du bronze et l'epoque archaique, Paris, Flammarion, 1980, p. 166). C9 (83).

Ancient Egypt & Black Africa, Karnak House, London, 1992, p. 83

"The earliest Greek scientist we know of lived in Miletus in the sixth century."

Sarah B. Pomeroy, Stanley M. Burstein, Walter Donlan, and Jennifer T. Robert, *Ancient Greece, A Political, Social and Cultural History*, Oxford University Press, New York, Oxford, 1999, p. 122

As one scholar puts it:

> "Miletus, in Caria on the coast of Asia Minor, was the cradle of Greek, and hence of European, philosophy; it was a flourishing city in the sixth century B. C. ...
>
> In Egypt, Miletus owned a whole section of Naucratis, the Greek settlement near today's Alexandria...."

Dr. Diop reminds us:

> "It must be said that, traditionally, philosophers and scientists were persecuted in the Greek Athenian state
>
> **...Most of the scientists**
> **who gave Greece its scientific fame**
> were persecuted and
> **had to flee from Greece**
> **to take refuge in Egypt.**
> **Almost all of them went to Egypt for training.**
> Anaxagoras, Socrates, Aristotle, Plato were persecuted or had to flee to escape persecution."

"Africa's Contribution To The World Civilization: The Exact Sciences," Nile Valley Civilizations Edited by Ivan Van Sertima

In fact, it is quite ironic that:

> "Socrates was executed by hemlock not for corrupting the bodies of young men but for corrupting their minds with knowledge both alien and frightening to Greek officials - - The Mystery System of the Black Egyptians - - so states Professor Williams of Rutgers University.
>
> A point which serves to prove that what we understand as "Greek Philosophy" was neither native nor natural to the Greeks.

Journal of African Civilization, April 1981

The Associate Curator of the Brooklyn Museum's

Egyptian and Classical Art Department, Robert S. Bianchi also mentions the Egyptian influence on Greek minds in his book *Museums of Egypt*:

- *Solon*, perhaps the wisest of the Athenians, visited Egypt in the sixth century B. C. and was much impressed by what he saw there.

- *Pythagoras* of Samos, visited Egypt in the sixth century B. C. as well. Initiated into the mysteries of the Egyptian religion, he is reputed to have evolved his theories about the transmigration of souls from the Egyptian concepts of the travels of the deceased through the Underworld.

- *Plato* himself did visit Egypt in the fourth century B. C. Plato's concept of the imperishability of...being was, in part, formulated with the help of the mythical gestures of eternity revealed to him by the priests of Egypt's sanctuaries.

"A group of Ionian wise men were the pioneers whose thought is to be regarded as a forerunner of both philosophy and science. One of them was *Anaximander* of Miletus in the sixth Century B. C...*Thales* preceded him; *Pythagoras* and *Heraclitus* came soon after, both founders of schools of thought that influenced minds for generations. One of the greatest was *Democritus*, who conceived the atom four centuries B. C. ...Yet the importance of this group of thinkers in the history of the human mind is great, for they were the first human beings to wonder about the universe, observe its doings, and attempt to understand how they came to pass."

Estes, J. Worth, *The Medical Skills of Ancient Egypt*, Science History Publications, U. S. A., 1989, p. 322

"They were called 'the Seven Wise Men.' They were the earliest statesmen and thinkers of Greece."

James Breasted, *The Conquest of Civilization*, Harper & Bros., New York and London, 1946.

Michael Wood, author of the book *Legacy* from the television program by the same name, said that the "Greeks believe Egypt possessed an inconceivable antiquity."

"For this reason, **Greeks of the highest repute for learning were eager to visit Egypt,** that they might gain knowledge of its noteworthy laws and customs.

For albeit the country of old was inhospitable to strangers for the reasons just mentioned, yet nonetheless in ancient times *Orpheus* and the poet *Homer* were anxious to voyage thither, as were many others as well in later days, including *Pythagoras* of Samos and even *Solon* the lawgiver. What is more,

the Egyptians assert that both the invention of writing and the observation of the stars originated among them, besides the discovery of geometrical principles and most of the arts, and the promulgation of the best laws.

And they say the surest proof of these claims is that most of the kings of Egypt for over four thousand and seven hundred years were natives, while the country was the most prosperous on the face of the earth.

This fortunate condition could never have existed had not this people possessed the most excellent laws, and customs, and those institutions concerned with all branches of learning."

Diodorus Siculus, *Diodorus on Egypt, Book I of Diodorus Siculus, Historical Library*, (trans. Edwin Murphy), McFarland & Company, Inc., Jefferson, North Carolina and London, 1985, p. 90-1

A similar example is presented by the author *of The History of Egypt*:

"Plato brought with him a cargo of olive oil, instead of money, to pay the expense of his journey. We can have no greater proof of the esteem in which the Egyptian schools were held than that these men, each at the head of his own branch of science, should have come to Egypt to finish their studies.

Here, **Eudoxus spent sixteen months, studying under the priests, and like them shaving his chin and eyebrows; and he may have learned from his tutor Ichonuphys,** who was then lecturing at Heliopolis, the true length of the year and month, upon which he formed his octaeterid, a period of eight years or ninety-nine months." (Samuel Sharpe, George Bell & Sons, London, 1876)

"Polycrates has been represented as a great encourager of learning, and the patron of eminent men, spending great part of his time in the company of persons of talent, among whom were Anacreon and Pythagoras. And his friendship with *Amasis* enabled him to recommend the latter to that monarch, when he visited Egypt, and to obtain for him those facilities

in studying the mysterious sciences and profound secrets of the Egyptians, which few foreigners were permitted to enjoy...

"Solon also visited Egypt during the reign of Amasis; and being much pleased with the laws of the Egyptians...he introduced many of them into the code established by him at Athens. (Herodotus 30.)

Thales is said, by Plutarch, in his Banquet of the Seven Sages,

to have been in Egypt in the reign of Amasis; and he mentions the improbable story of his showing the Egyptians how to measure the height of the pyramid by its shadow."

J. G. Wilkenson, *Manners and Customs of the Ancient Egyptians*, John Murray, London, 1887, p. 188-9

"Thales, the first who had the title of Wise man, traveled in Egypt

in about the fiftieth Olympiad, perhaps in the last reign.

He seems to have been chiefly in search of scientific knowledge,

and did not forget to inquire into the cause of the

Nile's overflow...

He is said to have been the first Greek that foretold an eclipse; and to have learned from the Egyptians the valuable mathematical truth that the angle in a semicircle is always a right angle; and he sacrificed an ox to the gods in gratitude for this increase of knowledge."

Samuel Sharpe, The History of Egypt, Vol. I & II, (6th Ed.), George Bell & Sons, London, 1876

In the book *A History of the World* the author, J. M. Roberts, expressed Egypt's great antiquity and impressiveness with these words:

"For nearly three thousand years – one and a half times the life of Christianity – Egypt was a historical entity, for much of it a source of wonder and focus of admiration." (p. 53)

To which he adds:

"...[the] Egyptian was later also to be reputed to have been great scientists; people could not believe that these huge monuments [the pyramids] did not rest on the most refined mathematical and scientific skill." (p. 58)

"So, the most ancient representative of Greek philosophy and science **(Aristotle affirms that Thales is the founder of natural philosophy: Metaphysics, Book 1, chap. III) is a former pupil of the Egyptians.**

Thales brought back from Egypt numerous cosmological, philosophical, mathematical, astronomical knowledge. The influence of Egypt upon Greece with the intermediary of Thales, is consequently real since

Thales had no other *masters*

but

Egyptian ones."

Theophile Obenga, *Ancient Egypt & Black Africa*, Karnak House, London, 1992, p. 84

The Ancient Greek Geographer, Strabo says this about the

Ancient Black Egyptian Priests of the City of Thebes:

"The Priests at Thebes are reputed to be the most learned in astronomy and philosophy."

(Strabo - Bk. XVII, Chap, 1 - Par. 22 - 816)

> "Herodotus ... says that the whole romance of the soul and its transformations was invented by the Egyptians, and propagated in Greece by men, who pretended to be its authors."

Count Volney, *Ruins of Empire*, p. 144

> "Concerning Egypt," Herodotus wrote, "there is no country that has so many wonders, nor any that has such a number of works which defy description."

Herodotus, "The Father of (European) History," reveals that the Greeks got the following from the Black Egyptians:

1. Almost all the names of the gods

2. Solemn assemblies and processions

3. Litanies to the gods

4. Astrology

5. Geometry

6. Correct calendar

7. Astronomy

Herodotus: THE HISTORIES, *In Great Books of the Western World*, Chicago, *Encyclopedia Britannica*, 1962, pp. 49, 50, 60-65 69, 70.

Strabo: THE GEOGRAPHY, Jones H. L. [trans.], In Loeb Classical Library, Cambridge, Mass., Harvard University Press, 1967, vol. 8, pp. 83, 85

As Professor Bernal noted:

...the Ancient Greeks... did not see their political institutions, science, philosophy or religion as original.

Instead they derived them – through the early colonization and later study by Greeks abroad – *from* the East in general and ***Egypt in particular.*** (*Black Athena,* vol. I, Rutgers University Press, New Jersey, 1987, p.120)

Professor at Corpus Christi College, Oxford, Robin Osborne says this of Herodotus:

> The earliest history in the western world is the work of Herododtus of Halikarnassos, written in the second half of the fifth century B. C...We can be fairly confident that Herdotus derived most of his information from live informants. He is thus an excellent guide to what the Greeks and others to whom he talked thought worth telling in the middle of the fifth century B. C.

Greece In The Making 1200 - 479 B. C., Routledge, London and New York, 1996, pp. 4-5

According to Professor Leo Hansberry:

> Herodotus... was aptly called by Cicero the *"historae patrem,"* or the "Father of History," and... has been rightly termed "the first artist in Greek prose."

> "As to the Greek writers, the most important is Herodotus."

Adolph Erman, *Life in Ancient Egypt,* H. M. Tirard, trans., Benjamin Blomdale, New York, 1969, p. 3

The author of the book *The Pyramids* makes a similar observation of Herodotus:

> Herodotus was a remarkable and reliable historian, a unique figure of antiquity. He is called the Father of History for producing the first comprehensive attempt at historical narrative based on scientific inquiry.

> His work marks the beginning of the Western approach to historical reporting. His writing shows superb analytical skills; it is anecdotal, charming, and entertaining.

Dr. Joseph Davidovits, Dorset Press, New York, 1988, p. 155

> "Herodotus remains our single literary source of any real importance. We may be grateful that so much of his work

survives, grateful too for his curiosity and interest in the affairs of countries outside Greece."

John Boardman, *The Greeks Overseas*, Thames and Hudson Limited, London, 1980. p. 21

"Herodotus combined the interests of cultural anthropologist, geographer, and naturalist with those of historian."

Richard D. Goff, George H. Cassar, Anthony Esler, James P. Holoka and James C. Waltz, *A Survey of Western Civilization*, vol. 1 West Publishing Company, New York, 1987

On November 11, 1953 *CBS* Radio broadcasted "The History of Herodotus," in which Lyman Bryson, Professor of Education, Teachers' College, Columbia University said of Herodotus:

"He told what he saw.

He wasn't afraid to say the Egyptians knew it before we knew it.

On the same broadcast, Professor Emeritus of History, William L. Westermann of Columbia University adds:

"...particularly with respect to Egypt where the Americans seem to have a real affection and understanding and belief in the antiquity of Egypt and **we wonder just as Herodotus did, at the immense age and wisdom that is represented here.**"

(*The Invitation to Learning Reader on the Roots of Civilization*, edited by George D. Crothers producer, Public Affairs Dept. CBS Radio, 1954)

Diodorus relates that during his stay in Egypt, certain Egyptian priests read to him this statement:

"...out of their sacred book" to the effect that many of the "wise and learned men [the bards who preceded *Homer* and from whom he is said by some to have derived some of his themes] among the Grecians journeyed to Egypt in ancient times" and that it was through their efforts that many of

the most distinguishing features

of early Greek civilization
were first transported
from Egypt to Greece.

In this connection,

> *Diodorus* remarks that he was specifically informed that among the most ancient of this group were

> *Orpheus*, who carried back to Greece the entire fable of hell, as well as many of the religious rites and ceremonies which later became well established in the land...

Diodorus Siculus, *Diodorus on Egypt, Book I of Diodorus Siculus, Historical Library*, (trans. Edwin Murphy), McFarland & Company, Inc., Jefferson, North Carolina and London, 1985

"... Egypt had always been recognized as a negro country,

Egyptian art itself was considered Negro art,
and therefore uninteresting.
This opinion did not change until the day it
was recognized with amazement that

Egypt was the Mother of all civilization."

Cheikh Anta Diop, *The African Origin of Civilization, Myth or Reality*, Mercer Cook, trans., Lawrence Hill books, Chicago Illinois, 1967, p. 167

In 1980, the editor of the book, *Museums of Egypt* by Robert S. Bianchi, the Associate Curator of Egyptian and Classical Art (Brooklyn Museum), said in the preface concerning ancient Egypt:

"It is sincerely hoped that . . .

Western Man's outstanding debt to

that great civilization of antiquity is

acknowledged in these pages..."

CREATORS OF RELIGION

Similarly, Dr. Albert Churchward, M. D writes:

" THERE IS EVERYTHING TO PROVE THAT *ALL RELIGIONS* HAD THEIR ORIGIN IN ANCIENT EGYPT..."

The Signs and Symbols of Primordial Man, George Allen & Company Ltd., London, 1913, p. 231

Count C. F. Volney in his book *Ruins of Empire* wrote:

"All religions originated in Africa."

"The Birth of Theology is also to be found in Egypt."

(H. Jaeger, a la naisssance de la theologie. Essai sur les Pre-socra-tiques. Paris, Les Editions du CERP, 1966, translated from German).

Theophile Obenga, *Ancient Egypt & Black Africa*, Karnak House, London, 1992, p. 86

> "What the average educated man of late antiquity thought he knew we might perhaps best summarize by quoting from the fourth-century Roman historian Ammianus Marcellinus:

> > 'If one wishes to investigate with attentive mind the many publications on **the knowledge of the divine** and the origin of divination, he will find that learning of this kind has **spread abroad** *from* **Egypt through the whole world.**

There, for the first time, long *before* **other men,**

they discovered the cradles...of the various
This book says Black people did not start
civilization!religions,

and now carefully guard

the first beginnings of worship, **stored up**

in secret writings.

Trained in this wisdom, Pythagoras, secretly honoring the gods, made whatever he said or believed recognized [the] authority [of the priests]...Solon too, aided by the opinions of the Egyptian priests, passed laws in accordance with the measure of justice...On this source Plato drew on, after visiting Egypt traversed higher regions of thought...gloriously serving in the field of wisdom.'(Ammianus xxii. 20ff. The translation is that of J. C. Rolfe, Loeb Classical Library vol ii, pp. 306f.)"

John R. Harris, (ed.), *The Legacy of Egypt*, 2nd ed., Oxford University Press, London, 1971, p. 140-41

"In certain aspects of knowledge of the Egyptians surpassed most of the nations of ancient times. They were famous for their medical knowledge, for their skill in divination and the interpretation of dreams by which they could declare the will of God;

their acquaintance with geography makes the Greeks look like ignorant barbarians;

they were

"the first **who introduced the names of the twelve gods, and the Greeks borrowed their names from them;**

they were *the first* to assign altars, images, and temples to the gods, and to carve the figures of animals on stone." They were *the first* to undertake large engineering works, and *the first* to erect large buildings in stone.

In almost every aspect of human life Egypt is found to have made the earliest advance towards civilization and to have reached a high standard in that subject.

The wisdom of the Egyptians became proverbial both in ancient and in modern times..."

Margaret A. Murray, *The Splendour That Was Egypt*, Philosophical Library, New York, 1957, p. xx

"Herodotus saw Egypt as the birth-place of Greek religion."

H. V. F. Winstone, *Uncovering the Ancient World*, Facts On File Publications, New York, Oxford, England, 1986, p. 121

In the words of the Dr. E. A. Wallis Budge:

"The **evidence derived from the Egyptian texts** also supplied information about several beliefs and characteristics of the Religion in all periods.

It showed...that the Egyptians believed in the existence of God Almighty...

There is no need to refer here to

the doctrines of reward and punishment, resurrection

and immortality, for the existence of these among the Egyptians

was demonstrated by E. de Rouge in 1860, and again by P. Pierret in 1881.

All these characteristics seemed to indicate that

the Egyptian Religion was of African...origin..."

Osiris, University Books, Inc., 1961, p. xviii-xix

Professor of Hieroglyphs at L'Ecole du Louvre in Paris and an Egyptologist in the Department of Egyptian Antiquties at the Louvre Museum, Guillemette Andreu wrote that:

"...there were constants, beliefs that sprung up at the beginning of the third millennium and persisted through the centuries, permanently underlying the attitude of the Egyptians toward their gods.

The explanation of the birth of the world was one of these lasting concepts, and it was accompanied by a major, enduring concern: the end of the world, or more precisely, the return to the original chaos, to the state that had preceded the creation of the universe.

In the beginning was Nun, a liquid, undifferentiated expanse, the dark, primordial ocean from which the first piece of land emerged by the will of

the self-actualized creator god. Thanks to the creator of the "first moment,"

 light appeared and the world was born, bringing with it humankind, plants, the river, the seasons, and all of nature's miracles...Each deity was an emanation of the creator, who divided and multiplied himself until he produced a sometimes extravagant, polymorphic, and complex pantheon that participated in the cosmic equilibrium. This perfect harmony of the world thus created, in which each thing had its place was defined by the notion of Maat...From the dawn of history, each locality had its deity, who was endowed with a specific myth and lirtugy."

Egypt, In the Age of the The Pyramids, David Lorton, trans., Cornell University Press, Ithaca & London, 1997, pp. 138-9

"What we have in the Memphite Theology is of the greatest importance. It is a search for the First Principle, the intelligence underlying the universe...But we must remember that

the Memphite Theology lies

two thousand years

before

the Greeks or Hebrews.

Its insistence that there was a creative and controlling intelligence, which fashioned the phenomena of nature and which provided, from the beginning, rule and rationale, was a high peak of pre-Greek thinking..."

The Culture of Ancient Egypt, The University of Chicago Press, Chicago and London, 1951, p. 60

The Jeremiah O'Connor Professor of Classics at the College of the Holy Cross, Thomas R. Martin suggested that:

Some nineteenth-century scholars wished to downplay or deny any significant cultural influence of the Near East on Greece, but that was plainly not the ancient Greek view of the question. Greek intellectuals of the historical period proclaimed that **Greeks owed a great deal to the older civilization of Egypt, in particular in religion** and art. Recent researches agree with this ancient opinion...

Ancient Greece, (From Prehistoric to Hellenistic Times), Yale University, New Haven & London, 1996, p. 21

The foremost American Orientalist James Breasted traces the development in Egypt of the world's first people of morality:

"The realm of family life reached a high development...Voices within began to make themselves heard, and moral values as we know them were discerned for the first time.

Thus both the organized power of man without and the power of **the moral imperative within, came to be early forces in shaping Egyptian religion.**

The surviving sources would indicate that the moral mandate was felt earlier in Egypt than anywhere else.

The earliest **known discussion** *of right and wrong in the history of man* **is embedded in a** *Memphite drama* **celebrating the supremacy of Memphis** and dating from the middle of the Fourth Millennium B. C. It is obviously a semi-theological, semi-philosophical discussion of origins, produced by a priestly body of temple thinkers..."

The Dawn of Conscience, Charles Scribner's Sons, New York and London, 1935, p. 19

"It was verified when a slab of basalt was unearthed in **Egypt** bearing an inscription with Cushitic script relating to a treatise on the **moral concept of RIGHT and WRONG** by King Ori in the year c. 3758 B. C. E. King Ori declared that they are 'Moral forces of God' (the Sun God - RA)."

Yosef Ben-Jochannan, *Black Man of The Nile And His Family*

The Western Heritage Holt, Rinehart and Winston, Inc., 1965 by Stewart C. Easton stated quite clearly that (page 33):

"The Greeks considered Egypt the repository of all ancient wisdom."

In the words of Herodotus:

"... the Egyptians *first* brought into use the names of the twelve days which the Greeks took over from them, and were *the first* to assign altars and images and temples to the Gods, and to carve figures in stone...

It was the Egyptians who originated and taught the Greeks to use ceremonial meetings, processions, and liturgies;

a fact which can be inferred from the obvious antiquity of such ceremonies in Egypt, compared with Greece, where they have been only recently introduced...

They were the first people to put forth the doctrine of the immortality of the soul."

The Histories, Trans. Audrey de Selincourt, Middlesex, England: Penguin Book, 1987, p. 146, 152

"Herodotus, puzzled by Egyptian customs and habits which were so different from those of his native Greece,

praises their fear of God, their cleverness and uncanny memory.

Diodoros pronounces them the most grateful nation on earth."

John Boardman, *The Greeks Overseas*, Thames and Hudson Limited, London, 1980

One of the most influential intellectual and cultural figures in 17th-century Rome: the German Jesuit Athanasius Kircher had no doubt about the great antiquity of Hermes Trismegistos, believing that he lived about the time of Abraham, and he was perfectly willing to accept

Egyptian prefigurations of Christ.

As he wrote:

"Hermes Trismegistos, the Egyptian, who first instituted hieroglyphs, thus becoming the prince and parent of all Egyptian theology and philosophy, was the first and most ancient among the Egyptians...

Thence, *Orpheus, Mousaios, Linos, Pythagoras, Plato, Eudoxos, Parmenides, Melissos, Homer, Euripides* and others **learned rightly of God and of divine things...**

Martin Bernal, *Black Athena,* vol. I, Rutgers University Press, New Jersey, 1987, p. 108-9

One writer wrote that even Alexander the Great when he came to Egypt "offered sacrifice to Apis and the other gods, then sailed down the Nile."

"Even though Greek interests dominated, there was no desire to eradicate Egyptian culture. The Macedonian people held the utmost regard for the Egyptians. *They admiringly traced their own architectural heritage and religion to Egypt.* Numerous Egyptian deities were identified with Greek gods."

Dr. Joseph Davidovits, *The Pyramids*, Dorset Press, New York, 1988

Eternal Egypt, a book by Professor Pierre Monte, contains the following statement:

"What impressed them (classical writers) most was

the very great antiquity of the Egyptian religion.

They realized that long before the Trojan War, the Egyptians had temples and priests, and that for this reason

Egypt should be called the mother of the gods."

The New American Library, New York, 1964, p. 228)

Dr. Walter A. Jayne makes us aware of how others viewed the Egyptians as recorded by an ancient Greek historian:

"...to a late observer (Herodotos)...

the Egyptians gained the reputation of being the most religious of all peoples.

The earliest glimpses of the life of the people, the evidences of the Pyramid Age, show that they were pious and devout (Herodotos, ii, 65), tenacious and

sincere in their beliefs, and with a high moral discernment for truth, righteousness, and justice.

These sentiments influenced their daily lives, and by such standards they were judged after death.

Moral purity and justice in this life gained for them a life after death..."

Walter Addison Jayne, M. D., *The Healing Gods of Ancient Civilizations*, Yale University, New Haven, 1925, p. 6

"The Greeks had at all times been forward in

owning the Egyptians as their teachers in religion....

we see clear proof that it was

in Egypt that the Greeks gained their first glimpse of the immortality of the soul, a day of judgment, and a future state of rewards and punishments;

and now that Rome was in close intercourse with Egypt,

the Romans were equally ready to borrow thence their religious ceremonies.

They brought to Rome the Egyptian opinions with the statues of the gods....and

though the Romans ridiculed their own gods they believed in those of Egypt.

> ...even Virgil, court poet, taught the Egyptian millennium, or the resurrection from the dead when the thousand years were ended; and **the cripple asking for alms in the streets of Rome would beg in the name of the holy Osiris.** (Dion Cassius, lib. liii)."

Samuel Sharpe, *The History of Egypt,* vol. I & II, (3th ed.), George Bell & Sons, London, 1876, p. 94

Professor Breasted, famous Egyptologist, also maintains that

the Ethiopians were the first to give religious thought and aspiration to the world.

> Speaking of the so-called Memphite Drama which is known only through a copy of it on a slab made by order of Sabacon, Ethiopian ruler of Egypt about 700 B. C."

J. A. Rogers, *Nature Knows No Color Line*

"The world's first religious principle

was substantiated.

A voluminous note, in which standard authorities seems to prove that this statement is substantially correct, and that we are in reality **indebted** to the

ancient Ethiopians,
to the fervid imagination of the persecuted and despised negro,
for the various religious systems

now so highly revered by the different branches of both the Semitic and Aryan races.

This fact, which is so frequently referred to in Mr. Volney's writings. . . "

Count Volney, *The Ruins of Empire*, Publisher's Preface

Dr. Albert Churchward in his book, *Signs & Symbols of Primordial Man* arrives at a similar conclusion:

"Öat all events the *fact* that we find

the same signs, symbols, doctrines, etc.,

practiced throughout

various parts of this world

would lead us to conclude that

they all had *one common origin*,

and all our research proves that

***in Egypt* was *the birthplace* and**

nowhere else can it be found .

In using the term 'in Egypt' we include the Nile valley and its sources.

In the work *A Book of the Beginnings*, **Vol. II**, the distinguished historian Gerald Massey clearly states the facts:

"Egypt is often called Kam, the Black land,

and Kam does signify Black; the name probably applied to the earlier inhabitants whose type is the Kam or Ham of the Hebrew writers....

the *OLDEST* mythology *RELIGION*,

symbols, language, had their

***BIRTHPLACE IN AFRICA*,**

that the primitive face of Kam came thence, and the civilization attained in Egypt emanated from that country and spread over the world. "

The Foundations of White Supremacy

(How White Supremacy is *"proven"* and *"justified"*)

Pillar #2

JUDEO-CHRISTIAN TRADITION

GAVE THE WORLD
THE TRUE RELIGION
& CONCEPT OF GOD

Translation:

The White man gave us the true God. [See Sistine Chapel and pictures of Jesus Christ]. The image of God is of a White Man. Therefore — "God is White." Consequently, the White man as a "superior being" is the closest thing to "God" on earth.

He is the "Chosen Race" to rule and to have special privileges and advantages based on his White skin. The White woman by extension is the most beautiful and precious woman on earth.

Because if it weren't for the White man, the rest of the non-Whites would still be uncivilized barbarians and savages ["inferior beings"]. And they would still be pagans worshipping trees, stones and rivers and other inanimate things —- forever destined to be savage worshippers of Satan, demons and evil. Not one genuine God-fearing Christian among them - with inferior "gods" and divinities to go along with their inferior nature and intelligence. In short, White ice is not only colder, but it is also *"holier,"* too. As a result, the White image of "God" rests —and rules— in the subconscious of anyone who is exposed to White supremacy.

What is the
COLOR OF YOUR GOD
[SUPREME BEING]
in your
Subconscious
Mind

What's wrong with this picture

Is "God" a White Man?

White People "Worshiped" Black Gods [Deities]

"Negroes were first worshiped in Greece and Rome.

White masses bowed down to Black deities.

The rites of Apollo were founded by Delphos and his Negro mother, Melainis; and

the worship of Black Isis and Horus were popular in Rome and the Roman colonies as far north as Britain.

When this later evolved into

the worship of the *Black Madonna*

and the *Black Christ*,

Christian Whites also bowed down to them.

Negroes, as was said, were *deified* in the early *Greece.*

They appear as gods in Greek mythology.

The chief title of Zeus,

greatest of the Greek gods,

was 'ETHIOPS,' that is 'BLACK'."

J. A. Rogers, *Nature Knows No Color line*

J. A. Rogers boldly proclaims that:

"the earliest Gods and Messiahs on all the continents were Black."

Sex and Race, Vol. 1.

Similarly, Godfrey Higgins Esq wrote:

"We have found the Black complexion or something relating to it whenever we have approached the origin of nations. The **Alma Mater**, the Goddess Multimammia**, the founders of the Oracles, the Memmon** or first **idols were always Black."**

Anacalypsis, Vol. I, p. 286

"In my search for the origin of the Ancient Druids, I continually found, at last, that my labors terminated with something Black.

Thus the Oracles of Dodona and of Apollo at Delphi were founded by Black Doves. Doves are not often, I believe, never Black. Osiris and his Bull were Black;

all the gods and goddesses of Greece were Black,

at least this was the case with **Jupiter, Bacchus, Hercules Apollo, Ammon. The goddesses Venus, Isis, Hecati, Juno, Metis, Ceres, Cybele were Black in the Campdoglio in Rome."**

Godfrey Higgins Esq., *Anacalypsis*, Vol. I

The First Gods IN ANTIQUITY WERE BLACK

The Ancients viewed the sacred image of divine as Black. And the holy race of the Gods was African.

"The GODS of Antiquity from Greece to Mexico were BLACK:

ZEUS OF GREECE

APOLLO OF GREECE

OSIRIS OF EGYPT

ISIS OF ROME

BUDDHA OF INDIA

HORUS OF ROME

FUHI OF CHINA

ZAHA OF JAPAN

QUETZALCOATL OF MEXICO

KRISHNA OF INDIA

to name a few ..."

[See: The works of J. A. Rogers]

In addition, J. A. Rogers' research has yielded an impressive amount of material on the subject, such as:

Sir Godfrey Higgins', *Anacalypsis*, (2 Vols. 1940)

Sir James Frazer's, *The Golden Bough*, 13 vols. 1928)

Albert Churchward's, *Origin and evolution of Religion*, (London, 1921)

Gerald Massey's, *Book of the Beginnings*, (2 Vols. 1930), and *Egypt, Light of the World* (New York, 1932)

Gaston Maspero's, *The Dawn of Civilization*, (3 Vols. London, 1888)

Count C. F. Volney's, *Ruins of Empire*, (France, 1792)

Sir E. A. Wallis Budge's *The Egyptian Book of the Dead and the Papyrus of Ani*, (2 Vols. edited and translated)

Professor George G. M. James' *Stolen Legacy*, (New York, 1954)

Professor John G. Jackson's Man, God and Civilization, (New York, 1973)

"In the Bible (Rev. 1:14)

'the Ancient of Days'

GOD

is described as having

Hair like the pure wool."

J. A. Rogers,*100 Amazing Facts about the Negro*

"The Earliest Deities,"

says J. A. Rogers,

"Were Woolly Haired Negroes ... The Pepper Corn Hair Was A Sign Of Divinity."

Pepper-Corn Buddha from early Thailand.

Contrast the hair style of the pictures at right Note the difference between how the hair would look for an African Bust—peppercorn—and that of a Caucasian (European)— straight or wavy below.

A picture from the *New York Times* (June 18, 1985) shows bust of Nero sculpted in A. D. 54, when the new emperor was a teenager. . .

Buddha, 7th Century Thailand Sandstone.

STRAIGHT AND WAVY

He cites the Greek god, Apollo, Jesus Christ and Buddha as examples located in his book *Sex and Race*, Vol. I on the following plates:

> "The Black hair of the Greek god, **Apollo**, whose rites were founded by a **woolly-haired, Negro,** Delphos (see Plate XXII) . . .

Little do people realize that the world famous **Apollo Theater in Harlem** is actually named after a Black god, with woolly hair [African features]... Apollo.

> **The same peppercorn** hair on the head of Christ on the coin (Bottom of Plate XXII). Likewise, of the Buddha ... (Plates XXVI and XXVII)"

A Book of the Beginnings (Vol. I) is a work written by the eminent scholar G. Massey; in it he states:

> "It is certain that the Black Buddha of India, was imaged in the Negroid type. In the Black Negro God, whether called Buddha or Sut-Nahsi we have a datum. They carry their color in the proof of their origin. The **people** who first fashioned and **worshiped the divine image in the Negroid mold of humanity** must, according to all knowledge of human nature, have been Negroes themselves. For Blackness is not merely mystical, **the features and hair of Buddha belong to the Black race** and Nahsi is the Negro name."

Colossal Buddha Head
(Musee Guimet, Paris)

"Found in Viet Nam 975 A. D. . . . At the Great Mahayana Temple at Duong..."

The historian and author David L. Snell Grove draws attention to the ... Flattened nose, powerful lips, the curling hair falling in locks." Their African origin is quite obvious.

Jesus Christ, The Son Of God, Was Black

Professor John Jackson *Man, God and Civilization* echoes a similar view:

"In early Christian art, *Jesus* is almost invariably represented as *Black-skinned*."

In the book of *Revelations* it reads:

"A throne stood in heaven, with one seated on that throne!

And be who sat there appeared

like jasper and carnelian.

Both of these are rare stones that are dark."

"About fifteen years ago *Life Magazine* ran a photograph of the Pope in his private chapel.

The Virgin and Child pictured on the wall of the chapel were Black."

K. A. Shabazz (Bruce Cosby), "On the Christ Color, Controversy," *The Black American* (Vol. 19, No. 52)

Albert B. Cleage, Jr., author of *Black Christian Nationalism: New Directions for the Black Church*, lists biblical evidence showing that:

Is "God" a White Man ?

"THE HEBREWS WERE DARK-SKINNED AFRICAN PEOPLE.

His *feet* were like burnt **brass**.... *(Rev.* 1:15)"

His *hair* was like *wool*... *(Rev.* 1:14)

My skin is **Black**... *(Job* 30:30)

Our skins were **Black**... *(Lam* 5:10)

They are **Black**... *(Jer.* 14:2)

Look not upon me because I am **Black**.

...(Solomon Songs 1:6)

"Josephus, the Jewish historian, wrote that

Christ 'was a man of simple appearance, mature age,

dark skin with little hair.' "

J. A. Rogers, *Nature Knows No Color Line*

Likewise, in the book, *The World's Sixteen Crucified Saviors*, Kersey Graves makes the following observation:

"In the pictures and

portraits of Christ by the early Christians,

is uniformly represented

as being Black."

"A coin of Justinian II in the British Museum, shows

Christ with the same tightly curled hair

as that of the earlier Buddhas.

The *Cambridge Encyclopedia* says:

'Whatever the fact,
this coin places beyond doubt that belief that
Jesus Christ was a Negro.' "

J. A. Rogers, *Sex and Race,* Vol. I

The MOTHER OF GOD, the Virgin Mary, was Black

"In fact, **the earliest statues of the Virgin Mary and Christ in Europe as far north as Russia were Black**. And even today, evidence can he found of this.

In **Poland**, she is called the **Black Madonna** of Czestochowa.

In **Spain**, there is a **Black Madonna** from Nuria called the 'Queen of the Pyrenees.'

In **Russia**, Notre Dame of Kazar is a **Black Virgin**.

One can find a **Black Christ**:

In **France**, the Cathedral of Millan.

In **Germany**, the Cathedral of Augsburg.

In **Italy**, the Church of San Francisco (at Pisa)."

J. A. Rogers, *Sex and Race*, Vol. I

Gerald Massey *Ancient Egypt* says,

"The Black Jesus is a well-known form of the child-Christ

worshiped on the continent (Europe)."

Jet Magazine (February 15, 1982) highlighted:

"THE MADONNA CONNECTION"

'Madonna' Links, Poles To Blacks, In America

"The Lady of Czestochowa has inspired millions of Polish citizens to fight tyranny. The most sacred religious shrine in the European country beset by Soviet Union troops is "The Lady," for centuries known as the Black Madonna."

"BLACK MADONNA

FROM

NURIA, SPAIN

WHO IS CALLED

'THE QUEEN OF THE PYRENEES'. "

Black Madonna of Czestochowa is revered in Poland. Pope John Paul II, a native of Poland, stands before the Madonna during a ceremony at Jasna Gora Monastery in Poland.

THE BLACK MADONNA

The New York, Sunday News, October 7, 1973, New York City, New York, by Ben Carruthers

Spain's Black Madonna Venerated for Years

"**The shrine of the Black Madonna**, high in the vastness of Montserrat, the Serrated Mountain of northeastern

Spain, has been a favored destination for Christian pilgrims for centuries.

A recent issue of Time Magazine (June 11, 1979), reported Pope Paul II's visit to Czestochowa's holiest shrine, which contains the painting of the Black Madonna. Time showed a good photograph of the Black Madonna and Child which has much value for historians.

In Volume I of Godfrey Higgins' *Anacalypsis*, he states that:

News photo by Jack Clarity

Replica of famed statue of Black Madonna and Child is admired by Ben Carruthers, secretary of Society of American Travel Writers."

"The first Black Buddhist people coming to Italy and bringing **the Black God and his Mother** along with them. And they not only brought the Black God and his Mother but they brought his house, the house at Loretto." (p. 264)

Conyers Middleton *("Letters from Rome")* agrees:

"The mention of Loretto puts me in mind of the surprise that I was in at

the first sight of the Holy Image for it is

as Black as a Negro."

"If the author had wished to invent a circumstance to corroborate the assertion that the **Romish Christ of Europe** is the **Christna** of **India**

how could he have desired anything more striking than the fact of the **Black Virgin** and **Child** being so **common** in the **Romish countries of Europe?**

A Black Virgin and Child

among the White Germans, Swiss, French."

Godfrey Higgins, *Anacalypsis*, Vol. II, p. 137-139

RUSSIA'S BLACK MADONNA

THE VIRGIN OF KAZAN,

This Ancient Black Madonna Is The Most Magnificent
of all The Russian Ikons.

Source: The Ancient Black Christians, Fr. Martin de Porres Walsh,
O. P.

"Tradition says that St. Luke who personally knew the mother of
Christ, carved with his own hand

the majority of these Black virgins.

It is highly interesting to know, therefore, if the mother of Christ
was not a Negro woman,

how it happens that she is Black
in France, Switzerland, Italy, and Spain?' "

("Romain Rolland, Intermediare des chercheurs et des curieux," Vol. 34, p. 192, Paris.)

Sex and Race, Vol. I

In the *Journal of African Civilization,* (Nov., 82), Dr. Finch summarizes:

"These Black Madonnas have been the holiest shrines of Catholic Europe and even

today millions of Europeans bow down to *worship*

an African goddess and her child."

The World's Earliest "Messiahs" were Black

BUDDHA WAS BLACK

"Japan B. C. 1000 ... Era of Buddha ...

as in most other images he is

represented with woolly hair

—a peculiarity that enables

his divinity to be traced under

all disguises of name and

caprices of art."

Cambridge Encyclopedia, pp. 126-127

"India B. C. 721 ... He was recognized as the Expected

One by the seers of Magi; his head was rayed,

his complexion was Black and his hair was woolly."

Cambridge Encyclopedia, p. 137

"The BUDDHA belonged to a culture that inhabited the INDUS VALLEY known as the Harappa. These people were of the BLACK RACE. It was within the rigid philosophical and scientific cultural structure of these people that gave birth to yoga, the Ayur-Veda (Eastern system of medicine), and a comprehensive understanding of the functionality of the Universe and how it relates to man." [1. *Philosophies of India* Heinrich Zimmer, Boligen Series XXVI Princeton pages 196, 221, 228-229; 281-282. 2. *The Wonder That Was India* A.0. Basham pages 26-43; 32 (paragraph 2); 305 (paragraph 2); pages 364-369.]"

Source: CLOVER INTERNATIONAL

Godfrey Higgins says:

"The religion of Buddha of India

is well-known to have been very ancient. In the most ancient temples scattered throughout Asia where his worship is yet continued,

he is found Black as jet with the flat face,

thick lips and

curly hair of the Negro.

Several statues of his may be met in the Museum of the East India Company."

Anacalypsis, Vol. I

Edward Moore, writing about two hundred years ago, makes a similar observation:

"Some **statues of Buddha** certainly exhibit

thick Ethiopian lips; but

all woolly hair."

Anacalypsis, Vol. I

MOSES WAS BLACK

"MOSES HIMSELF WAS BLACK.

When Jehovah wished to give Moses a sign, so runs the famous legend, he told him to put his hand into his bosom. The hand came out White, proving that it could not have been White before.

> The miracle lay in turning a Black skin White, and turning it Black again. Hence the perfect logic of the Mohammedan belief that

Moses was a Negro."

J. A. Rogers, Sex *and Race*, Vol. I

As Sir T. W. Arnold says,

> "According to Mohammedan tradition,

Moses was a Black man

> as may be seen from the following passage in the Koran,

> 'Now draw thy hand close to thy side; it shall come forth White but unhurt' - another sign (XX, 23). 'Then he drew forth his hand and lo! it was White to the beholders.

The nobles of Pharaoh said, "

> 'Verily this is an expert enchanter.' "

The Preaching of Islam, London, 1913, p. 358

MOHAMMED WAS BLACK

"Mohamet, himself was to all accounts

a Black man,"

as J. A. Rogers informs us.

In fact, "a contemporary of his describes him as 'large mouthed,' and 'bluish-colored,' with hair that was neither straight nor curly, that is, hair that was probably frizzy like that of the 'Fuzzy Wuzzy'." 'Bluish,' also happens to be the precise color of certain very Negroid natives of the Sudan.

Mohammed's *mother* was also *African*. His grandfather, Abd el Mottalib, is spoken of as being 'very dark.'

He might have been a slave, 'Abd' or 'aabd' originally meant 'slave.' " (Margoliovth, D. S. Mohammed, London, 1927, p. 63. See also J. A. Rogers)

Al-Jahiz asserts that *Abd Al-Muttalib,* **grandfather** of

the Prophet Muhammad,

was *"Black as the night* and magnificent."

The Book of the Glory of the Black Race, Preston Publishing Co., Los Angeles, 1981

LAO-TSE THE FOUNDER OF TAOISM

WAS BLACK

"China B. C. 667 ... Era of Lao-kuin or **Lao-Tsze** . . .

Lao-Tsze was a divine incarnation in a human form!

He was

'born of a virgin Black

in complexion and **as beautiful as jasper.'** "

Thornton: HISTORY OF CHINA, Vol. I , pp. 134-7

OSIRIS WAS BLACK

"Egypt B. C. 1350 ... Osiris was sun-rayed; his complexion was Black and his hair was woolly.

He was included in a slaughter of the innocents ordered by Typhon from which he, of course, escaped. His legitimacy was proved by numerous miracles; some of his doctrines appear in the *Book of the Dead*;

> the number of his disciples was ten; he was crucified on the vernal equinox; he descended to hell where he remained three days and nights to judge the dead and rose again and ascended bodily to heaven."

Cambridge Encyclopedia, pp. 107-108, See also: Diodorus Siculus on Osiris

ENOCH, THE FIRST PERFECT HUMAN BEING, WAS BLACK

From the book *Enoch the Ethiopian, The Lost Prophet of the Bible* we extract the following excerpts:

"ENOCH the Ethiopian, Patriarch-Prophet is the FIRST PERFECT HUMAN BEING in the Bible and the FIRST IMMORTAL MAN according to Moses the lawgiver (Gen. 5:18, 22, 24). And yet, he has been kept a virtual secret for over 1500 years.

The greatest revelation and Biblical mystery since the discovery of the Dead Sea Scrolls is Enoch the Patriarch (Gen. 5:18), the hidden Prophet, the First Ascender and Immortal (Gen. 5: 24).

This prophetic man, an outstanding spiritual leader before the Biblical flood was the Seventh Seed of Adam (Gen. 5:18) from "the godly line of Sethite," the great grandfather of Noah, the father of Methuselah and the son of Jared.

Enoch, the Ethiopian is **the first and greatest Patriarch-Prophet** and has been described as the second most powerful man in the Bible.

He has been referred to as

"an omniscient sage."

The Oxford Companion to the Bible, 1993, p. 184

Similarly, he has been described "as having assumed

astonishing superhuman traits."

Enoch and the Growth of An Apocalyptic Tradition, 1984, p. 135

In addition, he has been recorded as possessing

"superhuman knowledge."

The Universal Jewish Encyclopedia, Vol. 4, 1941, p. 179

> According to the Bible only two men have "walked with God" (Gen. 5:22, 24; 6:9); Enoch was the first and Noah, the second.

> The Bible also states that only three men ever ascended, body and soul, into heaven. Again Enoch was the first then Elijah and finally Jesus Christ. Enoch, however, is unique in that he was *the first* to have both "walked with God" and to have ascended into heaven without having experienced death.

> "Enoch was also said to officiate in paradise at the sanctuary before God. Elsewhere, certain religious laws are said to have originated with Enoch and his books.

> In some later parts of this literature, Enoch himself becomes a divine figure who dwells in heaven and executes justice...

Thus, Enoch combines the functions of prophet, priest, scribe, lawgiver, sage and judge."

The Encyclopedia of Religion, Vol. 5, 1987, p. 117

> Enoch lived so righteously that he did *not* die, but ascended into heaven, body and soul, **THE FIRST IMMORTAL MAN in Biblical history**. The first among men to enter paradise (heaven) in an earthly form.

> In Genesis (5:24), it is written that "God took him" which has been universally accepted to mean "into heaven." Meaning God took him up body and soul. He did not

know death like other mortal men because he never died.

Enoch is the first Immortal Prophet and the only Immortal Patriarch in the Bible.

Despite these facts, Enoch is the **Forgotten Prophet** of the Bible even though he is the first to prefigure Jesus Christ in Biblical history.

Enoch the Ethiopian was *greater* than Abraham and *holier* than Moses. Enoch was ***THE FIRST*** Patriarch and Prophet. Not even Abraham could make this claim.

The Bible shows that Abraham was not a prophet "....he did not make predictions about the future or in the name of God publicly call upon anyone to repent, as later prophets did..."

ABC's of the Bible, New York: Reader's Digest Association, Inc., 1991, p.39

> However, Enoch was also a prophet because it is said that he predicted, among other things, Noah's flood and the coming of the "Son of Man."
>
> Moreover, he wrote the story of Creation centuries *before* Moses wrote his story. In fact, Enoch came 400 years before Abraham. Enoch, therefore, becomes the 1st Prophet in the Old Testament. An example of Enoch preeminence lies in the fact that Enoch comes 21 generations *before* Abraham. Obviously, Moses comes even later; he was the 50th generation from Adam.
>
> Jesus Christ as the Son of God is more significant in the Bible; however, Enoch is Christ-like in that he conquered both death and sin.
>
> 'Ephraem of Syria (fourth century) stresses that Enoch, like Jesus, in conquering sin and death and in regaining paradise in spirit as well as body, is the antipode of Adam.'

The Encyclopedia of Religion, Vol. 5, Mircea Eliade, ed., New York: Macmillan Publishing Co., 1987, p. 117 "

> Many of us have only dim recollections or no recollection at all of Enoch although he is the most towering biblical character in history whose flawless credentials and heav-

enly achievements are recounted by Moses the lawgiver. Here, in the Bible, we have a **LEGENDARY HERO**, almost completely overlooked by everyone.

Why? That's the Mystery. Somehow a veritable *SUPERMAN* of early Christian history had gone practically unnoticed in the Bible.

The first Immortal Prophet

and the only

Immortal Patriarch in the Bible –

ENOCH THE ETHIOPIAN.

Let us remember that the Bible (from the Greek biblia, books) is for all Christians the most sacred of books, the source of truth, the revelation of God's word. No other book has been so lovingly reproduced. Yet precisely because it is held so sacred, the Bible has been the subject of unending debate.

The World's Great Religions, Henry R. Luce, ed., New York: Time Inc., 1957, p. 157

> The first written languages used for the Bible were the ancient African languages of Egyptian, Gecez, Amharic, Aramaic, Phoenician-Hebrew says Carl C. Nichols in his *Short History of the English Bible*.

> The logical extension is that the Bible must have originated in Africa along with practically everything else such as the human race, the first civilizations, the first religions, the arts, the sciences, and, as one European scholar put it, "even the use of the spoken word." All of this we will document in later chapters in this book.

According to *The World's Great Religions*:

> The Bible was written during some 1,400 years (1300 B. C. - 100 A. D.). Few of its many authors have been identified. No original manuscripts are known to exist - only copies of copies...

> However, in 1947, manuscripts pertaining to Enoch were found among the Dead Sea Scrolls in Jordan at Qumran Cave 4 which added to our knowledge of this Black

Ethiopian. In fact, one of the books discovered is from a larger work called 1 Enoch or Ethiopic Enoch.

Since the discovery of the Dead Sea Scrolls, a great deal of controversy has followed because no one has been able to see them for over 40 years, except for a small circle of chosen experts.

Geza Vermes, a Reader in Jewish Studies and Professorial Fellow of Wolfson College at the University of Oxford, asks in his book *The Dead Sea Scrolls*: "Can Qumran then be the parent of Christianity?"

One could also ask: What part does Africa play in this drama of Christian origins? These Scrolls experts certainly know something that the rest of the world does not. That is, the African origins of the Bible had another link to forge on the chain of Truth as to the real beginnings of Christianity and Scripture among the African Race.

How appropriate it is that some of this is found in the very book called Genesis which means "The Beginning" as in "In the beginning God created...(Gen. 1:1).

It is in Genesis that the man whom we call Enoch the Ethiopian is validated by

Moses the lawgiver.

It is Moses who refers to Enoch as a Patriarch (a head of a family) and Adam's 7th Seed (Gen 5:18). In addition, Enoch's lineage is detailed in Genesis Chapter 5 verses 18-32, and ironically this book written by Moses is

the "genesis" of Enoch's mantle of greatness in

Biblical history.

If Adam is the first Man according to Scripture then he must have been Black and if Enoch is his Seventh Seed then he, too, must have been an African.

In addition, Classical and contemporary writers attest through eye-witness accounts that term Ethiopic

[Kushite] extended to the regions commonly recognized today as the place where the Bible and the people of the Bible originated from, in the so-called "Arabian Peninsula" or (Asia Minor).

The people of this area are African (Black). [See Homer, Herodotus, Strabo, Ephorus, Budge 1902, Dunston 1992, McCray 1990, Felder 1994, Copher 1993, et. al.]."

Indus Khamit-Kush, New World Publications,

New York, 1996, introduction and pp.3-4

St. Maurice, the legendary Black "Savior," of White Germany & The Perfect Christian Warrior

According to *The Book The Image of The Black in Western Art*, (trans. W. G. Ryan, Harvard University Press, Cambridge, 1979), St. Maurice was **"A SANCTIFIED BLACK."**

It also notes that:

Charlesmagne...attributed to the saint the virtues of the perfect Christian warrior. (p.152)

Jean Devisse, *The Book The Image of The Black in Western Art*, (trans. W. G. Ryan, Harvard University Press, Cambridge, 1979)

The author Jean Devisse says that: "...rarely has a saint been accorded such manifestations of respect in different periods and in widely varying circumstances."

The scholar provides the following documentation:

...the Swiss confederation ...regards Maurice as a 'national saint...adopted his banner as the federal emblem...Maurice was venerated at Angers where King Ren created the Oder of Crescent in his honor and where the cathedral was named for him...Tours also venerated Maurice's memory and dedicated its cathedral to him...Northern Italy created a military order in honor of St. Maurice...Poland and Riga in Latvia venerated him ... (p.243)

In addition, the author states the following:

Otto I of Saxony borrowed the patronage of the saint from

the kings of Provence and assigned it to the royal (later imperial) crown. (p.153)

As Joel Augustus Rogers points out he was later to become the "Celestial Black Patron Saint of Germany," wearing the German eagle and a golden jeweled crown on his head. (*100 Amazing Facts about the Negro*)

St. Maurice

> In the tenth century it was the policy of the Ottoman rulers to establish St. Maurice as a common bond of veneration between the German and the Slavic peoples."

St. Maurice was so respected by Magdeburg, a German city, that:

> The city found another way to make Maurice known - the coining of money and tokens in his honor.

Jean Devisse, *The Book The Image of The Black in Western Art*, (trans. W. G. Ryan, Harvard University Press, Cambridge, 1979)

Says Devisse:

"Maurice was a Theban, and in the long run
the theme might be fruitfully exploited. **Egypt**...exerted a fascination on the European mind that was probably stronger and more conscious than has hitherto been recognized; From every point of view - economic, military, political, and cultural - Egypt was the land that drew the attention of Western Christians, Crusaders and merchants alike, the thirteenth century. If he could not conquer the country, Frederick (Henry VI) could at least demand that it furnish him the geographic, and

then the ethnic origin of St. Maurice."

(*The Book The Image of The Black in Western Art*, 1979)

In 1511 a "book of Relics" boldly ranked the city banner, which bore the name of St. Maurice, with the banner of Charlemagne.

Jean Devisse, The Book *The Image of The Black in Western Art*, (trans. W. G. Ryan, Harvard University Press, Cambridge, 1979)

In the same book another example of St. Maurice's preeminence is provided by a certain pilgrimage event:

> The pilgrims were...allowed to venerate precious objects called *Plenaria*, which were used in the liturgy: there were twelve of them at Halle. They were not reliquaries but objects in gold and silver plate on which images of Christ, the Virgin and the foremost saints...*Plenaria*, were exposed following a strictly determined hierarchical order, table by table and step by step on each table: the twelve were shown only on exceptional occasions. Maurice, we should emphasize, was given very special treatment; indeed, he was the only saint whose feast days, twice every year, brought out the whole group of *Plenaria*. (p. 199)

The writer also mentions St. Maurice's mother as a queen:

> ...in the midst of the universalist movement in which Otto of Freising took the initiative, when, too, there were manifestations of sympathy that reached **the Black queen Belakane, mother of a perfect knight.**

Lastly, this scholar would end this section by having to disclose what some would probably suspect:

In later times **Western Christendom**, despite efforts at rapprochement, **would betray its inability to convey**

the personality of the African through a vision as lofty and as true as the one offered by this image of man transfigured.

THE FIRST SAVIORS OF MANKIND WERE BLACK

The Saviors of Mankind from Buddha to Jesus were BLACK.

"The name of **KRISHNA** means **'THE BLACK ONE'**

and he thus in the first place comes into line with the deities of other faiths notably the Osiris of Egypt, to say nothing of the Black manifestations of Greek deities and of Jesus Christ."

John M. Robertson, *Christ and Krishna*, London, 1889, p. 16

Likewise, the distinguished historian, A. L. Basham, in his book *The Wonder That Was India*, describes

Krishna as "the Black one ... the name means Black."

There are Caucasians today, who still chant the name of this Black Man. They are known as the *"Hare Krishna"* organization to some. In fact, their leader has distinct African features if one looks at his picture on many of their books.

Both T. A. Buckley's *Cities of the Ancient World* and Professor T. Inman's *Ancient Pagan and Modern Symbolism* contain the following statement concerning the African origins of the earliest gods in human history:

"From the woolly texture of the hair,

I am inclined to assign to the **Buddha of India**, the *Fuhi* of *China*, the *Sommonacom* of the *Siamese*, the *Zaha* of the *Japanese* and the *Quetzalcoatl* of the *Mexicans*,

the same, and indeed an African, or rather Nubian, origin."

Quoting from the *Cambridge Encyclopedia* we have a 'New World' example of this fact:

"Quetzalcoatl was recognized as the Messiah

by seers and his hair was rayed;

his complexion was Black;

his hair was woolly,

he performed numerous miracles; he fasted forty days; he was tempted by the Evil One; he resisted, was persecuted and eventually crucified on the vernal equinox.'

"Bacchus

(according to Ovid, Pausanius, and Anacreon)

his complexion was Black and his hair woolly."

Cambridge Encyclopedia., p. 117 and p. 198, New York, 1899

J. A. Rogers, *Sex and Race,* Vol. I

Professor James in his incomparable work, *Stolen Legacy* states:

"All the great religious leaders from Moses to Christ were initiates of the Egyptian Mysteries.

This is an inference from the nature of the Egyptian Mysteries and prevailing custom.

(a). The Egyptian Mystery system was the

One Holy Catholic Religion

of the remotest antiquity.

(b)..This explains why all religions seemingly different have a common nucleus of similarity, the belief in God, belief in immortality and a code of ethics.

Read: *Ancient Mysteries*, C. H. Vail, p. 61, *Mystical Life of Jesus,* H. Spenser Lewis, *Esoteric Christianity*, Annie Besant, p. 107, 128-

9 also read note (2) Chapter III for branch lodges of ancient world."

In the words of Robert Brown Jr.:

> "**The mysteries of *all the other nations*** were quite similar to those of **Egypt**, and **were no doubt derived *from* them**."

(Stellar Theology and Masonic Astronomy.)

Professor Jackson: *Man, God and Civilization:*

> "Many ancient nations celebrate mysteries, but those of Egypt were the earliest."

R. A. Schwaller de Lubicz, the author of *Her Bak* and several books on Egyptian religion writes:

> "**About 3000 B. C. the Pyramid Texts were already speaking with authority**
>
> of the *constitution of man,* his *survival of death,* and
>
> his relation to the *life of the cosmos.*"

The Opening of the Way, New York: Inner Traditions International, 1981

Another fitting statement is made by Dr. Albert Churchward *(Signs and Symbols of Primordial Man):*

> "**The Egyptians had worked out all the architecture of the heavens**
>
> and their priests had carried the same with them to all parts of the world."

Professor Larkin:

> "**Every nation of antiquity from Gaul to India had esoteric mysteries**, secret societies, whose members were received by solemn rites of initiation."

"According to Dr. Martin Bernal of Cornell University,

the Greeks and Romans believed that their religion came from Egypt,

and they turned to Egyptian religion up until about 100 A. D.

Furthermore, Egyptian religion survives in Christianity itself. It is more accurate to view Christianity as a Judaeo-Egypto religion, rather than a Judaeo-Greek religion, though the New Testament was written in Greek and was influenced by Greek culture."

Lawrence E. Carter, "African Civilizations as Cornerstone for the Oikoumene," *Nile Valley Civilizations*

Professor Leo Wiener of Harvard University gives us a "New World" illustration of Professor James' main point by showing the connection between Egypt and the rest of the world:

"In his scholarly work **MAYAN AND MEXICAN ORIGINS**, he contended that groups of nine gods were frequently mentioned in the Pyramid Texts of ancient **Egypt**...'And, in **America**, we have the same Nine Lords of the Night frequently recorded in Mexico.' "

John Jackson, *Man, God, and Civilization*

Turning to the great religious leaders who studied in Egypt, R. A. de Lubicz (author of *Her Bak*) quotes the BIBLE (Acts 7:22) as saying that

"Moses 'was learned in all the wisdom of the Egyptians'
included in the Pentateuch as much of it as was suitable for his people; and
out of this tradition came Christianity."

St. Augustine, one of the founding fathers of Christianity, made this concession:

" I must admit that certain people other that the Greeks the Egyptians, for example, had before Moses' time a certain body of learning which might be called their wisdom.

Otherwise Holy writ could not have said
that

Moses was schooled in

all the wisdom of the Egyptians."

(Augustine, *City of God*, V. J. Bourk, ed., Image Books,

New York, 1958, p. 404)

The African Origin of Greek Philosophy, 1993, p. 53

"Egypt had inaugurated, for the first dynasties onward and probably before that, a system of cosmogony that the first Greek
philosophers, Ionians or Eleatics, reproduced
in its essential lines and from which Plato was not
loath to borrow the basis for his vast speculations, which
Gnostics, Christians, Platonists, Aristotelians and
Pythagoreans, all did only decorate with more or less pre-
tentious names and concepts, whose prototypes are
found in Egyptian works, word for word in the use of
both the Ennead and the Ogdoad, and almost that of the
Hebdoad."

Innocent C. Onyewuenyi, *The African Origin of Greek Philosophy*,
University of Nigeria Press, Nsukka, Nigeria, 1993, p. 163

Professor John Jackson shares a similar view:

"The Egyptian historian, **Manetho**, is our
authority for saying that Moses was an Egyptian
priest. His opinion was endorsed by

Strabo, who wrote:

**'Moses was one of the
Egyptian priests.' "**

Man, God, and Civilization

Sigmund Freud, himself a Jew, in his work **Moses and
Monotheism** agreed that

Moses must have been an *Egyptian priest.*

W. G. Waddell's translation entitled, **Manetho** (London, Harvard University Press, 1640) refers to the fact that Moses had an Egyptian name and lived in an Egyptian city:

> "The Egyptians titled two of their most important cities Annu; Hermonthis, in the south, and Heliopolis/On, in the north, where Re was the most important deity, and where the best educated of the Egyptians received their instruction.

> The fragments of Manetho say that **Osarseph** himself,

who later **changed his name to Moses,**

was a native of Northern Annu."

Another case in point is Jesus Christ, who also studied in Egypt.

The Aquarian Gospel Of Jesus Christ

SECTION XI, Chapter 47 and 48

Pages 87 - 98: Entitled

LIFE AND WORKS OF JESUS IN EGYPT

Jesus with Elihu and Salome in Egypt. Tells the story of his journeys. Elihu and Salome praise God. *Jesus goes to the temple in Heliopolis and is received as a pupil.*

And Jesus stayed in Zoan many days; and then went forth unto the city of the sun that men call Heliopolis, and sought admission to the temple of the sacred brotherhood. The master said, "Take then the vow of secret brotherhood." And Jesus took the vow of secret brotherhood.

CHAPTER 48

Jesus received from the hierophant his mystic name and number. Passes the first brotherhood test, and receives his first degree,

SINCERITY.

The chamber walls were marked with mystic signs, with hieroglyphs and sacred texts; and in this chamber Jesus found himself alone where he remained for many days.

He read the sacred texts; thought out the meaning of the hieroglyphs and sought the import of the master's charge to find himself.

As Professor Morton Smith of Columbia University from an article in The New York Times reminds us:

"Everybody knows there were a lot of apocryphal gospels besides the four canonical Gospels - Matthew, Mark, Luke and John."

Furthermore, from his two books published by Harvard University Press he goes on to make this revealing conclusion as highlighted in *The New York Times.*

In *The New York Times*, article (May 29, 1973) entitled:

A Scholar Infers Jesus Practiced Magic,

the reporter informs us that:

"Professor Morton Smith of Columbia University presents evidence that may alter understanding of the New Testament, of Christianity and of Jesus."

According to Professor Smith:

"What Professor Richardson suggested was that Mark 10:13 to 10:45 closely reflects the content of an early baptismal service:

'Once we have this report that Jesus administered a nocturnal secret initiation we naturally ask why nocturnal?'

Why secret? Particularly if this was only a baptism.

What was going on? "

Did not the Egyptians have initiation rites? Were they not in secret? Which explains, in part, why it was called the Mystery System.

The world renowned historian Cheikh Anta Diop also helps support Professor James' original point in his celebrated book, *African Origin of Civilization, Myth or Reality:*

"It would seem that **Buddha** was an **Egyptian priest** chased from Memphis by the persecutions of Cambyses. This tradition would justify the portrayal of **Buddha with woolly hair**.

Similarly, 'Koempfer, in his *Histoire du Japan* claims that the Sacya Buddha of India was a priest from Memphis who fled from Egypt when Cambyses invaded it...

Koempfer wanted to reduce everything to a dominant idea:

> *the diffusion of Egyptian doctrines in Asia by priests from Thebes or Memphis* exiled by Cambyses or fleeing his persecution...

A modern author gets the same results by another road. William Ward who published ... documents ... based on extracts from books in Sanskrit, included a biographical account of Buddha establishing that he would not have appeared until the sixth century B. C... (M. De Marles, Histoire generale de l'Inde. Paris, 1928. I, 470-472)"

Dr. Diop summarizes:

"There is a general agreement today on placing in the sixth century not only Buddha but the whole religious and philosophical movement in Asia, with Confucius in China, Zoroaster in Iran. This would confirm the hypothesis of a

dispersion of Egyptian priests at that time spreading their doctrine in Asia."

Creators Of Christianity

"Professor Churchward in his work *Origin and Evolution of Religion* holds that the African Pygmies and the

Negroes were the real originators of

Christian religion."

J. A. Rogers, *Sex and Race*, Vol. I

St. Augustine himself says:

> "What is now called the **Christian religion** has existed **among** the **Ancients** and was not absent from the **beginning** of the **human race** until Christ came in the **flesh** from which time the **true religion** which existed **already** began to be called Christian." (Retract 1, 13)

"The mystery of the resurrection," Prof. Churchward says, **"was** originally instituted by these Totemic Nilotic Negroes, **may be** seen still performed symbolically by the Arunta Tribes.

> Every native has to pass through certain ceremonies before he is admitted to the secrets of the tribe.

> The first takes place at about the age of twelve years; **the** final and most impressive one is not passed through **until** the native has reached the age of thirty years."

Origin and Evolution of Religion, London, 1924

He continues:

> "These two initiations thus correspond to, or represent **the origin of those mysteries** of the double Horus, or Jesus at twelve years of age; the child, Horus, or Jesus, makes **his** transformation into the adult in his baptism or other **kindred** mysteries. Horus, or Christ as the man of thirty years is **initi-ated** into the final mysteries of the resurrection."

He further remarks:

> "The doctrine of soul-making at puberty originated **among** the Nilotic Negroes as did many of the other Egyptian **mysteries.**"

Professor John Jackson *(Man God and Civilization)* supplies us with another example of Christianity's African origins:

> **"The resurrection of Osiris** is shown in a series of bas-reliefs on the walls of his Temple at Denderah. Another representation of this mystery is depicted in the Temple of Isis at Philae. Here there is an inscription, reading, 'This is the form of him whom one may not name, **Osiris** of the **Mysteries**, who springs from the returning waters.' "

Even in today's popular media sectors the African Origins of Christianity is a known fact as illustrated in the August 1997 issue of *Readers Digest* written by the historian Ralpoh Kinney Bennett who declared that:

"Christianity started in Africa.

It was hundreds of years later

before the European

encountered it."

"The Global War on Christianity," p. 50

To choose some examples among many:

> "In the appendix to *ANCIENT EGYPT*, Massey listed more than **200 direct parallels between the Jesus legend and the Osiris-Horus cycle. The earthly Jesus is equivalent to Horus: Jesus the Christ corresponds to Osiris, the resurrected god."**

Dr. Albert Churchward, one of Massey's disciples, has extracted a few of these parallels, which are listed below:

> *"Horus was with his mother, the virgin, until twelve years old, when he was transformed into the beloved son of God, as the only begotten of the Father in Heaven.*

Jesus remained with his mother, the virgin, until twelve years old, when he left her, to be about his Father's business.

Horus, at thirty years of age, became adult in his baptism by Anup.

Jesus, at thirty years of age, was made a man of, in his baptism by John the Baptist.

Horus in his baptism, made his transformation into the beloved son and only begotten of the Father, the Holy Spirit, represented by a bird.

Jesus in his baptism, is hailed from Heaven as the beloved son and the only begotten of the Father, God, the Holy Spirit, that is represented by a dove." *

* The data listed above is from *The Signs of Symbols of Primordial Man* pp. 422-3, by Albert Churchward. For correlative information, consult *Gerald Massey's Lectures*, pp. 1-25

Professor John Jackson informs us that:

"Gerald Massey, and his school, have argued persuasively for an

EGYPTIAN ORIGIN OF CHRISTIANITY,

claiming that *the whole Christian Bible,*

both Old and New Testaments are

traceable to the religious records of ancient Egypt."

"Egypt and Christianity," *Journal of African Civilizations*, Vol. 4. No. 2, Nov. 1982

" 'Gerald Massey (*Ancient Egypt, The Light of the World*) asserts:

'...that **the Gospels,**

like certain Old Testament accounts already alluded to, **were just the humanized** and historicized astronomical

mythology of Egypt instituted by

the early Christian canonizers

and

confirmed at the Council of Nicea.' "

Charles S. Finch, M. D., "The Works of Gerald Massey: Studies in Kamite Origins, "*Journal of African Civilizations*, Vol. 4. No. 2, Nov. 1982

As another instance take "Massey's lecture on 'The Historical Jesus and the Mythical Christ,' which shows that the **birthdays** of **Jesus** are the **same** as the **'Egyptian' Horus** who came **before** him.

Massey noted that

two birthdays had been assigned to Jesus by the Christian Fathers;

one at the Winter Solstice (Christmas), and the other at the Vernal Equinox (Easter); and he observed: 'These, which cannot both be historical,

are based on the two birthdays of the double Horus in Egypt.'

Plutarch, a renowned ancient Western historian, tells us that Isis was delivered of Horus the child, about the time of the Winter Solstice, and that the festival of the second or adult Horus followed the Vernal Equinox.' "

John Jackson, "Egypt and, Christianity" *Journal of African Civilizations*, Vol. 4 No. 2, 1982

Signs of Symbols of Primordial Man is a masterful work researched by Dr. A. Churchward; in it he lists the different names or attributes of Horus and Amsu, the risen Horus or Horus in spirit. Note the fact that

the TITLES OF HORUS ARE ALMOST EXACTLY THE SAME AS THOSE CREDITED TO JESUS CHRIST.

A point which Dr. Churchward has so skillfully uncovered. Below are a few examples:

HORUS -   The Manifesting Son of God.
HORUS -   The First Man-God.
HORUS -   The Anointed Son of the Father.
HORUS -   As "I am the Resurrection and the Life."
HORUS -   Prince of Peace.
HORUS -   The Good Shepherd With The Crook Upon His Shoulder.
HORUS -   The Light of the World.

HORUS - As Child of the Virgin.
HORUS - Who Gives the Waters of Life.
HORUS - The Divine Healer.
HORUS - God Of Light.
HORUS - The Master.
HORUS - Who Descends into Hades.
HORUS - As the Lamb.
HORUS - The Exorcist of Evil Spirits, as the Word.
HORUS - The Lord of Resurrection From the House of Death.
HORUS - The Raiser of the Dead.
HORUS - One with His Father.
HORUS - Transfigured on the Mount.
HORUS - On The Cross.
HORUS - Who Exalted His Father In Every Sacred Place.

Professor Jackson (*Journal of African Civilization*, November, 1982) presents further evidence:

"On the inner walls of the holy of holies, in the Temple of Luxor, inscribed by King Amenhotep III (1538-1500 B. C.),

the birth of Horus is pictured in four scenes, very much like Christian representations of the Annunciation and the Immaculate Conception of the Virgin Mary, and the Birth and Adoration of the Christ Child.

These four consecutive scenes, as **engraved** on the **walls of the Temple of Luxor**, are reproduced in Gerald Massey's **Ancient Egypt: The Light of the World**, Vol. II, p. 757, and may he described as follows:

1. *The ANNUNCIATION*
    The god Thoth is shown announcing to the Virgin Isis the impending birth of her son Horus.

2. *The IMMACULATE CONCEPTION*
    The god Kneph (the Holy Ghost), and the goddess Hathor are shown mystically impregnating the virgin by holding crosses (symbols of life), to the head and nostrils of the mother-to-be.

3. *The BIRTH OF THE CHILD GOD*
    The mother sits on the midwife's stool, and the new-born infant is held by attendants.

4. *The ADORATION*
   The infant Horus is shown receiving homage from gods and men including the 3 Kings, or Magi, who are tendering him gifts. In this scene the cross symbol again appears."

"In this picture," as the Egyptologist Samuel Sharpe noted, "we have the Annunciation, the Conception, the Birth and the Adoration as described in the first and second chapters of Luke's Gospel."

Sharpe further states:

> "And as we have historical assurance that the chapter in Matthew's Gospel

> which contains the miraculous birth of Christ are later additions not the earliest manuscripts,

> it seems probable that these two poetical chapters in Luke may also be unhistorical,

> and borrowed from the Egyptian accounts of the miraculous birth of their Kings."

From the work, *Egyptian Mythology, and Egyptian Christianity*, (p. 19)

> "The Egyptian influence on Orthodox Christianity is far more profound than most people realize.

> All of us have seen the CHI (X) - RHO (P) emblem, displayed in many Christian churches, reputed to be the sacred monogram of Christ.

> This monogram, originally sacred to Horus, was known in Egypt thousands of years before the beginning of Christianity.

THE WHOLE CHRISTIAN BIBLE WAS *DERIVED*

FROM THE SACRED BOOKS OF EGYPT,

SUCH AS:

THE BOOK OF THE DEAD, THE PYRAMID TEXTS

AND THE BOOKS OF THOTH.

In the words of a distinguished American disciple of Gerald Massey, Dr. Alvin Boyd Kuhn:

> "The **entire Christian creation** legend descent into and exodus *from* **Egypt**, ark and flood allegory, Israelite history, Hebrew prophecy and poetry, Gospel, Epistles and Revelation imagery,
>
> all are now proven to have been the transmission of ancient Egypt's scrolls and papyri into the hands of later generations which knew neither their true origin nor their fathomless meaning.
>
> **From the walls of the temple of Luxor** ... there faces Christianity a group of four scenes that spell the non-historicity of four episodes purveyed as history in the Gospel's recital of the Christ nativity:
>
> the angel's pronouncement to the shepherds tending their flocks by night in the fields; the annunciation of the angel to the virgin; the adoration of the infant by three Magi; and the nativity scene itself.
>
> **Egypt had used the symbol of a star rising** in the east as the portent of coming deity **for millennia *anterior* to the Christian era.'** "

The present essay has been excerpted from a large manuscript entitled *Christianity Before Christ* that Professor John C. Jackson is preparing for publication.

From the pen of Gerald Massey:

> "The original foundational matter of the Mosaic writings is not, was not, historical at all, but entirely mythical...**The myths of Egypt will be found to have been copies and reproduced. The Hebrews took them from the Egyptians**, with other stolen goods, and were unable or did not choose to render a true account of them."

Ancient Egypt, Light of the World

For Example:

The 10 COMMANDMENTS originally came from the 42 NEGATIVE CONFESSIONS OF BLACK EGYPTIANS.

"NEGATIVE CONFESSIONS (4100 BC)

From the BOOK OF THE DEAD and PAPYRUS OF ANI

1. I have not committed theft.

2. I have not slain man or woman.

3. I have not uttered falsehood.

4. I have not defiled the wife of a man.

TEN COMMANDMENTS (700 BC)

1. Thou shalt not steal

2. Thou shalt not kill.

3. Thou shalt not bear false witness against thy neighbor

4. Thou shalt not commit adultery."

SOURCE: *Tutankhamen's African Roots, Haley, et al., overlooked* by Yosef A. A. ben-Jochannan

In the book *The African Origin of Civilization, Myth or Reality*, Dr. Diop makes a related point concerning:

> "the famous passage from the **Book of the Dead**, in which the deceased renders an accounting of his earthly acts before the Tribunal presided over by the god Osiris.
>
> > *It is readily seen that **Judaism**, Christianity, and Islam, later religions, have taken the dogma of the last Judgment from this text."*

Similarly, a connection between THE NEGATIVE CONFESSIONS and THE TEN COMMANDMENTS is made by the Associate Curator of the Brooklyn Museum's Egyptian and Classical Art Department, Robert Bianchi who said:

> "Some indications of accepted modes of behavior are also preserved in the '**Chapter of Negative Confessions**' from *The Book of the Dead*.
>
> > The deceased is asked a series of questions about activities in which he is not supposed to have engaged.
>
> > He asserts:
>
> > > I have not known evil; I have not acted wickedly; I have not despised God;

I have not caused misery. I have not caused pain. I have not killed. I have not stolen. . .

In many respects, *these sentiments echo the Ten Commandments* and

place the ancient Egyptians much closer to the Judeo-Christian ethos than is generally admitted."

THE ARK OF THE COVENANT

"The Ark of the Covenant, built and set up by Moses in the wilderness, according to the Sacred volume - and which has not been seen - is precisely similar in all measurements to the 'Stone Chest' still to be seen in the King's Chamber of the Great Pyramid

and which is undoubtedly the original, although the contents are gone. According to the ritual, it should have contained the 'Coffined One,' and we know that miniatures of this used to be carried around the Egyptian temples at Memphis on stated occasions during their religious rites."

Yosef A. A. ben-Jochannan, *Blackman of the Nile and his Family*

Another case in point:

The Proverbs of Solomon came from the Wisdom of the Black Egyptian named Amen-En-Eope.

"SOLOMON'S PROVERBS

——-Beware of **robbing the poor**...

——-And of oppressing the afflicted.

——-Consider these **thirty chapters**...

——-They delight, they instruct...

——-**Knowledge** how to answer him that **speaketh**...

AMEN-EN-EOPE

——-**Rob not the poor** for he is poor...

——-Neither oppress the lowly gate...

——-Have I not written for thee **thirty sayings**.

——-Of counsels and knowledge...

——-That thou mayest make **known truth** to him that **speaketh**."

Yosef A. A. ben-Jochannan, *Blackman of the Nile and his Family*

A similar view is given by Professor Breasted in the classic *Dawn of Conscience*:

"...The publication of papyrus... in the British Museum.... revealed the author...

Amenenope! All old Testament scholars of any weight or standing now recognize the fact that this whole section of about a chapter and a half of the Book of Proverbs, is largely drawn verbatim from the Wisdom of Amenenope; that is the Hebrew version is practically a literal translation from the Egyptian.

It is likewise obvious that in numerous other places in the Old Testament not only in the Book of Proverbs but also in the Hebrew law, in Job, as we have already noticed in Samuel and Jeremiah, Amenenope's wisdom is the source of ideas, figures, moral standards, and especially certain warm and humane spirit of kindness."

Egypt, an exquisitely illustrated art book, by Ceres Wissa Wassef, contains a similar connection:

"The Book of Proverbs has much in common with Egyptian collections of wise sayings; it contains in particular several profound ideas adapted from the Teachings of Amenemhet (first millennium B. C.)"

"The earliest examples of Egyptian ethical philosophy were maxims of sage advice similar to those of the Book of Proverbs and the Book of Ecclesiastes in the Old Testament."

Edward Burns and Philip Ralph, *World Civilizations,* 5th Ed., W. W. Norton, N. Y., p. 37

"One of the greatest **African Ethiopian temples** was **located** at Abu Simbel, or Ipsambul, **in Nubia**.

When an English Traveler named Wilson visited this temple, he **saw sculptured on its walls the story of**

the Fall of Man

as told in Genesis.

Adam and Eve were shown in the Garden of Eden as well as the tempting serpent and the fatal tree.
Commenting on this fact, Godfrey Higgins asked:

'How is the fact of the mythos of **the second book of Genesis being found in Nubia**, probably a thousand miles above Heliopolia, to be accounted for?'

Anacalypsis, Vol. I , p. 403

Higgins then added that:

The same mythos is found in India. For evidence he cited Colonel Tod's *History of Raputans* as follows:

> 'A drawing brought by Colonel Coomba, from a sculptured column in a cave-temple in the south of *India represents the first pair at the foot of the* ambrosial *tree,* and a *serpent* entwined among the heavily laden boughs, presenting to them some of the *fruit from his mouth'* " [*Anacalypsis*, Vol. I , pp. 403-404]

John G. Jackson **"Krishna and Buddha of India: Black Gods of Asia, "African,Presence in Early Asia,"** p. 106, Ed.: Ivan Van Sertima

Bamber Gascoigne who wrote the book, **The Christians**, (which also appeared as a television program) speaks of Ethiopia this way:

"There is only one country in the world today, which has been Christian almost from the start,

and in which one can still find monks living with something of the early simplicity: Ethiopia.

Until 1974 **Ethiopia** was still essentially its own small **Christian empire, with a tradition longer than any,**

Christianity had penetrated its mountain vastness as early as about 340.

The imperial title 'Lion of Judah' is one of the phrases used for Christ himself in Revelation, and Haile Selassie - - the name which Ras Tafari chose for himself in 1920 means 'Might of the Trinity'."

In other words,

"...Ethiopia, a Black country,

is the oldest Christian country

in the world! "

Father Martin de Porres Walsh, O. P., *The Ancient Black Christians* p. III

THE FIRST GREAT MOTHER

[MADONNA] WAS BLACK

[White People "Worshiped" Black Images in Antiquity]

In the newspaper, *The Washington Post* (May 4, 1979), a similar view is expressed.

"Many of the Madonnas painted

in the earliest centuries of Christendom

were BLACK,

according to historians, and it wasn't **until the Renaissance that it became popular to give the Mother of Christ the features of a Florentine Maiden [a *White* woman]."**

Describing Isis, the author Bonwick in his Book *Egyptian Beliefs* expressed this view:

"We may be surprised that as Europe has Black

Madonnas,

Egypt had Black images and pictures of Isis. At the same time it is odd that **the Virgin Mary** copies most honored should not only be **Black,** but have a decided **Isis** cast of **features.** And elsewhere he declares: 'The Black Osiris? with a decided *Ethiopian* appearance was a mystery as was *the Black Isis.*' " ("The Rosicrucians," p. 134.)

In Everyman's *Dictionary of Non-Classical Mythology*, Egerton Sykes notes:

"With the advent of Christianity many of the chapels of Isis were taken over, and the representations of the goddess with the infant Horus in her arms became pictures of the Virgin Mary carrying the Holy Child.

Florentine Maidens

As Isis was dark-skinned
they became
the famous Black Virgins.

Notre Dame in Paris was built on the remains of a Temple of Isis; the original name of the city was Para Isidos, the Grove of Isis.

There are **Black Virgins**

near *Marseilles,*

near *Barcelona,*

at *Czestochowa* **in** *Poland,*

and

in numerous other cities in *Europe."*

Says the English scholar, Jocelyn Rhys:

*"...***in the catacombs of Rome,**

Black statues of this Egyptian divine

Mother and Infant

still **survive**

from **the early Christian worship of the Virgin and Child** to which they were converted.

In these the

Virgin Mary is represented as a Black Negress

and often, with the face veiled in the true Isis fashion.

Statues of the goddess Isis with the child Horus in her arms were common in Egypt, and were exported to all neighboring and to many remote countries,

where they are still to be found with new names attached to them—Christian in Europe, Buddhist in Turkestan, Taoist in China and Japan.

Figures of the Virgin Isis do duty as representations of Mary, of Hariti, of Kuan-Yin of Kwannon and of other Virgin Mothers of Gods."

SHAKEN CREEDS: THE VIRGIN BIRTH DOCTRINE

Biblical Anthropology is a work written by H. J. D. Astley. In it, he concludes:

"We have seen Isis and Horus, Cybele and Attia, Astarte and Merodach, **everywhere** the **Great Mother** of all the gods and of life, and her Son which we enshrined at length in the Virgin and Child of Christianity.

She (the Church) utilized the gods by making their festivals the days of commemoration of the Christian saints or even took them over bodily and adopted them so that

Isis and Horus

became the

Virgin Mother and her son..."

In the *Story of Civilization*, Vol. IV, Will Durant writes:

"Statues of Isis and Horus

were renamed

Mary and Jesus;

the Roman Lupercalia and the Feast of the Purification of Isis became the Feast of the Nativity; the Saturnalia were replaced by Christmas celebration ..."

The late keeper of the Egyptian and Assyrian Antiquities at the British Museum, Sir Ernest A. Wallis Budge, in his discussion of "**Isis** and the **Virgin Mary**" draws this conclusion from the evidence:

"There is little doubt that in her character of the loving and protecting mother she appealed strongly to the imagination of all the ... peoples among her cult...and that the pictures and sculptures wherein she is represented in the act of

suckling Horus formed the foundation for the Christian paintings of the Madonna and Child.

Several of the incidents of the wanderings of the Virgin and the Child in Egypt as recorded in the Apocryphal Gospels reflect scenes in the life of Isis ... and **many of the attributes of Isis**, the God-mother, the mother of Horus ...

are identical with those of Mary

the Mother of Christ."

The Gods of the Egyptians, New York, Dover, 1969

Professor James, in the classic *Stolen Legacy*, explains:

"The statue of

the Egyptian Goddess Isis

with her child Horus in her arms was

the first Madonna and Child."

The words of Edward Carpenter:

"But it is well-known as a matter of history, that

the worship of Isis and Horus

descended in the early Christian centuries to Alexandria where it **took** the **form** of

the worship of the Virgin Mary and

the Infant Savior,

and so passed into the European ceremonial."

Pagan and Christian Creeds, Edward Carpenter, pp. 32-33

Lucius Apuleius, a Roman philosopher of the second century A. D., in his classic *Metamorphosis* quotes the goddess Isis as saying to him:

"I who am Nature, the parent of things, queen of all the elements . . . Phrygians called me Pressinuntia, the mother of the gods; the native Athenians...Minerva; the floating Cyprians...Venus...the inhabitants of Eleusis the ancient goddess Ceres. Some again have invoked me as Juno, others as Bellona, others as Hecate...

and those who are enlightened by the emerging rays of the rising sun, the Ethiopians...and Egyptians, powerful in ancient learning, who reverence my divinity with ceremonies perfectly proper, call me by my true appellation, Queen Isis." (Doane's BIBLE MYTHS, Note, p. 41 81)

Similarly, "Isis," says *The Encyclopedia Britannica*, was worshiped in Egypt, Greece, Rome, Gaul almost all the remainder of Europe and England (See Isis)."

Sex and Race Vol. I

William MacQuitty makes a related point concerning the universal worship of Isis:

"It was, incidentally, from Alexandria that **Horus** and Isis entered the legend that surrounded **Buddha** in Gandhara in northern **India** and thence **traveled to China**, where the goddesses Isis resembled the Chinese Queen of Heaven, **Kwanyin**, who, like Isis, was also Queen of the Seas. In Japan she was called **Kwannon**."

Island of Isis, Charles Scribner's Sons, 1976) New York:

Larousse Universal Dictionary, in referring to Isis says: "One of the most ancient of the divinities of Egypt, **she formed with Osiris**, at the same time for **son and husband**, a **mythical trinity** in which is to be found the **Holy Trinity of** the **Christian religion**. Isis was the force of life itself."

Sex and Race Vol. I

In the Report by **British Association for the Advancement of Science** (1916), Sir Arthur Evans declares:

"The worship of a **Mother Goddess** predominated in later (prehistoric) times generally associated with **a divine child** - - a worship which later survived in a classical guise **influenced** *all* **later religions.**"

Frank Snowden, **Blacks in Antiquity**, suggests the African origin of Isis:

"A substantial Ethiopian influence on Isis worship in Greece and in Italy is strongly suggested, if not proved, by the tradition of Ethiopian association with the cult, by the Negroes depicted in Isiac ritual..."

Didorus Siculus is of the same opinion as to Blackness of Osiris: "This Osiris was Mizraim, the son of Ham." (Book I, chap. 2)

One of the most notable historians, Godfrey Higgins Esq. spells it out:

> "*No person who has considered well the character of the temples in India and Egypt are of the same race of people; and this race evidently Ethiopian.* The Worship of the Mother and Child is seen in all parts of the Egyptian religion. It prevails everywhere. It is the worship of Isis and the Infant Horus or Osiris. It is the religious rite which was so often prohibited at Rome but which prevailed in spite of all opposition, as we find from the remaining ruins of his temple." (*Anacalypsis* Vol. 1)

He goes on to explain:

"It was perhaps from this country

Egypt, that the worship of the Black Virgin and Child came into Italy

and where it still prevails. It was the worship of the mother of God, Jesus, the Savior; Bacchus in Greece; Adonis in Syria; Christna in India; coming into Italy through the medium of the two Ethiopians she was, as the Ethiopians were, Black, and such she still remains."

A similar view is taken by T. W. Doane:

> "The Egyptian *Isis* was also worshiped in Italy many centuries before the Christian era and all images of her with the Infant, *Horus,* in her arms have been adopted as we shall presently see by the Christians even though they represent her and *the child as Black as an Ethiopian in the same manner as we have seen that Devaki and Chrishna were represented.*" ("Bible Myths," Chap. XVIII, New York, 1882.)

> "In fact, both the Greeks and the Romans identified major Egyptian deities with their own gods, and even absorbed some of the ancient religious beliefs, notably the cult of Isis."

Robert S. Bianchi, *Museums of Egypt,* (Newsweek, Inc., 1980, p. 162)

"The cult of Isis continued when the other gods and goddesses of antiquity had been forgotten. Pilgrims from Greece and the Roman empire came to worship her, heaping her shrine at Philae with offerings as late as the fifth century A. D." - - - According to William MacQuity,

Island of Isis (Charles Scribner's Sons, 1976 New York:)

The scholar Edward Carpenter touches on a similar point:

"Finally, we have the curiously large number of Black virgin mothers who are or have been worshiped.

Not only cases like Devaki the Indian goddess, or

Isis the Egyptian, who would naturally appear Black-skinned or dark,

but the large number of images and paintings of the same kind yet extant — especially in the Italian churches — and passing for representations of Mary and the infant Jesus.

Such are the well-known images in the chapel at Genoa, Pisa, Padua, Munich and other places ... At Paris, far on into Christian times there was, it is said, on the site of the present Cathedral of Notre Dame, a Temple dedicated to 'our lady' Isis."

Pagan and Christian Creeds, New York, 1920

"Maya, the mother of Buddha, and Devaki the mother of Chrishna, were worshiped as virgins, and represented with the infant Saviors in their arms, just as the virgin of the Christians is represented at the present day.

Maya was so pure that it was impossible for God, man, or Asura to view her -with carnal desire . . .

Chrishna and his mother are almost always represented as Blacks, and the word Chrishna means the '*Black.*' "(New York: pp. 326-327).

T. W. Doane, *Bible Myths*, New York, 1970

The **Washington Post** newspaper (May 4, 1979) talks about this same Black Madonna (of Czestochowa), declaring that:

"It is also one of the most haunting and beautiful works of religious art in the world...Art experts believe the Madonna was painted between the 6th and 8th centuries and say the style is reminiscent of early **Egyptian Christian**."

Joseph R. Ledit, S. J. Professor of Russian History, Oriental University, Rome, contributes an article on the various Black Virgins in *"The Chronicle,"* St. Louis, Mo., (1932), and quotes St. Francis:

"Our Lady shows Herself as a familiar Virgin, kind to all who come before Her.

She is a sister to **the Black Virgins of Moulins, of Dijon, of Bourg, of Liesse, of Rocamadour, of Chartres,** and it seems that **the Virgins of this color, who are older than our White Madonnas,** are more **our grandmothers than our mothers.**"

Sex and Race, Vol. I

In 1980, the Brooklyn Museum's Associate Curator of Egyptian and Classical Art, Robert S. Bianchi made this interesting point in his book, **Museums of Egypt**:

"As time passed, Egypt played a significant role in the history of the early Church.

The pharaonic image of

Isis nursing the child Horus

was translated into Christian iconography

as the Virgin and the Christ Child."

THE FOUNDING FATHERS

WERE BLACK

The Founding Fathers of Christianity were Black:

1. Tertullian - First of church writers who made Latin the language of Christianity.
2. Cyprian - Bishop and martyr.
3. St. Augustine - One of the most famous, "Fathers of the Church."

Mrs. Stewart Erskine in her work, *The Vanished Cities of Northern Africa*, helps support this fact when she says:

> "The three great names that bring honor to the African Church are Tertullian, the first of the Church writers who made Latin the language of Christianity; Cyprian, Bishop and martyr; and Augustine, one of the most famous of the Fathers of the Church."

J. A. Rogers' text agrees:

> "The first great leaders of Christianity...were all born in parts of Africa where Negro strain was abundant in the population, and were very likely Negroes themselves.
>
> This is true of St. Augustine, Tertullian, Origen, Cyprian, and Clement of Alexandria.
>
> Tertullian and St. Athanasius (293-373 A. D.), for whom the Athanasian Creed is named, are definitely said to have been Negroes."

Sex and Race, Vol. I

THE FIRST CHRISTIAN MARTYRS

WERE BLACK:

1. Felicitas

2. Perpetua

3. Nymphano

Professor ben-Jochannan in his massive work *Black Man of the Nile*, indicated that:

"The African Emperor, SEPTIMUS SERVERUS, mounted the throne of Rome, which did not occur until three years after the death of FELICITAS, PERPETUA, and NYMPHANO — the alleged 'FIRST CHRISTIAN MARTYRS.'

Strange as it may seem, the 'FIRST CHRISTIAN MARTYRS' were also indigenous **African women** — so-called 'Negroes, Bantus, Africans south of the Sahara.' "

C. P. Groves in his four-volume work, *The Planting of Christianity in Africa* wrote:

'A certain *NYmphano*, claimed as the first martyr, also, came from Numidia, the name in this case being Punic. The Church of Rome, in its official history, stated that on July 19 A. D. 189, *Felicita* and *Perpetua* were mar-tyred by the soldiers of Emperor Septimus Severus.' (See also: Yosef ben-Jochannan, *Black Man of the Nile*)

BLACK POPES

1. Pope Victor (186 A. D. - 197 A. D.)

2. Miltiades (311 A. D. - 314 A. D.)

3. St. Gelasius (492 A. D. - 496 A. D.)

The New York Voice (July 2, 1980) featured an article entitled, "BLACK POPES PLAYED STRONG ROLE IN CHRISTIAN HIS-TORY," written by Mark Hyman in which he reports that:

"Victor was the fifteenth pope and a native of Black Africa .... He was buried near the body of apostle Peter, the first pope in the Vatican.

He served during the reign of Emperor Septimus Severus, also an African, who had led Roman legions in Britain."

As for the second Black pope:

"It was Miltiades who led the church to final victory over the Roman Empire. Miltiades was buried on the famous Appian Way."

Concerning Pope **Gelasius**, he is said to have "delivered the city of Rome from the peril of famine."

Lastly, Mr. Hyman mentions that: **"There were Black fathers of the church:** Men like St. Augustine (the son of a Black African woman) Tertullian and Cyprian, both of these men were Carthaginians ... and *they were as Black as Hannibal."*

"In his book *The Saints Go Marching In*, Robert Fulton Holtzclaw, M. A., made a very important statement in the Preface:

'Roman Africa was Roman in name and government, but not in population. The names of the gods and people became Latinized because Latin was the language of the masters of commerce. But the majority of the people were Black and the Punic language was spoken until the Islamic invasion of the Eighth Century.' African influence was far-reaching in those very early times. The earliest and most renowned authors in Rome were African, from Terrence to Apuleius. Several of the early saints of the Church were African Robert Holtzclaw goes on to state that:

'Africa did its part in the spiritual history of mankind. One of the most zealous churches of early Christianity came into being in Africa.'

From Africa came Neo-Platonic thought and the first experiments in monasticism.

Three of the early popes were Black: See S.s. Gelasius, Miltiades and Victor I.

They were Africans and they contributed immeasurably to the propagation of the Gospel and the establishment of the Kingdom of God on earth.' " [*]

[*] Edward Scobie, "African Popes," JOURNAL OF AFRICAN CIVILIZATIONS, April 1982, Vol. 4 No. 1

For African birth of the Popes see:
LIBER PONTIFICALIS (Book of the Popes), L. R. Loomis, translator, New York, 1916, p. 17. For Pope Victor and Melchiades, sometimes called Miltiades, p. 40. for Gelasius, p. 110. Also see: *100 AMAZING FACTS ABOUT THE NEGRO*, J. A. Rogers

Conclusion

THE PERCEPTION OF THE WHITE SUPREMACIST

"There is *No* Reality, only perception."
The White supremacist practices the following levels of "perception"

1. Selective Perception: here the White supremacist only lets in that which reinforces his/her racist [White supremacist] point of view. They filter the world through its own racist, White supremacist "eyes." For example, the Supreme Court ruling on affirmative action, O. J. Simpson trial reaction, and the Million Man March have all pointed out they, Blacks and Whites, still live in different "realities".

    They practice projections in that they project their own feelings of inadequacy onto others. They are plagued by many "demons" not the least of them are "fear" demons.

2. Perceptual Defense: Here they feel that equality and justice for all can not be right or good because it doesn't fit their White supremacist view of the world. Justice and equality are mere words to be used and spoken to fool others, not something that should be institutionalized or actually put into practice in a fair and non-discriminatory way. White privilege must reign supreme; others are not so entitled.

3. **Cognitive Consistency: In this case, they are only comfortable with ideas, beliefs and practices that reinforce White supremacy and promote White superiority. Which explains why they will pay almost $40 for a book like *The Bell Curve* that is filled with math charts and statistics, something they will never read but what reinforces their belief in White intellectual superiority and Black inferiority. They can not step up unless they can put someone else down. The White supremacist considers every Black person a sub-human species without a history— 3/5 of a man [or human].**

4. **To this day we are still considered only 3/5 of a man by the United States Constitution. There was a written amendment [correction?] made to confer equality, but if you look objectively at their actions, we are not even represented on social, political or economic levels with just 3/5 status. For instance, out of 100 senators only one is Black that's less than 1/100 of a man even though we are at least 12 per cent of the population.**

The principles of White supremacists in the United States are described in the *Progressive* magazine (June 1995) in an article entitled "In the Land of White Supremacy" by June Jordan:

`I came to recognize media constructions such as "The Heartland" or "Politically Correct" or "The Welfare Queen" or "Illegal Alien" or "Terrorist" or "The Bell Curve" for what they were: multiplying scattershots intended to defend one unifying desire —to establish and preserve White supremacy as our national bottom line.

Racism means rejecting, avoiding belittling, or despising whatever and whoever differs from your conscious identity.

White Supremacy means to put you on the planet to rule, to dominate, and to occupy the center of the national and international universe because you're "White."

Anything or anyone appearing to challenge your center-stage and its privileges becomes ungodly, or the Devil, or the Devil Incarnate ... "The Niggers"...

By the same token, Professor Martin Bernal once said, "racism is so pervasive it can hardly be underestimated...We all have it."

PROBLEM & SOLUTION: HOW TO GET TO OUR RIGHTFUL PLACE IN HISTORY & SOCIETY

If you have "no facts" to prove that you are equal and have made important contributions to mankind, then what is your subconscious mind supposed to think? It will conclude that you are inferior, and you will act —and think— that way. Even if you don't realize it.

As long as the image of God in your subconscious is White you are not the equal of the White man nor will you act like one because you can not defeat or compete with "God" or "His" human representation.

The self-hatred and self-defeating attitudes and actions will have both obvious and subtle ways of showing itself. For example, it is this image that makes us not co-operate and unite fully with each other. Deep down our subconscious tells us "who wants to bind with an inferior being"? Definitely not you! This explains in part why so many of us seek to mate with White people. Notice how, on general levels, Black men marry or have relationships with more heavily endowed White women. Seldom are they the best the White race has to offer in terms of class or social status.

It is the subconscious image of a White "God" which we hold as "sacred," "right" and unchangeable that causes us — and our children — to self-destruct as a people. Following the lead of the so-called "superior race" some of our youth now worship sex [look how they dress and act], money [it's all about the "Benjamin"], drugs [near epidemic proportions] and death—"physical and mental." On a physical level, this is the first generation outside of a war situation that does not believe they will live past 30 years of age. On a mental level, if you are smart in school then you are trying to be "White." Intelligence now has a "color" – and it's definitely not Black.]

Everything that works against us in our community is directly related to the "God-Image" in our subconscious. Notice how we often work harder for White people than we work for ourselves. Well, who wouldn't work harder for "God" than for themselves? If this sounds like an uncomfortable truth it should be.

Moreover, there are those who are out to control this "God-Image" of themselves and the "inferior-image" of others. They start very early with a pervasive programming and conditioning that stretches everywhere where "White" is seen as *better than* "Black." This wasn't always the case. It all started with slavery and now a modern version of it is in the form of "volunteer" slavery to the White "Image of God" in our minds.

Thus we remain chained with a mental bondage that acts beyond our conscious mind. We will voluntarily serve others before we serve ourselves. We will put the interest of "others" before our own, and as incredible as it sounds, we will believe it was the "right" thing to do because White is innately "better"...

For instance, in a national study entitled, "A Different World: Children's Perceptions of Race and Class in the Media," [1998] the findings showed the following:

"Children more often associate positive qualities – financial and academic success, leadership, intelligence – with White characters and associate negative qualities — law-breaking, financial hardship, laziness, goofy behavior – with minority characters.

Children of all races say the new media tends to portray

Blacks and Hispanics more negatively than Whites…particularly in reports about young people."

That is why when a Black man was portrayed as Jesus in a play in New Jersey some White supremacists wanted to kill him, and he received death threats. Apparently, the "color" of Jesus does mean something to someone. The image that mentally controls and directs our thoughts and actions must be maintained at all costs.

And, we will never be able to unite and be an independent, self-respecting people until that "Image" is permanently changed.

Why does the Nation of Islam sound so "progressive" when they say, "We must do for ourselves? "The point is so obvious it is almost painful.

Why do Black youth kill each other so readily? It's not because they see worthwhile, valuable human beings in front of them. They see other inferior beings like themselves so who cares if they are "stuff" or "pop." Their "God-Image" is subconsciously "White"; therefore, something "Black" cannot be of any real value. It must be "naturally" inferior and worthless.

Why do Black youth dress with their underwear on top of their heads? Is this a fitting symbolism for where they believe their brain exists? Someone has their minds in their hip pocket and clearly it is not they because their Black minds are **under** [read: lower or inferior] to the superior [read: higher or better] White mind. No one chooses to insult and denigrate him or herself. This only happens when his or her "God-Image" is a picture of someone else.

In addition, they wear their pants down so "low" that they show [reveal] their underwear. The subconscious is again acting automatically on the information it has about the current status and worth of the individuals in question. The reading is — here is an inferior, someone of "low" and inferior position. Conclusion: let it dress in ways that reveal its image and concept of one who is "low" and inferior.

Notice what they are stressing their underwear. Look at the word underwear — under denotes something located or positioned down, low or underneath something else. The inferior is under the superior. Clearly, the subconscious makes its point in both obvious and subtle ways.

They also dress with in their shoes untied, another statement the subconscious makes about the general state of their mind. They can not "tie" things together or make the necessary connections that would leave them in control of their own "reality." One that is "tied" to an higher status in the world

If you are still not convinced then why do Black men willingly call themselves "dog" in a "brotherly" way? Notice the spelling of D O G, it is the opposite of G O D just as Black is the opposite of White, and inferior is the opposite of superior. The White "God-Image" is at work in a most revealing way. This "reality" exposes the state of the subconscious mind and the inferior and low view it takes of the individual.

If you are Black, you cannot beat them or compete with them or defeat them. How can one defeat or beat "God"? The subconscious mind will not accept that as a possibility and you will act accordingly. This is why some Black people look to others – superiors – to do for them that which they should do for themselves. The "I-want-something-for-free" mentally persists among those who believe that their inferior nature cannot get it themselves. The White image of "God" shackles their abilities and their motivation. The White "God" will provide for "His" creation; therefore, we expect White people to provide for us. A position we should take is one of true equality, We invested in America, all we want is a fair return on our investment. Calculate 200 million people dead, hundreds of millions working for free over 300 years and you get some idea of what we are entitled to.

However, high self-esteem is not possible under these conditions of no self "God-Image" and no worthwhile history of racial contributions to mankind. High self-delusion and denial are very probable given the circumstances of an oppressed and repressed "consciousness".

White supremacy also retards the growth and development of White people who will remain dependent and addicted to the artificial "excellence" that preferential treatment created based on their White skin privilege. This only promotes White mediocrity as a "universal" standard.

If one could get into their minds you would see that their image of "God" is White. Thus being a different color than "God" they do not see a relationship between this Supreme Being and themselves. Therefore, they have no divine standards of behavior for themselves. Black is less, inferior, unworthy and "cheap." The natural consequence of this is seen in their words and actions.

WHITE SUPREMACY is a drug. It makes a person drunk with power and evil. It robs them of their humanity and their soul. For one has to be a soulless creation to rape little girls, engage in lynching, castrating grown men's body parts, burning people alive, dehumanizing fellow human beings by calling them inferior and 3/5 of a man, a savage sub-human, and then to sell them for money. White Supremacy robs White people of their basic humanness that they themselves can barely be called "humans" in any complimentary sense of the word. Look at how they ripped apart the body and decapitated the head of an innocent Black man by dragging him in the back of a truck in Texas.

Is there a greater sin than to sell other human souls for money based on race or the color of one's skin?

"Race is a source of America's shame. It's the great sin of our culture. People are afraid of it because we engaged in the ungodly act of subjugating a race of people for 250 years. We built our culture on a premise of race that is ungodly," says Jesse Jackson as reported in the *Christian Science Monitor*, October 23, 1995.

When will the WHITE SUPREMACISTS gain enough confidence in themselves so that there is no need to put down others artificially in order to raise themselves higher? Overcompensation and projection make a poor case for self-development. Many of the hidden ills that exist within their own communities, those that are not generally publicized could be alleviated by their refusal to continue the heinous practice of White Supremacy. Ills like drug abuse, child abuse (sexual, physical and mental), spousal abuse (sexual, physical and mental), hatred for parents, alcoholism, to name a few. You can't have peace at home if you're raising hell everywhere else.

As long as White supremacy sets up unfair advantages based on the superficial "qualifications" and "merits" of a White skin, mediocrity and evil will rule. Because White people will not allow themselves to compete without unfair privileges; therefore, whatever mediocre standards they set up based on skin preference will ward off any real levels of excellence. For example, the press recognizes Larry Byrd as a great player primarily because he had to compete with everyone not just White men. His skills got better due to the fact that he played against everybody.

Solutions to our problems

1.   Remove the White image of "God" from our subconscious. [Note: God equals Supreme Being. The understanding that goes with the word God is "Supreme" as in White "Supremacy." You can not get a more powerful "superior" image in mind than to view someone else as "God"]. You can not *act* as their equal if that image rules your subconscious thoughts and actions.

2.   Your "God-Image" must reflect you or you will forever be handicapped mentally by a foreign image in your mind that robs you of self-confidence, self-worth and self-esteem. There is no Self if you are Black but your "God" is White. With this image and "reality" there is no logical connection there for self-development or elevation. These opposite images play a subtle and obvious role in our everyday lives. There is no room for Black Contribution in a White supremacist mind set. It destroys the basic foundations of White supremacy.

3. Because that "God-Image" is of someone that is always better and greater than you are. Thus you will remain forever weak and defenseless against the onslaught of White supremacy in all its various manifestations in this society. Which is how many of us act today. You can not exist in America and not see an Image of "God" that is White in your mind. The programming and conditioning is everywhere. The real question is: What color is your "Supreme Being" in your subconscious mind? And if you say that you do not have one then you might have already lost the battle and "reality" because you can not be honest with yourself. All of us have a White image of "God" in our subconscious but if we do not admit to the "cancer" that eats away at our self-worth than we will never be truly free or independent.

How can you rid yourself of this image? By studying your history, it can offer you intellectual proof of your equality with all other races. It will also offer proof that the subconscious mind will eventually accept, if you keep and maintain positive reinforcements of the truth.

Get a "God-Image" that reflects YOU. Every other ethnic and racial group does this except African-Americans and now even some Africans.

3.   Put pictures around your home and environment that affirm and confirm achieving Black people past and present.

4.   Support businesses that uphold your self-image thus your self-esteem. Help other Blacks once you get into a position to do so. If we have a reputation as a people of helping each other, then this will work against our greatest internal enemy— envy and jealousy.

5.   Destroy all "egotism" that prevents and hinders Black progress and development.

6.   Read books, magazines and newspapers that speak to Black accomplishments past and present.

7.   Make all of the above a way of life and not just a "fad."

Summary:

Where in the psyche of the White supremacist is there room for significant Black contribution in history?

How is it that the people they held in contempt as the "inferiors" were in fact the ones who taught them, the "superiors"? The Truth, for most of them, is just too hard to bear.

How is it that Jesus Christ just happens to look like the enslavers, the White supremacist?

And how is it that Jesus Christ is in fact the color of those they considered "inferior"?

One can appreciate the dilemma. If God is in fact "Black," then the Supreme Being of the universe is "inferior" according to their belief. How can they —or you— worship something that is an "inferior" being to them? That means "God" is "inferior." How does the Creator become "inferior" to its creations? The contradictions are mind boggling!

Why is it that on money it reads: IN GOD WE TRUST and in the middle there is a picture of some White man who was president.? The subconscious message is that "God" also is a White man, and that we should trust him.

The standard for White is "better" and superior for Blacks "less" and inferior. That is why young Blacks have a saying "no disrespect" because to be an inferior is to be insulted and disrespected on a regular basis in this society. And, this is not just reserved for young Blacks [See the new racism called "stealth racism"].

White supremacists lie often, convincingly and with a straight face to ensure that they are perceived as having a divine right to rule as in "Manifest Destiny." Their "superior" and privileged positions and advantages must remain intact, justice and truthfulness not- withstanding. The White supremacists, though missing logic, have an agenda. It is to make us all feel and act inferior. And they want to justify and rationalize their evil and mean spirited behavior. To make sure that they are given special, preferential treatment, privileges and advantages.

THOMAS JEFFERSON, the exemplary apostle of American 'democracy' and 'author of a well-known document' which laid down 'as a 'self-evident truth' — 'that all men are created *equal*, and endowed by their Creator with certain inalienable rights; that among these are life, *liberty*, and the pursuit of happiness.'

Replying to Douglas in Springfield in 1857, Abraham Lincoln noted the same phenomenon. There was a time, he said, when 'our Declaration of Independence was held sacred by all, and thought to include all; but now, to aid in making the bondage of the negro universal and eternal, it is sneered at...

The First President of the United States was a "Black Man, A Moor. His name was John Hanson. He served as president from 1781-1782 A. D.

He was president of the Continental Congress under the Articles of Confederation. John Hanson was elected a month after the Revolutionary War had stopped.

John Hanson appointed a commanding general in the war, George Washington. So the true founding father was a Moor.

If God is White, then you can not beat them, defeat them or even compete with them. This is why you don't really try. Some Black people are doing for others what they could be doing for themselves. Other communities have jobs and opportunities for their children. They are building institutions for themselves.

During the summer their children have work opportunities within their own communities. They make jobs available to their youth. But we have none for our youth.

Because we believe in the "White-image-of-God," few expect White people to provide jobs for them and for us.

If your ultimate spiritual Image is White, but you are Black, then what does that mean?

It means White is right, White ice is colder; White is best or better. This theme is played out everyday in our lives. Can you give examples of this in what your have personally experienced? If White is spiritually high then Black must be spiritually low.

The White Supremacist War for our MINDS is being waged on two Fronts. One is Spiritual [God is White.] The other is intellectual [White people are more intelligent]. The cancer of White Supremacy is eating and destroying the White community from within. It permits child, spouse, drug and alcoholic abuse as well as all kinds of sexually deviant behavior.

Despite the "hype" many White people do not and can not live in peace. Not with all the Hell they are raising in other people's lives. It gives them a sense of Absolute Power and it has corrupted them absolutely.

If White supremacy was to stop today, the White community would be its first immediate beneficiaries. It is what their "prophets" are trying to tell them but most of them are not listening. Selfishness reigns Supreme.

The White Supremacist as he seeks to make others inferior, he becomes more inferior himself. He is chained by a monstrous link to the dark, hellish world of negativity. The world of intolerance, inequality, injustice and enslavement. Trapped in a world of self-delusion he becomes that which he despises the most —an inferior being.

His fear of inadequacy and some say genetic annihilation (See the Cress Theory of Color) reduces his chance of any real development or growth to a higher level.

How can one be superior if he seeks to oppress and enslave others? This was a question Captain Kirk in Star Trek asked a race of so-called "pure" intellectual beings.

Among high and advanced cultures and "beings" hatred is an absolute contradiction of spiritual, divine principles. Only the most insecure of individuals would seek to raise himself /herself by lowering others. Where is the greatness in that? But the White Supremacy lies and denies to the extreme. To himself, his family and finally to the world.

He is not what he thinks he is and deep down he knows it. Therefore, he clings to the belief that the "hype" and myth of White Supremacist is better than the Reality itself.

His greatest gamble is that God, the Supreme Being, the Creator does not exist. Or He is a White Supremacist. Because one can not commit the demonic, satanic, devilish and inhuman crimes against innocent human beings without eventually expecting that "what you sow, you shall reap."

Who would want that type of holocaust on themselves? How can he believe the God who is all-powerful, all-seeing and all present "mentally" challenged (omnipresent) and will somehow not exact due justice and punishment for the acts committed against Him and His creations of all colors.

The White Supremacist bets against himself and basic common sense. They believe that God just might be a racist like them, and He created White people to be better than all others. How ironic it is for him to see that the very things he believes in will challenge all of his inhuman, racist views.

HERE ARE THE 10 FUNDAMENTAL TRUTHS A *White Supremacist* MUST OPPOSE:

I.   THE TEN COMMANDMENTS

1.   тḫou sḫalt пot kill.

    a. Killing hundreds of millions of Africans in Africa, the Middle passage, and in America itself.

    b. The almost complete genocide of the aboriginal of the Western Hemisphere.

II. Thou shalt not covet thy neighbor's goods

    a. Stole and are still stealing all the resources from other people of color, non-Whites throughout the world, especially in Africa.

    b. Colonialism, imperialism and neo-colonialism.

    a. Raping African women in Africa and America and other non-White people.

III.   The Bible – Genesis "The Story of Adam and Eve" – All races from one source.

III.   The Declaration of Independence – "All men are created equal."

IV.   The Son of God, Jesus Christ's commandment to "Love thy neighbor as thyself"

V.   The Bible warning, "as a man soweth, so shall he reap."

VI.   God is all-knowing, all-present, all-powerful

VII.   God is not a "respecter of people."

VIII.   Justice is an eternal principle in the universe.

IX.   "All Men atre endowed with certain inalienable rights."

X.   God is TRUTH

There is a wide gap between what a White Supremacist says, and what he does. Look more at his actions and less at his words. Despite the fact that the world has been dominated by these White supremacists, there still exist a few radical White writers who spoke the truth of what they saw and knew.

This is an almost miraculous occurrence when one considers that Africa has been under attack for centuries by those who sought to dismiss it, call it a "dark" continent, a continent without a history, unworthy of respect. This was a continent basically populated by inferior savages and barbarians. White Supremacist's conclusion: Africa was fair game for whatever practices it sought to inflict. As Dr. John Henrik Clarke said, "Everyone who came into Africa waged war against African culture."

As J. California Cooper elegantly expressed it in her beautifully written book *The Wake of the Wind*:

I am Africa. I am a place. I am a state of mind. Hundreds of years ago my children lived free. We had our skirmishes, within my shores, even small wars that did not disturb my great and sprawling land. We were not perfect. But …we never lift our shores to seek to destroy and rob any other culture or people; to steal the fruit of their land or minds and leave the land and people ravaged. Nor did we seek to steal any people's love of themselves. Nor tell other peoples they were ignorant savages and inferior while we were superior, as the whitish ones said to us. They lied so much and long they began to believe it themselves. They cried "GOD" with their mouths while holding a knife in one hand and a gun in the other, slicing and firing at a vibrant life. They also brought with them other diseases including endless greed, envy and hate our nations changed…They kill for land, women or gold spreading their savageness to all others, even among themselves. And…they have now influenced others. Anathema! (Doubleday, New York, 1998, prologue)

After you have shackled, enslaved a people, branded, castrated, lynched, burned, tortured them. Then you call them 3/5 of a man, sub-species, an ape, a monkey and a general inferior creation. How then can you admit they are your teachers and the ones who gave you civilization?

There is no room in a White supremacist psyche for Black contributions to civilization or world progress. This reaches too far into the consciousness of the so-called "objective" White scholars of academia and their Black-skinned counterparts.

This is like asking a Nazi to accept the Jewish origins of Nazism and of Hitler if that were the case. They couldn't accept it if it were true any more than White supremacists can accept the African origins of Civilization.

But you must view Africa with a new "God-consciousness." A new spiritual and cultural awareness must be attained. Humanity's roots are African roots. They will perish without her. Know yourself, know your history. The ancestors are waiting…"

Philadelphia New Observer, November 18, 1998 reported a letter allegedly written by an engineering student from North Carolina. It is quite instructive in hearing it from the proverbial horse's mouth:

Dear Black Americans:

After all of these years and all we have been through together, we think it's appropriate for us to show our gratitude for all you have done for us. We have chastised you, criticized you, punished you, and in some cases even apologized to you but we have never formally nor publicly thanked you for you're never-ending allegiance and support to our cause. This is our open letter of thanks to a unique people, a forgiving people, a steadfast people, and a brave people: Black Americans.

We will always be in debt to you for your labor. You built this country and were responsible for the great wealth we still enjoy today. We thank you for your diligence and tenacity. Even when we refused to allow you to even walk in our shadows, you followed close behind, believing that someday we would come to accept you and treat you like men and women. Your strength in the face of adversity cannot be understated. You are truly a great people, and we thank you so much.

We publicly acknowledge Black people for raising our children, attending to our sick, and preparing our meals while we were occupied with the trappings of the good life even during the times. When we found pleasure in your women and enjoyment in seeing one of your men lynched, maimed and burned, some of you continued to watch over us and our belongings. We simply cannot thank you enough. Your bravery on the battlefield, despite being classified as three-fifths of a man, was and still is outstanding and beyond the call of duty. We often watched in awe as you went about your prescribed chores and assignments, sometimes laboring in the hot sun for 12 hours, to assist us in realizing our dreams of wealth and good fortune.

You were always there and we thank you. Now that we control at least 90 percent of all of the resources and wealth of this nation, we have Black people to thank the most. You were there when it all began, and you are still with us today, protecting us form those Black people who have the temerity to speak out against our past transgressions. How can we thank you for your dedication? You warned us about Denmark Vessey. You let us know about Gabriel Prosser's plans; you called our attention to Nat Turner. And you even sounded the alarm when old John Brown came calling Harper's Ferry. Some of you still warn us today. Thank you, thank you thank you!

Now, as we look out upon our enormous wealth, and as we assess our tremendous control of the resources of this country, we can only think of the sacrifices you and your families made to make all of this possible. You are indeed fantastic, and we will forever be in your debt. Oh think of how you have looked out for us for hundreds of years and to see you still doing the same thing today is simply amazing. Thank you for continuing to bring 95 percent of what you earn to our businesses. That is gracious of you.

Thanks for buying our Hilfigers, Karan, Nikes, and all of the other brands you so adore. Your purchase of these products really makes us feel that we are at least giving something back to you for your patronage. After all, in the past, the brands we put on you were quite painful, but those of today can be proudly worn because they give you a sense of self-esteem, right? But it's the least we can do for a people who have treated us so well. Your super-rich athletes, entertainers, intellectuals, and business persons (both legal and illegal) exchange most of their money for our cars, jewelry, homes, and clothing. What a windfall they have provided for us! The less fortunate among you spend all they have at our neighborhood stores, enabling us to open even more stores. Sure, they complain about us, but they never do anything to hurt us economically. You are a very special people. Thank you.

Oh, yes. Allow us to thank you for not bogging yourselves down with the business of doing business with your own people. We can take care of that for you. Please don't even trouble yourselves with it. Yes, you were very successful at it after slavery ended and even as recently as 1960, but you know what happened when you began to build your own communities and do business with one another. Some of the "lower ones" of our kind burned you out time and time again. So, why bother? In today's business environment, your own people will not support you anyway. You just keep doing business with us. It's safer that way. Besides, everything you need, we make anyway, even Kente cloth. You just continue to dance, sing, fight, and get high, go to prison, backbite, envy and distrust and hate one another. Have yourselves a good time, and this time we'll take care of you. It's the least we can do, considering all you've done for us. Heck, you deserve it,. Black people.

For your labor, which created our wealth, for you resisting the messages of trouble-making Blacks like Washington, Delaney, Garvey, Bethune, Tubman and Truth, for fighting and dying on our battlefields, we thank you. For allowing us to move into your neighborhoods, we will forever be grateful to you. For your unceasing desire to be near us and for hardly ever following through on your threats due to our lack of reciprocity and equity we thank you so much. We also appreciate your acquiescence to our political agendas, for abdicating your own economic self-sufficiency, and for working so diligently for the economic well-being of our people.

You are real troopers. And, even though the relatives died for the rights described therein, you did not resist when we changed those Black rights to civil rights and allowed virtually every other group to take advantage of them as well. Black people, you are something else! Your dependence upon us to do the right thing is beyond our imagination, irrespective of what we do to you and the many promises we have made and broken.

But, this time we will make it right we promise. Trust us. Tell you what. You don't need your own hotels. You can continue to stay in ours. You have no need for supermarkets when you can shop at ours 24 hours a day. Why should you even think about owning more banks? You have plenty now. And, don't waste your energies trying to break into manufacturing. You've worked hard enough in our fields. Relax, have a party. We'll sell you everything you need. And when you die, we'll even bury you at a discount 20%. Now how's that for gratitude?

Finally the best part. You went beyond the pale and turned your children over to us for their education. With what we have taught them, it's likely they will continue in a mode similar to the one you have followed for the past 45 years. When Mr. Lynch walked the banks of the James River in 1712 and said he would make you a slave for 300 years, little did we realize the truth in his prediction. Just 13 more years and his promise will come to look forward to at least another 50 years of prosperity. Wow! Things could not be better and it's all because of you. For all you have done, we thank you from the bottom of our hearts, Black Americans. You're the best friends any group of people could ever have!

Sincerely

All other Americans

Selected Bibliography

Jackson, John G., "Egypt and Christianity," Journal of African Civilizations

Jackson, John G. 'Krishna and Buddha of India: Black Gods of Asia,' African Presence in Early Asia Editor: Ivan Van Sertima, New Brunswick (U. S. A.) and Oxford (U. K.): Transaction Books

Scobie, Edward, 'African Popes,' Journal of African Civilizations,

Sertima, Ivan Van. Editor. Nile Valley Civilizations,

Hunter, Adams III 'African Observers of the Universe, The Sirius Question,' Journal of African Civilizations

Smith, Elliot, G. The Influence of Ancient Egyptian Civilization in the East and in America. The John Rylands Library (reprinted by Dr. G. K. Osei)

Hilliard, Asa G. "Kemit Concepts in Education," Nile Valley Civilizations

Rogers, Joel A., Sex and Race, Vol. I , New York, .

Sauneron, Serge. The Priests of Ancient Egypt. Grove p.

Rogers, Joel A. World's Great Men of Color ,Vol. I . New York: Collier Books. .

Spady, James . 'Black Space,' Journal of African Civilizations, September, .

Selected Reading

John G. Jackson, *Introduction to African Civilization; Man, God And Civilization*, The Citadel Press, Secaucus, New Jersey

Cheikh Anta Diop, *The African Origin Of Civilization: Myth Or Reality & Civilization Or Barbarism*, Lawrence Hill A Co., Riverside Avenue, Westport, Conn.

J. A. Rogers, *Sex and Race* (Volumes I, II, III) Helga M. Rogers, Fifth Avenue, New York, NY ,

From Superman To Man; Amazing Facts About The Negro; Nature Knows No Color-Line; Africa's Gift To America; Five Negro Presidents

Yosef ben-Jochannan, Black *Man Of The Nile And His Family,   Our Black Seminarians And Black Clergy Without A Black Theology*, Alkebu-lan Books and Education Materials Association W. th St., Suite New York, NY & See also Black Classic Press

In Pursuit Of George G. M. James' Study Of African Origins In "Western Civilization"

About the Author

He has a B. A. from City University [Herbert H. Lehman] and a Masters in Teaching from Fordham University.

Having taught mathematics for the last years, he has also written three math books.

He has taught mathematics at a junior college in the Bronx.

Concerning his book, he has appeared on TV [cable] and New York radio stations such as, WLIB, WBAI, WWRL.

To correspond, please write:

Luxorr Publications

Indus Khamit-Kush

Published by Luxorr Publications.

Index

A

Abu Simbel, 271
Adventure Of Mankind, The, 111
Aegean Sea, 171
Africa's Gift To America, 67, 304
African Exodus, The Origins of Modern Humanity, 73
African Genius, 55
Agassiz, Louis, 47
Al-Jahiz, 242
Allen, George, 88, 154, 160, 209
Allman, G. T., 163
Amasis, 165, 203
Amazing Facts About The Negro, 225, 249, 284, 304
Amenhotep III, 265
America: Latin, 25
American Historical Review, 180
American Journal of Anatomy, 44, 47
American Journal of Psychology, 36
American Museum of Natural History, 38, 61, 66, 69
Ammianus Marcellinus, 209
Amunothph, 91
An Introduction to the History of Medicine, 157, 199
Ancient Egypt & Black Africa, 86, 154, 199, 201, 209
Ancient Egypt in Light of Modern Discoveries, 97, 112, 188
Ancient Egypt Under the Pharaohs, Vol. I, 106
Ancient Egypt, The New World, The, 132, 155, 188
Ancient Egyptians, 78-79, 81, 84, 90, 96-98, 123, 154, 160, 166-167, 184, 191, 203, 215, 269, 278
Ancient Greece, A Political, Social and Cultural History, 116, 188, 198
Ancient History, The, 121
Ancient History: From Rollin and Other Authentic Sources, Both Ancient and Modern, vol. I., 135
Andreu, Guillemette, 211
Anglo-Saxons, 22, 52
Aquarian Gospel Of Jesus Christ, 258
Arizona, University of, 136

Armana Letters, 191
Armenians, 176
Art Through The Ages, 120
Arthur, J., 45
Asia Minor, 96-97, 115, 170, 180, 199-200, 248
Asians, 53, 72
Astley, H. J. D., 276
Atlantic Monthly, 11, 36
Australopithecus, 61, 66, 68-70
Autobiography of Benjamin Franklin, The, 50

B

Babbitt, Frank C., 151
Baikie, James, 134
Baldwin, James, 8
Baldwin, John, 97, 129, 131
Balls, Lawrence W., 99, 130
Bambino, Gesli, 302
Bankruptcy Of Christian Supernaturalism, The, 180
Barbados, 34
Barnes Review, The, 39, 41
Barringer, Paul B., 50
Bartholdi, Frederic Auguste, 17
Basel, University of, 190
Basham, A. L., 253
BBC, 94, 118, 168
Bean, Dr. Robert Bennett, 44, 47
Bell Curve Debate: History, Documents, Origins, The, 24, 26, 285
Bell Curve, The, 32
Ben-Jochannan, Yosef, 5, 138, 171, 214, 268-270, 283, 304
Benjamin, Park, 132, 155, 188
Benn, Alfred, 198
Bérard, Victor, 162
Bernal, Martin, 5, 78, 138, 162, 188, 215, 256, 286
Besant, Annie, 254
Black Athena, 138, 142-143, 162, 164, 188, 206, 215
Black Christian Nationalism: New Directions for the Black Church, 228
Black Enterprise, 303
Black Image in the White Mind , The, 33
Black Madonna, 222, 232-236, 273, 280
Black Madonnas, 237, 273
Black Man of The Nile And His Family, 214, 304
Black Spark, White Fire, 196

Blackamoors, 22
Blackwell, Basil, 142, 161
Blomdale, Benjamin, 102, 156, 160, 206
Blowmink, Barbara, 89
Boardman, John, 115, 120, 192, 207, 215
Boaz, Noel T., 58
Bonwick, James, 133, 187
Book I of Diodorus Siculus, 159, 184, 189, 202, 208
Book of Ecclesiastes, 271
Book of Proverbs, 270-271
Book of The Beginnings, A, 58, 81, 218, 224, 226, 312
Book of The Dead, The, 191, 194, 224, 243, 266, 268
Book of the Life Beyond, The, 187
Bourk, V. J., 257
Brace, Charles Loring, 52
Breasted, James, 90, 117-118, 131, 171, 178, 198, 201, 213
Breuil, Abbe, 97
Bridges, Marilyn, 78
British Broadcasting Corporation *see* BBC,
British Museum, 135, 230, 270, 276
Brodrick, Mary, 129, 148, 155
Brooklyn College, 76
Brooklyn Museum, 200, 208, 268, 281
Brown University, 191
Brown, Bishop William Montgomery, 180
Brown, John, 298
Brugsch-Bey, Henry, 95
Brunet, J., 115
Bryson, Lyman, 207
Buchanan, James, 16
Buchanan, Pat, 26, 36, 43
Buckler, John, 119-120
Budge, E. A. Wallis, 211, 224
Bunsen, Christian, 102
Burckhardt, Jacob, 185, 190
Burgess, John, 31
Burke, Edmund, 34
Burns, E., 188
Burns, Edward McNall, 106, 122, 169
Burns, Edward, 105-106, 115-116, 122, 144, 169, 271
Burstall, Christopher, 94, 118, 168, 192

Bush, George, 16
Byrd, Larry, 290

C

Caesar, Julius, 2, 76
Calhoun, John C., 32, 34
California Institute of
    Technology, 46
California, University of, 45, 65,
    107
*Cambridge Encyclopedia of
    Africa, The,* 53
Cambridge Encyclopedia, 55,
    230, 237, 243, 253-254
Cambridge University, 55, 124,
    140, 151, 162, 205, 248-250,
    303
Campanis, Al, 23
Capart, Jean, 85
Carpenter, Edward, 277, 280
Carruthers, Ben, 234-235
Cartell, B., 50
Carter, Jimmy, 16
Carter, Lawrence E., 256
Carter, Michael, 64, 119
Carthage, 96, 137
Carthaginians, 134, 144, 147, 284
Caselli, Giovanni, 79
Caspian Seas, 176
Cassar, George H., 181-182, 207
Cassius, Dion, 217
Casson, Lionel, 128, 186
Cathedral of Augsburg, 232
Cathedral of Millan, 232
Cathedral of Notre Dame, 280
CBS Radio, 207
Celts, 22, 31, 145
Ceram, C. W., 146
*Challenge of Facts and other
    Essays, The,* 50
Champollion, Jacques, 102
Charlemagne, 250
Cheops, 89, 128, 171
Chicago, University of, 73, 100,
    117, 125, 148, 213
Chrishna, 279-280
Christian Science Monitor, 46,
    290
Chronicle, The, 281
Church of Rome, 283
Church of San Francisco, 232
Churchward, Albert, 61, 88, 110,
    150, 160, 188, 209, 218,
    224, 255, 262-263
Cicero, 206
Cimmerians, 176
Cincinnati Reds, 23
City University, 76, 109, 305
Civil War, 23, 28-29
Civilization of the Ancient

Egyptians, The, 95, 184
Civilization Or Barbarism, 82,
    124, 154, 187, 304
Clarity, Jack, 235
Clark, J. Desmond, 65
Clark, Josiah, 41
Clarke, John Henrik, 5, 8, 78,
    112, 138, 170-171, 197, 296,
    312
Cleage, Albert B., 228
Cleveland Cavaliers, 23
Clinton, Bill, 15
Coast of Guinea, 34
Cobern, Camden M., 99, 112,
    189
Colonel Coomba, 272
Colonialism, 295
Colton, Joel, 168, 183
Columbia University, 33, 107,
    109, 207, 259
Columbus, Christopher, 312
Confucius, 158, 260
Conquest of Civilization, The, 90,
    116, 118, 131, 171, 184, 201
Constant, Benjamin, 142
Cook, Mercer, 171, 208
Coon, Charles, 27, 42
Cooper, J. California, 296
Coors, William K., 33
Cornell University, 5, 78, 138,
    152, 212, 256, 302
Corpus Christi College, 116, 206
*Correspondence of Theodore
    Parker,* 44
Corry, John, 20
Cosby, Bruce, 228
Cosgrove, Kevin, 25
Cottrell, Charles, 102
Cox, Jacob D., 11
Cradles of Civilization Egypt,
    144
*Credibility of Herodotus' Account
    of Egypt in the Light of the
    Egyptian Monuments, The,*
    140
Cress Theory of Color, 294
Crete, 128, 169, 179-180
Crick, Francis H. C., 46
Cro-Magnon Man, 65
Crothers, George D., 207
Crusaders, 249
*Cultural Unity of Black Africa,
    The* 101, 173
Culture of Ancient Egypt, The,
    120, 124, 211
Cumston, Charles Greene, 157
Czestochowa, 232-235, 275, 280

D

Daedalos, 159

Dagurerreotype, 14
Daily Challenge, 17
Daily News, 25
Dakar, University of, 82
Dante, 182
Daphnae, 141
Dark Ages, 118-119, 164, 181
Darwin, Charles, 49, 55
Davidovits, Joseph, 206, 215
Davidson, Basil, 55, 85, 88, 97,
    140, 156
Davies, Norman, 181
Davies, V., 135
Davies, Vivian, 136
Davis, Charles H. S., 99, 112,
    189
Dawn of Civilization, The, 105,
    224
De Bow, 34, 43
Dead Sea Scrolls, The, 243, 246-
    247
Democritus of Abdera, 157
Denderah, 262
Denon, Vivant, 85
Descent of Man, The, 45, 55
Desert: Sahara, 283
Detroit Institute of Art, 77
Deuel, Leo, 167
Devisse, Jean, 248-250, 303
Diallo, Armadou, 48
Dickens, Charles, 22
*Dictionary of Non-Classical
    Mythology,* 273
Dinesh D'Souza, 46
Dionysian, 139
Dionysus, 126, 184
Diop, Cheikh Anta, 5, 64, 67, 82,
    101, 104, 124, 154, 167,
    171-172, 183, 208, 259, 301,
    304
Discovery of Egypt, The, 91, 132,
    144
Djoser, 89
Doane, 278-280
Donlan, Walter, 116, 180, 200
Dorians, 115
Dover, Kenneth, 94, 118, 168
Dubois, W. E. B., 112
Durando, Furio, 119
Durant, Will, 123, 144, 155, 157,
    163, 276
Dutton, E. P., 111
Duyn, Janet Van, 138
Dynasties, 79, 133, 159, 177, 257
Dynasty, 79, 89, 98, 131, 146,
    158, 167, 197

E

*Early Advanced Humans And
    Their Lifeways,* 68

East India Company, 239
Ebony, 28
Eden, Garden of, 271
Edfu Text, 79
Edinburgh College, 39
Edwards, A. B., 141
Edwards, Amelia B., 75, 96, 130, 141, 160
Egypt and Its Monuments, 130, 158
Egypt of the Egyptians, 99, 129
Egypt Revisited, 138
Egypt Uncovered, 136
Egypt's Place in Universal History, 102, 125
Egypt, Antiquities From Above, 77
Egyptian Belief and Modern Thought, 133, 187
Egyptian Beliefs, 273
Egyptian Mysteries, The, 154
Ehrlickman, John D., 12
Eisenhower, Dwight D., 11
Eliade, Mircea, 245
Ellis Island Foundation, 18
Emperor Septimus Severus, 283
Empire: Assyrian,130
Encyclopedia Britannica, The, 205, 278
Encyclopedia of Religion, 244-245
End of Racism, The, 46
Engels, Friedrich, 19
Enoch and the Growth of An Apocalyptic Tradition, 244
Enoch the Ethiopian, The Lost Prophet of the Bible,, 243
Enopides, 158
Entertainment Network, 88, 97
Environment and Race, 61
Ephorus, 248
Ephraem of Syria, 245
Epicurean, 167
Epicurus, 198
Erastosthenes, 141
Erman, Adolph, 102, 156, 160, 206
Esler, Anthony, 181-182, 207
Esoteric Christianity, 254
Essai, 209
Essence, 8
Euclid, 185
Eudoxos, 148-149, 159, 215
Euphrates River, 107
Eurasia, 68
Eurasian, 171
Euripides, 215
Eurocentrism, 77
Evolution of Religion, 188, 224, 261

F

Fabre, M., 28-29
Farr, Edward, 134, 137
Farrand, Max, 50
Faure, 82
Favorinus, 190
Fawcett-Major, Farrah, 19
FBI, 25
Federal Bureau of Investigations, see FBI
Felicita, 283
Felicitas, 282-283
Fideler, David, 196
Fifth Dynasty, 158
Finch, Charles S., 263
Finch, Dr., 237
Fitzgerald, F Scott, 22
Five Negro Presidents, 304
Ford, Gerald R., 16
Fordham University, 305
Fourth Millennium, 104, 124, 128, 214
Franklin, Benjamin, 12, 25, 50
Franklin, John Hope, 47
Frederick County, 14
Fredrickson, George M., 33
Freedman, E. B., 36
Freeman, Charles, 140, 145
Freemasons, 16
French Mission, 18
Führer, 21

G

Galileo, 38
Galton, Francis, 39
Gandhara, 278
Gardner, Helen, 120
Garfield, James A., 11
Garfield, James, 11, 16
Garrison, Dr. Fielding H., 199
Garside, E. B., 146
Gascoigne, Bamber, 272
Gaul, 255, 278
Gecez, 246
Gelasius, 283-284
Genealogies, 191
Georg, Herr Eugen, 111
Germany, 72, 78, 232, 248-249
Ghalioungui, Paul, 142
Giddings, Franklin Henry, 33
Giotto, 38
Gizeh Pyramid, 302
Glasgow Museum, 55
Glauberman, Naomi, 26, 28, 35
Gliddon, George R., 132, 155, 187
Global War, 262
Glory That Was Greece, The, 119, 122
Gnostics, 257

Gobineau, 45
Goddard, E. H., 116
Gods, Graves, and Scholars, 144
Good Morning America, 25
Gosse, Bothwell A., 96, 184
Gothic, 89
Graglia, Lino, 46
Graham, Billy, 19
Gralnick, Jeff, 25
Grand Michigan, 196
Grant, Ulysses, 12
Granville, Dr. S., 124
Gratiolet, 47
Graves, Kersey, 230
Gray, Basil, 302
Great Black Women of Antiquity, 302
Great Britain, 34, 79, 147
Great Map of mankind: British perception of the world in the age of Enlightenment, The, 37
Great Men of Color, 301
Great Philosophers of the East, 138
Great Seal, 14-15
Greece In The Making 1200 - 479 B. C., 114, 206
Greek Civilization, 6, 114, 142, 156, 185, 190, 196, 208
Greek Islands, 156, 179
Greek Isles, 121
Greek Society, 182
Greene, Larry A., 26-28, 35-36, 43, 45, 50
Greener, Leslie, 91, 132, 144
Griffin, Jasper, 115, 120, 192
Grove, David L. Snell, 227
Groves, C. P., 283
Guinea, 34, 48
Guthrie, Kenneth Slyvan, 196

H

Habilis, H., 66
Hades, 184, 265
Halberstam, David, 24
Hall, G. Stanley, 36
Hamilton, Alexander, 12
Hamilton, Edith, 198
Hamites, 39, 41, 61, 103
Hamitic, 39
Hannibal, 284
Hanson, John, 13-15, 293
Harding, Warren, 16
Hare Krishna, 253
Harlem, 7, 226, 312
Harris, John R., 156, 210
Harrison, John B., 109
Harvard University, 107, 123, 151, 205, 248-250, 256,

258-259, 302-303
Hathor, 265
Hatzfeld, Jean, 116
Hawkes, Jacquetta, 83, 102
Hecataeus, 189, 191-192
Hecate, 278
Hecateaus, 158
Hecati, 223
Heeren, Arnold Hermann
    Ludwig, 110
Heliopolia, 271
Helipolis, 153
Helipolitan, 188
Hellwald, 190
Helper, Hinton R., 50
Henry VI, 249
Heordotus, 142
Her Bak, 255-256
Heraclides, 198
Heraclitus, 201
Hercataeus of Miletus, 191
Herdotus, 206
Herlihy, D., 107
Hermapion, 188
Hermippus, 194
Hermonthis, 258
Hermopolis, 191
Hermopolitan, 191
Herod, 93
Herodotos, 216
Hesiod, 118
Heston, Charlton, 19
Hierakonpolis, 135
Hieroglyphics, 92, 151
Higgins, Geoffrey, 5
Higgins, Godfrey, 58, 63, 223-
    224, 235, 239, 271, 279
Higgins, K., 126
Higgins, Kathleen M., 126, 150
Hill, Bennett D., 119-120
Hindus, 158
Hipprocrates, 198
*Historical Researches into the
    Politics, Intercourse, and
    Trade of the Carthaginians,
    Ethiopians, and Egyptians*,
    134, 144, 145
Histories Book II, 155
History of Ancient Civilization, A,
    40, 42, 63
History of Ancient Egypt, 161
History of Ancient Greece, 116
History of Civilization, A , 106,
    108
History of Egypt, 84, 91-92, 95,
    101, 123, 130, 149, 161,
    164, 175, 190, 202, 204, 217
History of Europe, A, 114, 172,
    182, 192
History of Greece, A, 117-118

History of Nations, 67
History of Philosophy, A, 73, 120,
    126, 150
History of Raputans, 272
History of Science, A, 123, 150,
    163
History of the Modern World, A ,
    113, 121, 168, 169, 180
History of World Societies, A ,
    119, 120
History of World Societies, A,
    119-120
Hitler, Adolph, 26
Hoffman, Frederick, 50
Hoge, Warren, 16
Holland, 63
Holoka, James P., 181-182, 207
Holt, Frank L., 161
Holy Spirit, 263
Holy Trinity, 278
Homer, 91, 102, 118, 135, 139,
    152, 159, 184, 202, 207,
    215, 248
Hominid Evolution, 54
Hominids, 61, 73
Homo Erectus, 55, 64, 66-67, 69,
    71
Homo Sapiens, 54, 57, 67-69, 74
Homo-Erectus, 61
Homo-Habilis, 61
Hoover, J. Edgar, 25
Horus, 79, 222, 224, 261-262,
    264-266, 273, 275-279, 281
Hottentot, 39
Houston, J., 34
Houston, James, 34
Howard, O. O., 41
Huggins, Willis N., 77-79, 127
Hughes, Howard, 20
Hume, David, 40
Hunter College, 191
Husley, Elpseth, 37
Huxley Memorial lecture, 65
Hyman, Mark, 283
Hypatia, 185

I

Iamblicus, 196
Iberia, 111
Ichonuphys, 203
Ignatius Donnelly, 150
Iliad, 114, 118
Illiad, 159
Illinois, 148, 171, 208
Imprimerie De L, 90
In the Name of Eugenics, 46
Indianapolis, 100, 138, 143
Indo-Europeans, 5, 114, 117,
    171-172
Institut Francais D, 90

*Intimate matters: A history of
    sexuality in America*, 36
Ionia, 115, 120, 156, 199
Ipsambul, 271
Iran, 260
Iraq, 107
Isis, 101, 132, 184, 222-223, 262,
    264-265, 273, 275-281
Islamic, 142, 284
Island of Isis, 278, 280
Isocrates, 165
Israel, 80, 92, 173
Israelite, 267
Israelites, 80

J

Jabbar, Kareem Abdul, 26-27
Jackson, Andrew, 12, 16
Jackson, Jesse, 290
Jackson, John G., 77-79, 107,
    152, 224, 272, 301, 304
Jackson, John, 5, 77-79, 107,
    110, 152, 174, 224, 228,
    256-257, 262-264, 267, 272,
    301, 304
Jaeger, H., 209
Jamblicus, 165
James River, 300
James, George G. M., 5, 183,
    193, 196, 224, 304
Jarvis, Dr. Edward, 35
Jayne, Dr. Walter A., 216
Jayne, Walter Addison, 90, 216
Jehovah, 93, 241
Jensen, A. R., 45-46
Jerusalem, 93
Jet , 25, 28, 33, 232
Jet, 25, 28, 33, 63, 232, 239, 303
Jeune, Champollion Le, 132, 173
Jim Crow, 22
John Hopkins University, 68-69,
    186, 192
John Jay College, 109
Johnson, Lyndon B., 12, 16
Jomard, 141
Jordan, June, 286
Josephus, 230
Journal of African Civilization,
    200, 237, 265
Jr., Louis Gates, 45
Jung, C. G., 36
Justinian II, 230

K

Kant, Emmanuel, 45
Katz Radio Group, 24
Kemp, B. J., 162
Kenrick, M. A., 106
Kenya, 58, 66-70
Kenya, National Museum of , 69
Khayats, 129

Khephren, 89
Khufu, 89
Kidd, Benjamin, 52
Kilpatrick, James J., 8
King James, 3
King, Casey, 303
King, Martin Luther, 25
Kircher, Athanasius, 215
Kirk, Captain, 294
Kirk, G. S., 151
Kitemè, Dr. Kamuti, 71
Kneph, 265
Knox, Henry, 27
Koempfer, 260
Koran, 167, 241
Kuan-Yin of Kwannon, 276
Kuhn, Alvin Boyd, 267
Kush, 2-3, 105
Kushite, 248
Kushites, 107
Kwannon, 276, 278

L

*Leopard's Spots: Scientific
    Attitudes Toward Race in
    America, 1815-1859, The*,
    27, 32, 34, 35, 40, 42, 43
Life of the Ancient East, The, 135
L'Afrigue Noire, 129
L., Jones H., 205
Lady Liberty, 18
Laerce, Diogenes, 164, 166
Lane, Allen, 114, 172, 182, 193
Lao-Tsze, 242
Larousse Universal Dictionary,
    278
Larson, Arthur, 11
Las Vegas, 28
Lassalle, 19
Latin American, 8
Latvia, 248
Leakey, L. S. B., 8
Lectures on Egyptian Art, 98
Ledit, Joseph R., 281
Lefever, Ernest W., 12
Lefkowitz, Mary, 78, 170, 196
Lehman, Herbert H., 305
Leibovitch, J., 90
Leipzig, Philosophie, 159
Lengyel, Emil, 166
Les Nouvelles, 97
Leslie, Connie, 7
Lewis, H. Spenser, 254
Library, John Rylands, 301
Lick, Dale, 24
*Life and Times of William
    Howard Taft, The*, 11
Life of Plato, 153, 166
Life of Pythagoras, 165, 196
Light Of Egypt, The, 75, 147

Like It Is, 6, 152, 197
Lincoln, Abraham, 10, 14, 18,
    293
Lion of Judah, 272
Literaries, 97
Living Pageant of the Nile, The,
    100, 138, 143
Livingston, 37
Lloyd, A. B., 162
Locke, John, 40
Loeb Classical Library, 155, 205,
    210
Logos of Heracleitus, 195
Lombrosos, 29
Long, Edward, 27, 116
Loom of History, The, 115
Loomis, L. R., 284
Lord Raglan, 50, 178
Loretto, 235
Lorton, David, 212
Los Angeles Dodgers, 23
Louvre Museum, 211
Lovejoy, Owen, 44
Luce, Henry R., 246
Lucius Apuleius, 277
Lucy, 65, 67, 70
Lycorgos, 159, 189
Lycurgus, 151
Lydians, 2
Lyell, Charles, 34
Lyon, 87

M

Maat, 212
Macedonian, 215
MacQuity, William, 280
Madonna, 222, 232-236, 273,
    277, 280, 302
Magdeburg, 249
Magi, 237, 266-267
*Magic and Medical Science in
    Ancient Egypt*, 142
Maillet, 86
Maillet, Benot de, 86
Malay, 41
Malek, Jamomir, 145
Man, Rises to Parnassus, 59
Manetho, 187, 257-258
Manifest Destiny, 293
*Manners and Customs of The
    Ancient Egyptians*, 81, 202
Manual of Ethnology, 52
Margoliovth, 242
Mariette, Auguste, 128, 147, 155
Marles, M. De, 260
Marseilles, 275
Marshall, P. J., 37
Martyrdom of Man, 152
Marx, Karl, 19, 93
Maryland Gazette, 14

Maryland Public Television, 162
Maryland, 14, 162, 192
Maspero, Gaston, 84, 105, 149,
    224
Massey, Gerald, 5, 58, 81, 166,
    218, 224, 232, 263, 265,
    267, 312
Maya, 280
McCabe, Joseph, 62, 174
McKay, John P., 120
Mckinley, William, 16
McMahan, Ian, 76
McNeil, William H., 117
Mead, 125, 158
Medes, 176
Medicine, A Historical Outline,
    58, 131
Melainis, 222
Melampos, 159
Melbourne, 99, 131
Melchiades, 284
Melissos, 215
Memmon, 223
Memphis, 151, 158, 175, 191,
    196, 213, 260, 269
Menkaure, 89
Menozzi, Paolo, 53
Merodach, 276
Mesopotamian, 105-106
Mesraim, 105
Metamorphosis, 277
Methuselah, 243
Mexicans, 253
Mexico, 223-224, 256
Miami Heat, 24
Michigan State University, 109
Michigan State, 24, 109
Michigan, University of, 107
Middle East, 2
Middle Nile, 105
Middlesex, 214
Milesian, 192
Miletus, 167, 185, 191, 199-201
Million Man March, 285
Miltiades, 283-284
Minerva, 102, 153, 192, 278
Minoans of Crete, 128
Mississippi Valley, 181
Mizraim, 110, 279
Mohamet, 241
Mohammed, 241-242
Mohammed, D. S., 242
Mohammedan, 241
Mohammedanism, 40
Monastery, Jasna Gora, 234
Mongolian, 41, 61, 178
Monotheism, 80, 82, 257
Monroe, James, 16
Moore, Edward, 239
Moralis, 165

Moslem, 167
Muller, Herbert J., 115
Muller, Herbert, 115
Munich, University of, 72
Murphy, Edwin, 159, 184, 189, 202, 208
Murray, Dr. Margaret A., 148
Murray, John, 81, 95, 203
Murray, Margaret A., 75-76, 99, 128, 140, 148, 211
Murray, O., 185, 190
Murray, Oswyn, 115, 120, 192
Museum of Natural History, 38, 61, 66, 69-70
Museums of Egypt, 201, 208, 279, 281
Mycenae, 115-116
Mycenaean, 116
Mycenaeans, 116
Mycerinus, 89

N

Napoleon, 143, 145, 177
Nation of Islam, 288
National Enquirer, 19
National Geographic Society, 69, 85
National Review, 46
Nativity, 267, 276
Natural History Museum, 38, 61, 66, 69-70, 72, 74
Nature Knows No Color Line, 217, 222, 230, 302
Naucratis, 186, 200
Naukratis, 141
Naydler, Jeremy, 79
Nazi, 6, 297
Nazism, 297
Negro: What is His Ethnological Status, The, 51
Nelson, Jill, 8
Nevada, University of, 28
New Dimensions in African History, 170
New Haven, 90, 135, 213, 216
New National Black Monitor, 8
New Science and the Story of Evolution, The, 174
New Science, 80, 174, 303
New Testament, 256, 259, 312
New York Times , The, 10, 18, 20, 22, 24, 44, 46, 54, 56, 58, 60, 64, 68, 72, 102, 224, 256
New York Times Science Times, 54, 56, 303
New York Voice, 283
Nichols, Carl C., 246
Nicklaus, Jack, 24
Niger Expedition, The, 22
Nile Valley Civilizations, 64-65,

193, 200, 256, 301-302
Nineveh, 127
Nisbet, James, 87, 96
Noble, Gil, 152
Nojoque, 50
North Carolina, 100, 159, 184, 189, 202, 208, 297
Northern Annu, 258
Northern Europe, 89, 171
Northern Italy, 248
Not Out of Africa, 196
Notes on Virginia, 27, 29, 45
Notre Dame, 232, 275, 280
Nott, J. C., 34
Nsukka, 151, 157, 191, 195, 198, 257
Nubia, 110, 271
Nubian, 253
Nubians, 2, 104
Numidia, 283
Nuwaubian Moors Newsletter, The, 13, 16
Nuwaubian, 13, 16, 302
Nymphano, 282-283

O

Observations Concerning the Increase of Mankind, 1753, 25
Observer, The, 74
Odyssey, 114, 118, 184
Oenopides of Chios, 159
Oenopides, 159, 186
Oenuphis of Heliopolis, 151
Oeuvres, 45
Ogdoad, 257
Oklahoma, 145
Old Kingdom, 89, 125
Old Testament, 80, 245, 263, 270-271
Olduvai Gorge, 66, 70
Olivet, 174
Olympiad, 203
Olympiads, 21
Olympiodorus, 153, 166
Olympiodorus, Life of Plato, 151, 164
Onyewuenyi, Innocent C., 151, 156, 190, 195, 198, 257
Opening of the Way, The, 254
Orientalism, 143
Origin and Evolution of the Human Race , The, 88, 150, 160
Origin of Civilization, The, 50, 81, 98
Origin of Civilized Societies, 105
Origin of Greek Civilization 1100 - 650 B. C., The, 118
Origin of Races, The, 44

Origins, Kamite, 263
Orpheus, 139, 152, 159, 184, 202, 208, 215
Osarseph, 258
Osborn, 38, 61, 88
Osborn, Dr. Henry Fairfield, 38
Osborn, Henry Fairfield, 38, 61
Osborne, Linda Barrett, 303
Osburn, William, 95
Osei, Dr. G. K., 301
Osei, G. K., 174, 301
Osiris-Horus, 262
Osler, 132
Otto I of Saxony, 248
Otto of Freising, 250
Ottoman, 249
Our Black Seminarians And Black Clergy Without A Black Theology, 304
Out of Africa, 5, 37, 67-68, 73, 196
Out of Egypt, 93, 144, 157, 184
Outlines of Ancient Egyptian History, 129, 148, 155
Oxford Companion, 243
Oxford History of the Classical World, The, 119, 196
Oxford University, 54, 58, 111, 115-116, 120, 125-126, 150, 156-157, 170, 180, 192, 200, 210, 247
Oxford, University of, 58, 126, 150, 157, 170, 247

P

Paabo, Dr. Svante, 71-72
Paleoanthropology, 55, 74
Paleolithic, 65, 97
Paleontological Institute of Paris, 65
Palestine, 133
Pappademos, J., 148
Papyrus of Ani, 224, 268
Papyrus, 191, 224, 268, 270
Para Isidos, 275
Paris, University of, 40, 42, 103, 160
Parmenides, 215
Parnassus, 61
Parsons, Geoffrey, 117-118, 122, 130, 170
Parthenon, 94, 121
Pausanius, 254
Payne, Buckner H., 51
Payne, Elizabeth, 177
Peck, William H., 77, 85
Pennsylvania, University of, 42
Pentateuch, 256
People of the Nile, 86, 181
Perpetua, 282-283

Perry, W. J., 150
Persian, 106, 135, 189
Persians, 123, 176, 193
Petrarch, 38
Petrie, Flinders, 83, 141
Pharaoh, 2, 134, 163, 173, 241
Pharaohs of Ancient Egypt, The, 181
Pharaohs, Fellahs and Explorers, 86, 94, 141
Pharaonic, 161-163, 281
Pharoahs, 89
Pharonic, 132
Philadelphia New Observer, 297
Philadelphia, 199, 297
Philae, 262, 280
Philanthropist, 52
Phillipson, Dr. David W., 55
Phillipson, Dr. Laural, 55
Philosophies of India, 238
Phoenicia, 146
Phoenician, 198
Phoenician-Hebrew, 246
Phoenicians, 2, 82, 145
Phrygians, 176, 277
Physiognomy, 97
Piazzas, Albert, 53
Pierret, P., 211
Pindar, 160
Planting of Christianity in Africa, The, 289
Poland, 232, 234, 248, 275
Polk, James, 16
Polycrates, 203
Pope Gelasius, 283
Pope John Paul II, 234
Pope Paul II, 234-235
Pope Victor, 283-284
Porphyrius, 164-165
Porphyry, 125
Pre-Historic Nations, 96, 110, 128, 131, 163
President Nobody Knew, The, 10
Presocratic Philosophers, The, 155
Pressinuntia, 277
Priests of Ancient Egypt, The, 139, 145
Principles of Geology, 34
Pringle, Henry F., 11
Professor A. H. L. Heeren, 110, 134, 146
Professor A. R. Jensen, 45
Professor Alan Gardiner, 159
Professor Ashley Montagu, 62
Professor Basil Davidson, 85
Professor C. Seignobos, 103
Professor Charles Seignobos, 40, 42, 63
Professor Daniel J. Kevles, 46

Professor Donald Johnson, 67
Professor Emeritus of History, 207
Professor Emile Amelineau, 183
Professor Erwin H. Ackerknecht, 192
Professor Innocent C. Onyewuenyi, 156, 190
Professor J. M. Roberts, 172
Professor John D. Ray, 140, 145
Professor John Jackson Man, 224, 228, 262
Professor Leo Hansberry, 206
Professor Leon J. Kamin, 46
Professor Lionel Casson, 128, 186
Professor Louis Agassiz, 47
Professor Margaret A. Murray, 75
Professor Pierre Monte, 215
Professor R. B. Cartell, 50
Professor Richard Wilkinson, 136
Professor Samuel G. Morton, 32, 40, 42
Professor Sauneron, 123, 148, 165
Professor T. Inman, 253
Professor Theophile Obenga, 199
Professor William Sinnegen, 191
Professors Edward McNall Burns, 169
Professors R. Solomon, 126
Professors Willis N. Huggins, 79
Prophet Muhammad, 242
Prosser, Gabriel, 298
Psammetichus, 189
Ptah, 194
Pyramid Age, 104, 216
Pyramid Texts, 191, 255-256, 266
Pyramids and Sphinx, The, 103, 105
Pyramids, 77, 83, 85, 89, 98, 100, 102-103, 105, 126-127, 130-131, 133, 136, 140, 147, 150, 162, 169, 175, 177, 204, 206, 212, 215

Q

Quetzalcoatl, 224, 253-254
Qumran, 246-247

R

Race, The History of an Idea in America, 8, 10, 26, 28, 35, 36, 44, 46, 52
Races of Mankind, The, 136
Races of Men: A Fragment, The, 38
Races of the Old World: A Manual of Ethnology, The, 52

Racial Stereotypes, 36
Ralph, P., 188
Ralph, Philip Lee, 106, 122, 144, 169
Ralph, Philip, 105-106, 115-116, 122, 144, 169, 271
Ramapithecus, 66
Rameses, 86, 91, 130
Ramesside Stela, 191
Ras Tafari, 272
Rationalist Annual, The, 177
Raven, J. E., 151
Rawlinson, 107, 125, 155, 158
Rawlinson, George, 125, 158
Reader, Herbert Thompson, 140
Readers Digest, 262
Reis, Dr., 88
Renan, 88
Rensberger, B., 71
Rensberger, Boyce, 66
Review X, 34, 43
Rhys, Jocelyn, 275
Ridley, Mark, 58
Rinehart, 214
Rise of Christian Europe, The, 37
River: Ganges, 179
Robert, Jennifer T., 116, 180, 200
Roberts, J. M., 114, 172, 182, 185, 192, 204
Robertson, John M., 253
Robinson, Charles, 191
Robinson, Cyril E., 117-118
Robinson, Jackie, 24
Robinson, Victor, 174
Rocamadour, 281
Rochester, 80
Rockefeller Center, 109
Rogers, J. A., 64, 67, 178, 217, 222, 224-225, 230-232, 241-242, 254, 261, 282, 284, 301-302, 304
Rolfe, J. C., 210
Rollins, Charles, 121
Roman World, 114
Roman, Bernard, 152, 192
Romer, John, 86, 180
Roosevelt, Franklin D., 16
Rosicrucians, The, 273
Rostoutzeff, M., 109
Royal African Company, 34
Royal Anthropological Institute of Great Britain, 79
Ruins of Empire, 86, 103, 205, 209, 218, 224
Ruins of Empire, The, 103, 216
Rushton, 45
Russia, 28, 232, 236
Ryan, W. G., 248-250, 303

S

S., Henry, 82, 246
Sabacon, 217
Saggs, H. W. F., 134
Said, Edward, 142
Saints Go Marching In, The, 284
Sais, 151, 155
Salome, 258
San Francisco, 93, 232
San Juan, 8
Sarton, George, 123, 163
Saturday Review, 45
Saunders, M., 122
Savior, 0, 248, 277, 279
Saviors, 230, 253, 280
Schoch, Dr. R. M., 102
Schoch, Dr. Robert M., 102
Schomburg Center, 8
Schomburg, Arthur A., 7-8
Schott, Marge, 23
Schweitzer, Albert, 20
Scobie, Edward, 284, 301, 312
Scrolls, 243, 246-247, 267
Scythians, 176
Secaucus, 304
Secret Medicine of the Pharoahs, The, 89
Secrets of the Pharoahs, 76, 92
Seelig, Dr. M. G., 58
Seelig, M. G., 58, 133
Seignobos, Charles, 40, 42, 63
Seiss, Joseph A., 93
Selassie, Haile, 272
Selincourt, 214
Semite, 179
Semites, 39, 61
Semitic, 39, 134, 176, 217
Senstuttgut, Hegel, 40
Sertima, Ivan Van, 5, 148, 197, 200, 272, 301-302, 304
Seymour, D., 95
Shabazz, K. A., 228
Shaler, Nathaniel Southgate, 27
Shaw, Ian, 161
Shelly, Percy Bysshe, 113
Sherman, Dennis, 109
Shimbun, Yomiuri, 46
Shockley, William, 45
Short History of Philosophy, A, 126, 150
Short History of Western Civilization, A, 105, 109
Siculus, Didorus, 279
Signs and Symbols of Primordial Man, 61, 154, 209, 255
Signs and Symbols of Primordial Man, The, 154, 206
Simpson, O. J., 285
Sistine Chapel, 219

Sixteen Crucified Saviors, 230
Slant of the Pen, The, 31
Slave Trade, 22, 34
Slavery, 17-18, 26, 32, 34-35, 50, 287, 299, 303
Slaves, 1, 10, 12, 17, 24, 28, 32, 34-35
Slavic, 249
Slosman, Albert, 187
Smith, G. Elliot, 98, 301
Smith, John Augustine, 43
Smith, W. Stevenson, 301
Snowden, Frank, 278, 302
Socrates, 94, 158, 194, 200
Sorbonne University, 160
South Africa, 54, 66-67, 69-70
Soviet Union, 233
Spain, 232-235, 237
Spartan, 159
Spencer, Herbert, 35
Sphinx and the Lotus:The Egyptian Movement in American Decorative Arts, The, 89
Spiegelberg, Wilhelm, 142
Spirit of Ancient Egypt, The, 129
Splendor of Greece, The, 21, 62
Splendour That Was Egypt, The, 74, 98, 126, 140, 148, 208
Sports Illustrated, 24
Sprewell: case, 25
Springfield, 293
St. Athanasius, 282
St. Augustine, 256, 261, 282, 284
St. Francis, 281
St. Gelasius, 283
St. Louis, 281
St. Luke, 236
St. Paul, 60
Stace, William, 198
Stanford University, 7, 45
Stanton, William, 27, 32, 34-35, 40, 42-43
Star Trek, 294
Starr, Chester G., 111, 114
Statue of Liberty, 17-18
Steele, Claude, 7
Steinberg, Alan, 26-27
Stellar Theology and Masonic Astronomy, 252
Stellar Theology, 255
Stetter, Cornelius, 89, 135
Stevenson, Karen, 28
Stewart, Desmond, 103, 105
Stobart, J. C., 119, 122
Stolen Legacy, 5, 183, 193, 195, 224, 254, 277
Stolen Legacy, The, 192
Stone Age, 98, 113, 170
Stonehenge, 171

Story of Evolution, 65, 174
Strasbourg, University of, 168
Straw, Jack, 16
Stringer, C., 54
Stringer, Chris, 74
Stringer, Christopher, 71-73
Study of History, A, 100
Sudan, 2, 87, 242
Sudani, 79
Sullivan, Walter, 62
Sumeria, 144
Sumerian, 96, 107-108
Sumerians, 96, 106-107
Sumner, William Graham, 52
Sunday News, 234
Superman To Man, 304
Supreme Court, 15, 285
Survey of Western Civilization, A, 181-182, 207
Sut-Nahsi, 226
Sweden, 78
Swiss, 235, 248
Switzerland, 237
Sykes, Egerton, 273
Syria, 63, 180, 245, 279

Taft, William Howard, 11, 16
Talboys, D. A., 147
Tanzania, 58, 66, 70
Taoist, 275
Tasso, 38
Taung, 66
Taylor, Griffith, 61, 63
Telos , 24, 25, 26, 33, 36, 40, 45, 50
Temple of the Cosmos, the ancient Egyptian experience of the Sacred, 80
Terrasson, Jean, 161
Texas, University of, 126, 150
Thailand, 225
The African Origin of Civilization, The, 67, 82, 104, 166, 169, 208, 268
The African Origin of Greek Philosophy, The, 149, 159, 196, 191, 195, 197, 255
The Book of the Glory of the Black Race, 242
The Great Pyramid: A Miracle in Stone, The, 93
The Healing Gods of Ancient Civilizations, The, 90, 216
The History and Geography of Human Gene, The, 53
The Image of The Black in Western Art, The, 248, 249, 250
The Invitation to Learning Reader on the Roots of

Civilization, The, 207
The Legacy of Egypt, The, 124, 140, 144, 156, 157, 170, 210
Story of Civilization, The, 82, 144, 158, 162, 276
Story of Medicine, The, 172
Story of Philosophy, The, 155
Stream of History, The, 118, 122, 130, 170

T

Transitions from Ancient Egyptian to Greek Medicine, The, 122
Traveler's Key to Ancient Egypt, The, 141
Theban, 91, 189, 249
Thebes, 82, 85, 91, 103, 167, 174, 177, 205, 260
Theophrastus, 125, 194
Third Dynasty, 79
Thompson, John, 10
Thorndike, E. L., 35
Thoth, 86, 265-266
Thothmosis, 91
Tiber, 128
Tigris-Euphrates, 63, 105-108
Time Frame, 57
Time, 235
Time-Life Books, 57, 128
Timeaus, 186
Timotheus, 160
Tirard, H. M., 102, 156, 160, 206
Titian, 38
Tomlin, Frederic, 138
Toynbee, Arnold, 40
Trevor-Roper, Hugh, 37
Trigger, B. G., 162
Trismegistos, 215
Trojan War, 174, 198, 216
Tropical Dependency, A , 87, 96
Troy, 102, 115
Trübner, 95
Turkestan, 275
Turner, Nat, 298
Tutankhamen, 268
Tyrannio, 194
Tyre, 146

V

Vail, C. H., 254
Van Hook, 165
Vanished Cities of Northern Africa, The, 282
Vatican, 283, 312
Vermes, Geza, 247
Vermont, 80
Versailles, 17
Versluis, Arthur, 154
Vessey, Denmark, 298
Viet Nam, 227

Vinci, Leonardo da, 38
Virgin Mary, 232, 265, 273, 275-277
Virgin Mother, 262, 276
Virginia, University of, 50
Volney, Count C. F., 86, 209, 224
Voyages en Syrie et en Egypte, 76

W

Waddell, W. G., 258
Wake of the Wind, The, 296
Washington Post, The, 71, 72, 270, 280
Western Experience, The, 106, 114
Wisdom of the Egyptians , The, 75, 140
Wonder That Was India, The, 253
Works of Gerald Massey, The, 263
World's Great Religions, The, 246
Walker, Alan, 68-69
Waltz, James C., 181-182, 207
Ward, William A., 129
Ward, William, 129, 260
Washington Post, The, 71-73, 273, 280
Washington University, 82
Washington, George, 10, 12-16, 293
Wassef, Ceres Wissa, 271
Wayne, John, 19
Weech, W. N., 120
Weightman, Doreen, 168
Weiss, John, 44
Wellesley University, 170
Wells, H. G., 175
Weltfish, Gene, 137
Wendt, Herbert, 154
Werbruck, Marcelle, 85
West Africa, 48
West, John Anthony, 141
Westemann, William L., 207
Weulesse, Jacques, 129
White on Black, Images of Africa and Blacks in Western Popular Culture, 1992, 21, 25, 28
White, Charles, 28-29, 42-43
White, Dr., 27, 42-43, 65
Whitehead, Alfred North, 181
Widney, J. P., 179
Wilbour, Charles Edwin, 106
Wilford, J., 69
Wilford, John, 54, 57, 68, 73
Wilkenson, J. G., 81, 203
Williams, G., 37
Wilson, Allan C., 54
Wilson, John A., 100, 125
Wilson, Woodrow, 10-11

Winchester, J., 132, 155, 188
Winslow, C., 99, 112, 189
Winstone, H. V. F., 211
Wister, Owen, 10
Woloch, I., 107
Wood, Michael, 53, 143, 162, 201
Woodson, Carter G., 48, 99, 312
World Civilizations, 104, 106, 114, 116, 120, 144, 166, 270
World History of Art, A, 114, 121, 131
Worth, J., 201

Y

Yoga: birth of, 238

Z

Zaha, 224, 253
Zimmer, Heinrich, 238
Zoeller, Fuzzy, 24